The Asia-Pacific Century

Challenges and Opportunities

T0295676

Edited by Adam B. Lowther

CRC Press
Taylor & Francis Group
Boca Raton London New York

CRC Press is an imprint of the
Taylor & Francis Group, an **informa** business
A TAYLOR & FRANCIS BOOK

CRC Press
Taylor & Francis Group
6000 Broken Sound Parkway NW, Suite 300
Boca Raton, FL 33487-2742

First issued in paperback 2019

© Taylor & Francis Group, LLC
CRC Press is an imprint of Taylor & Francis Group, an Informa business

No claim to original U.S. Government works

ISBN-13: 978-1-4822-1840-4 (hbk)
ISBN-13: 978-0-367-37954-4 (pbk)

Visit the Taylor & Francis Web site at
http://www.taylorandfrancis.com

and the CRC Press Web site at
http://www.crcpress.com

Contents

Foreword

In 2002 Pres. George W. Bush proclaimed that the twenty-first century would be the "Asia-Pacific Century." While I am not sure he was the first person to use that phrase—and it has been often used by others over the past 10 years—for those of us who study the region and/or have more than a casual familiarity with the region, the proclamation rings true. In a November 2011 article in *Foreign Policy* magazine, Secretary of State Hillary Clinton went so far as to say, "The future of politics will be decided in Asia, not Afghanistan or Iraq, and the United States will be right at the center of the action." These are powerful words, underscoring the fact that Asia matters, and it matters a great deal.

For those who are interested in national security affairs, the question is not whether Asia matters but what our country should do about the fact that Asia matters. How should we posture ourselves to best advance our national interests in a region that will have so much to do with our future security and prosperity?

Certainly, there will be much study and many well-considered judgments concerning these important questions, and most of this work will contribute to advancing our collective ability to successfully confront the scores of challenges that lie ahead. In this regard, I was pleased to learn that the Air Force Research Institute was undertaking a year-long study of the Air Force strategy in the Asia-Pacific region.

While it is clear that all instruments of national power will play critical roles in our national strategy for the region, the military instrument will underpin all of our efforts in the region. The US Air Force will play an especially key role, with its ability to rapidly span the vast distances in the Pacific while engaging our allies, partners, and friends in the region through forward presence and exercises.

By addressing issues from economic integration to a potential nuclear arms race and key regional actors (China, North Korea, India), this book provides a broad perspective on the topics that will shape the future of US involvement in the region. I was especially interested in the chapter on building partnerships because my experience tells me we will need to increasingly leverage the capabilities of other nations if we are to achieve our objectives in an affordable manner.

The Asia-Pacific region is neither generally at war nor completely at peace. This is a region that holds the promise of multilateral cooperation that can lead to greater economic prosperity, as well as the ability to deal constructively with many of the most significant security challenges of our time. These include the areas of nuclear proliferation, international criminal activity, terrorism, environmental degradation, pandemic diseases, natural disasters, and more. This is a region whose future is not preordained but that will be shaped by the actions of the Pacific nations themselves, and the United States will continue to be a leading member of this group of nations. This is also a region where both hard and soft power will be required to maintain stability and achieve progress.

During the three years I lived in Japan, it struck me that the people who felt most viscerally positive about the relationship between our countries were those who were children during the post–World War 2 period. The lesson they could have taken from that time was one associated with the trauma resulting from the utter devastation our country had brought to theirs. Instead, the lesson many of them took away was one of gratitude for the vast effort we made to help them stand back up after the national tragedy that befell them. Much of that immense effort was undertaken by the US military forces stationed there after the war. This combination of hard power during the war and soft power after the war demonstrates the versatility of the military instrument of our national policy, a flexibility that will continue to be required in the years and decades to come.

This book does an admirable job of addressing both the hard power and soft power challenges we will face in the region. I am confident readers will find this to be a worthy addition to their literature collection on the Asia-Pacific.

EDWARD A. RICE, JR.
General, USAF
Commander
Air Education and Training Command

About the Authors

Dr. Stephen J. Cimbala is a distinguished professor of political science at Penn State Brandywine. He is the author of numerous works in the field of national security studies, defense policy, nuclear arms control, deterrence, and other subjects. Dr. Cimbala is an award-winning Penn State teacher. His recent publications include *Nuclear Weapons in the Information Age* (Continuum International Publishing Company, 2012) and his edited volume, *Civil-Military Relations in Perspective: Strategy, Structure and Policy* (Ashgate Publishers, 2012).

Dr. Chad Dacus is a research professor of economics at the Air Force Research Institute (AFRI), Maxwell AFB, Alabama. His current research interests include defense acquisition, economics and strategy, and cyberspace risk modeling. Before joining the AFRI staff, Dr. Dacus worked for the Center for Naval Analyses as a research analyst in readiness and infrastructure and then as a field representative to US Fleet Forces Command.

Dr. Thomas P. Dolan is a professor and chairman, Department of Political Science, and chairman, Master of Public Administration Program, Columbus State University. Rated as a naval flight officer and mission commander in the P-3 Orion, he also served as an intelligence analyst with the Combined Forces Command, US Forces, Korea, and with the War Plans Division, Forces Command.

Dr. John P. Geis II is director of research, Air Force Research Institute, Maxwell AFB, Alabama. He is a retired US Air Force colonel with an Air Force career spanning training and combat operations. He flew the T-37, AT-38B, T-43, two variants of the F-111, and the AC-130H special operations gunship and was director of long-range planning for all US Air Force special forces. Dr. Geis served for eight years as director, Air Force Center for Strategy and Technology, where he advised national leadership on strategic implications of emerging technologies.

Dr. Kimberly Gill is an assistant professor, Department of Political Science, and director, Master of Public Administration Program, Columbus State University. She serves as a mediator for the Third Judicial District of Georgia and is a court-appointed special advocate. She also assists the US Army Sniper School, Fort Benning, Georgia, in course development.

Dr. Sanu Kainikara is the airpower strategist at the Air Power Development Centre of the Royal Australian Air Force and also a Visiting Fellow at the University of New South Wales. He is the author of many books and is a former fighter pilot of the Indian Air Force who retired as a Group Captain after 21 years of commissioned service. He has two bachelors' degrees, a master's degree in defence and strategic studies from India's University of Madras, and a PhD in international politics from the University of Adelaide in South Australia. He is currently conducting his PhD research on the law of armed conflict and military strategy at the Australian National University.

Justin Logan is the director of foreign policy studies at the Cato Institute. He is an expert on US grand strategy, international relations theory, and American foreign policy. His current research focuses on the shifting balance of power in Asia—specifically with regard to China—and the formation of US grand strategy under unipolarity. He has lectured on a range of foreign policy issues to the J-5 (Strategic Plans and Policy), on Capitol Hill, and at universities throughout the United States and world.

Dr. Adam Lowther is a research professor at the Air Force Research Institute (AFRI), Maxwell AFB, Alabama. The editor of *Terrorism's Unanswered Questions* and the author of *Americans and Asymmetric Conflict: Lebanon, Somalia, and Afghanistan*, he has also published in the *New York Times*, *Boston Globe*, *Joint Force Quarterly*, and *Strategic Studies Quarterly*. Dr. Lowther was an assistant professor of political science at Arkansas Tech University and Columbus State University. He served in the US Navy aboard the USS *Ramage*; at the office of the commander in chief, US Naval Forces, Europe; and with Naval Mobile Construction Battalion 17.

Dr. Rajeswari Pillai Rajagopalan is a Senior Fellow at Observer Research Foundation (ORF), New Delhi. Dr. Rajagopalan joined ORF after five years as assistant director at the National Security Council Secretariat. Previously, she was a research officer at the Institute of Defence Studies and Analyses, New Delhi, as well as a visiting professor, Graduate Institute of International Politics, National Chung Hsing University, Taichung, Taiwan, in early 2012. She is the author of three books on Chinese, US, and Asia-Pacific military strategy. Her latest book, *Clashing Titans: Military Strategy and Insecurity among Asian Great Powers*, was published in 2012.

Dr. Simon Reich is a professor of global affairs and political science at Rutgers University–Newark. He formerly served as director of the Division of Global Affairs, Rutgers, and the inaugural director of the Ford Institute for Human Security, University of Pittsburgh. Reich worked at the US Congressional Office of Technology Assessment and was the director of research and analysis, Royal Institute for International Affairs (Chatham House), London. He has published 10 books and is the author of a forthcoming book with Richard Ned Lebow, *Goodbye Hegemony! Power and Influence in the Global System* (Princeton: Princeton University Press, 2014). His work has been translated into Dutch, German, and Japanese and includes over 40 articles or book chapters.

Dr. Brooks B. Robinson has served since December 2007 as economic advisor for US Pacific Command (USPACOM), where he surveys economic conditions in 36 countries comprising USPACOM's area of responsibility. He produces the annual *Asia-Pacific Economic Update*, conducts economic research, and participates in domestic and international conferences and seminars. Dr. Robinson spent most of 2007 as senior research economist for analysis, Institute for Triple Helix Innovation, Honolulu. For the previous two decades, he was an economist with the US Department of Commerce, Bureau of Economic Analysis (BEA). He also served as director, market research, US and Foreign Commercial Service, New Delhi, India, and as acting director, US-Asia Environmental Partnership program, during a two-year hiatus from BEA.

Dr. Sheldon W. Simon has been a professor in the School of Politics and Global Studies at Arizona State University since 1975. A specialist in US national security and Asian international politics, he is the author or editor of 10 books and over 150 scholarly articles and book chapters. Professor Simon has also taught at the Universities of Kentucky, British Columbia, and Hawaii as well as George Washington University, the Monterey School of International Studies, and Carleton University (Ottawa). In 2009–10, Dr. Simon held the Visiting Asia Mentor Professorship at the US Naval War College. Simon consults regularly with the State and Defense Departments; in 2012 he led an interagency study on the future of the South China Sea conflicts for the US Department of State.

Dr. Dhirendra K. Vajpeyi is a professor of political science at the University of Northern Iowa and chair of the International Political

Science Association Research Committee on Technology and Development. He has authored or coauthored 16 books and numerous chapters and articles. His major publications include *Indira Gandhi's India*; *Civil-Military Relations, Nation-Building, and National Identity*; *Modernizing China*; *Globalization, Governance and Technology*; and *Water Resource Conflicts and International Security: A Global Perspective*. Dr. Vajpeyi has lectured at universities in Moscow, St. Petersburg (Russia), the People's Republic of China, Chile, and Klagenfurt (Austria). He was a Senior Research Fellow at the Hoover Institution, Stanford University.

Chapter 1

Why Asia Matters

Dr. John P. Geis II
Director of Research, Air Force Research Institute

Introduction

In 1900 Britain was the richest country in the world. It had the planet's largest military and was the center of global business, information, finance, and commerce. Its education system was second to none, and its currency was the world's reserve currency. In fact, the dictionary definition of *sterling* as having fine quality is an outgrowth of the intrinsic trust the world placed in the British pound as recently as 80 years ago.[1] In the early part of the twentieth century, the British Empire was comprised of one-fifth of the land area and a quarter of the people on Earth. It was called "the Empire on which the sun never sets."[2] Yet, in only a few decades, this empire crumbled,[3] and the era in which Britain ruled the seas gave way to what historians term "the American Century."[4]

This shift occurred as America emerged from the two world wars with the world's largest economy, gold reserves of more than 20,000 metric tons, and the world's most advanced commercial infrastructure. The US economy grew nearly 50 percent during the 1940s, and America was, for a brief time, the world's only nuclear superpower.[5] For the rest of the twentieth century the United States remained the world's preeminent nation-state, as it continues to be going into the second decade of the twenty-first century. In fact, after the collapse of the Soviet Union in 1989, the word *hyperpower* was used to describe the United States' position in the world, giving rise to comparisons between modern-day America and the great empires of Rome and Greece.[6]

Yet, a new shift is under way. First noticed in the 1960s, Asian demographics, even then, portended a significant shift in economic might. The earliest such prediction was by German scholar and polymath, Wilhelm Fucks, in his economic essay *Formeln zur Macht (Formulas for Power)*. He predicted that both China and India would rise in the first half of the twenty-first century to surpass the United States in economic strength.[7] In the last 15 years, many other forward-looking studies have come to the same conclusion. The *Air Force 2025* study concluded that among the possible outcomes before 2030 was the rise of an Asian colossus that would become "the largest economic power the world has ever known."[8] More recently, economists at the International Monetary Fund (IMF) projected that the crossing point between China's economy and that of the United States will occur in 2016.[9] By the end of this decade, by their prediction, the United States will have fallen to the world's *third* largest economy—behind the European Union and China.

This chapter seeks to examine the shift that is under way. It explores the contention that the "American Century" is giving way to the "Asian Millennium."[10] In short, it asks the question, Does Asia really matter, and, if so, in what way? To explore this question, this chapter first looks at economic growth across the Asia-Pacific, examining not just China and India but the rest of the region as well. It then looks at the geological and geophysical makeup of the region and what this means for issues of humanitarian concern. Lastly, it examines the recent predilection of Asian nations for bolstering their militaries and attempts to discern what this may mean in the decade ahead. In the end, this chapter will show that the Middle Kingdom of the world's largest continent is regaining a level of importance that it has not enjoyed for centuries and, moreover, that this newfound importance will likely last for a long time to come. As a result, like the president's foreign policy, American attention must now "pivot" toward Asia.[11]

The "Asian Tigers," Pandas, and Elephants

The rapid growth of the economies of the East Asian "Tigers" began in the 1960s and would continue more or less unabated for approximately 35 years. While the term "Tigers" usually is applied to Hong Kong, Singapore, Indonesia, and South Korea, other countries in East Asia also enjoyed substantial, even spectacular, growth. In the time frame from 1960 to 1995, Japan, Hong Kong, South Korea, Singapore, Taiwan, Indonesia, Malaysia, and Thailand all maintained a growth rate at least double that of the rest of East Asia.[12]

By the mid-1990s, some cracks in this growth pattern began to emerge. Economist Paul Krugman wrote in 1994 that "popular enthusiasm about Asia's boom deserves to have some cold water thrown on it. . . . Future prospects for growth are more limited than almost anyone can imagine."[13] While not readily apparent to many investors who continued pouring money into Asia hoping for massive returns, Krugman's essay foretold of a crash that was three years away. However, the crash was shorter in duration than Krugman foresaw.

East Asia's growth was interrupted in 1997 by a combination of cyclical economic forces and overstimulation of the economies, exacerbated in parts of the continent by endemic corruption, cronyism, and poor IMF policies.[14] The crisis of the late 1990s was severe. Thailand saw growth rates plummet from over 4 percent per year to negative 3.5 percent per year. Indonesia's stock market plunged over 50 percent in only a few months, and this was on top of a currency devaluation which took the rupiah from 2,400 to the US dollar to over 17,000 in only a few months.[15] Before the crisis ended, the IMF would find itself bailing out some of the world's largest economies and imposing on them stringent lending and spending restrictions.

Of note is that the bailout eventually cost tens of billions of dollars, much of which came from the United States. Further, the IMF-imposed austerity measures led to regional deflationary spirals that briefly threatened to spread to the United States and Europe.[16] In short, during three decades of prosperity, the Asian Tigers had grown large enough that serious problems in their economies could now adversely affect the global economy in ways unlikely to be noticed before. Even at their 1997 size, the Asian Tigers mattered. Further growth was on the horizon.

With the exception of Japan, which was in its "lost decade," economic growth across Asia was only briefly interrupted. Even the lost decade was not totally lost, as Japan's economy grew in the 2000s—even if at a slower rate. Figure 1.1 shows the growth of selected Asian nations in comparison to that of the United States. The graph, logarithmic in scale, shows that exponential economic growth continued across Asia in spite of the recession of the late 1990s, with several countries having gross domestic products (GDP) in excess of one trillion dollars.

As the new millennium dawned, the economic landscape had changed. By 2000 Asia had a greater GDP than North America, and by 2005 East Asia alone had a GDP of $12.8 trillion—outstripping North America's $12.7 trillion GDP.[17] Today, collectively, the Asian continent's GDP is just under twice that of North America and is more than 50 percent larger than the combined economies of the nations of Europe. For comparison purposes, figure 1.2 shows the relative size of the GDPs of the earth's six inhabited continents.

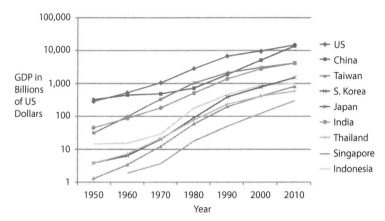

Figure 1.1. GDP of selected countries 1950–2010. (Data comes from Kristian S. Gleditsch, "Expanded Trade and GDP Data," *Journal of Conflict Resolution* 46 [2002]: 712–24. Gleditsch uses IMF data to build his database. The 2010 statistics come directly from the IMF report *World Economic Database*, September 2011, http://www.imf.org/external/pubs/ft/weo/2011/02/download.aspx.)

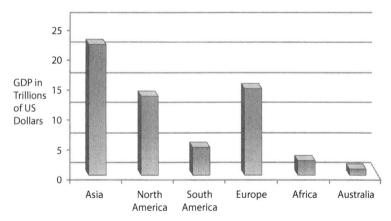

Figure 1.2. GDP of Earth's six inhabited continents. (Developed by the author using data from Central Intelligence Agency, *The World Factbook* [New York: Skyhorse Publishing, 2005], https://www.cia.gov/library/publications/the-world-factbook.)

The size of various regions' GDP might be merely an intellectual curiosity except that the growth of Asia has translated into direct relevance for the United States' economy. Beyond America's own shores, Asia is now this country's major trading partner, with 58 percent of recent trade growth directly related to North America and Asia. The remaining 42 percent is split among the other continents. As shown in figure 1.3, Asia contains six of the United States' top 15 trading partners, with China in second place.

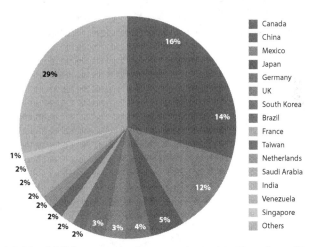

Figure 1.3. Total US imports and exports in 2010. (Developed by author using data from the United States Census Bureau website on foreign trade, http://www.census.gov/foreign-trade/statistics/highlights/top/top 1112yr.html, as of 1 March 2012.)

The trends clearly show Asia as an increasingly important trading partner. These trends are likely to accelerate in the future. Recent studies by Goldman Sachs, among others, indicate that the rise of the Asian economies, especially China and India, will continue for the foreseeable future. The predictions made by these brokerage firms indicate that China will eventually surpass the United States economically—though some suggest the crossing point will be later than the 2016 date given by the IMF.[18] In addition, India has been growing its economy at a rate analogous to that of China during the early phase of its "industrial revolution." India's growth rate for the past decade has been over 8 percent per year and, with a population of 1.2 billion people, is translating into rapidly increasing consumption and production of materials, both of which will lead to greater trade.[19] In fact, by midcentury, Goldman Sachs forecasts India's economy to be as large as that of the United States, with a growth rate twice that of China. India's growth is expected to be buoyed by her democratic system of governance, open economy, and population exceeding 1.8 billion people.[20]

Already a major factor in the US economy, the Asian economies appear likely to grow for years to come. As they do, trade between the United States and its Asian partners should increase, intertwining East and West further. Asian trade, however, currently flows through narrow chokepoints, and in asking why Asia matters, it is useful to understand this economic geography.

Getting International Trade "Strait"

The Strait of Malacca has been part of major shipping routes since the earliest days of trade between the Middle East and China. In the early 1500s, Portugal took control of the stronghold of Malacca, a key trading center in the early sixteenth century and the place for which the strait was named. Control of the passage shifted to the British Empire in 1867, lasting until Malaysia and Singapore gained their independence.[21]

While the Strait of Malacca remains crucial for shipping, it is not ideal. Bordered by three nations—Singapore, Malaysia, and Indonesia—the strait can be subject to international disagreements. In addition, it is quite narrow. While the strait is almost 600 miles wide between northern Sumatra and Thailand, it narrows to a width of approximately 3,000 meters between southern Sumatra and Singapore in what is called the Phillips Channel.[22] In addition, at this point, it has a depth of only 25 meters, making it barely capable of handling large oceangoing tankers and cargo vessels in the 300,000-ton class. While this means the strait occasionally requires dredging, as of 2009, it was handling over 60,000 cargo vessels annually, many carrying oil or petroleum products crucial to the East Asian economies with which the United States conducts considerable business each year.[23] In fact, almost all of Japan's oil and much of the oil for China—some 13.6 million barrels a day—transited the Malacca Strait in 2009.[24]

As of 2007, the latest year for which a comprehensive analysis is available, the world's busiest shipping routes were in Asia. Two of the world's busiest ports, Singapore and Shanghai, are in the Asia-Pacific region. While figure 1.4, below, shows evidence of dense transatlantic trade, the area highlighted by the yellow tracks is concentrated around the Strait of Malacca and then across the South China Sea, making them the most strategic places of ocean real estate in the world.

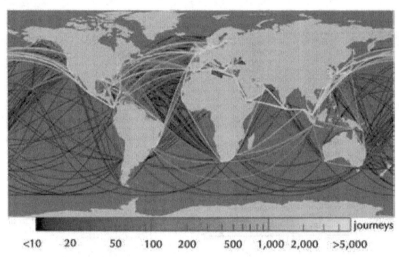

Figure 1.4. Global shipping in 2007. (*Reprinted from* Pablo Kaluza et al., "The Complex Network of Global Cargo Ship Movements," *Journal of the Royal Society Interface 7*, no. 48 [6 July 2010]: 1093–1103, http://rsif.royalsocietypublishing.org/content/7/48/1093.full.pdf+html. Used by permission.)

This real estate is strategic not merely due to the narrowness of the chokepoints but also due to the resource-rich nature of the Asia-Pacific region. East Asia has some of the world's largest reserves of fossil fuels and minerals on the planet. More than 140 minerals are found here, to include gold, silver, uranium, iron, boron, cadmium, nickel, vanadium, and zinc. Outside of Siberia, central Asia contains an estimated 3 trillion barrels of oil and nearly 5 percent of the world's natural gas reserves.[25] As one moves north into China and Russia's Siberian province, the in-ground resource pool becomes even richer. China contains the world's largest reserves of tungsten, tin, antimony, rare earth minerals, tantalum, and titanium. In vanadium, molybdenum, niobium, beryllium, and lithium—elements all crucial to physics research—China ranks second. China also has large coal reserves.[26] Further north, Siberia holds over 80 percent of Russia's oil, natural gas, coal, precious metal, and diamonds. In many cases, these quantities are estimated to be roughly a quarter of the world reserves.[27]

Further to the south, the region is also resource rich, but the resources are different. South Asia, while not containing vast mineral resources, is rich in arable land and because of its climate is able to produce large quantities of tropical fruits, rice, and other foodstuffs, as well as various hardwoods and lumbers. Because of its major rivers and precipitation, this section of the continent is rich in freshwater.[28]

The vast resources of Asia along with its geography and economic strengths combine to produce a region crucial to global trade. The straits around Singapore, Malaysia, and Indonesia are the busiest in the world and are indispensable to the economies of India, Japan, China, and many of the smaller island nations of the Pacific. Oil, minerals, and lumber, all key components in modern manufacturing, flow through these chokepoints. As such, freedom of navigation and efficient trading mechanisms are of vital interest to many nations in the region.

A Place Where It Is Natural to Have Problems

The importance of the Asia-Pacific region is primarily economic, but at times, US interests are focused on populations. In the past several years, Asia has experienced multiple natural disasters caused by both geological and meteorological phenomena. US interests during and after these events are due, first, to the United States' capacity and desire to supply humanitarian aid. Exhibiting this behavior is one way in which international relations are improved, and Asia abounds in opportunities to display these behaviors. Second, from a standpoint of self-interest, helping partners recover from disasters also prevents economies from collapsing, which, in turn, prevents the disaster from seriously or adversely affecting the regional and global economy. As such, the United States has a multifaceted interest in helping Asia face adversity in all its forms. Asia faces two primary sources of natural disasters: weather and geology.

Among the most severe weather problems in the region are typhoons. So numerous are these that the World Meteorological Organization standard for naming storms is different in this part of the world. In the Atlantic Basin, the presumption is that a single alphabetical list will suffice for each season, and every year the first storm begins with an "A." In the Pacific, the naming of storms merely continues where the last storm left off, with new lists started as needed as a single list would almost never suffice for a season. In May 2008, Cyclone Nargis hit Myanmar. It peaked as a category-four storm on the Saffir-Simpson Scale for tropical systems, though it is depicted as a category-two storm in figure 1.5, below. Nargis made landfall on 2 May 2008, killing a minimum of 80,000 people, with 54,000 more never found.[29] This was not unique. Major storms routinely displace thousands in the region. In December 2011, for example, tropical storm Washi produced heavy rains that eradicated villages and caused tens of thousands to flee their homes.[30]

Figure 1.5. Cyclone Nargis before landfall in Burma. (Photo courtesy of the National Aeronautics and Space Administration.)

Nargis and Washi are not the worst storms to hit the region. On 29 April 1991, a category-four cyclone struck Bangladesh, killing an estimated 138,000 people—a death toll held down by the recent building of storm shelters. These shelters were built in the wake of an earlier cyclone that killed half a million people in Bangladesh in the 1970s.[31] In the case of these cyclones and storms, most of the deaths and destruction were due to flooding, which can also occur in conjunction with the annual monsoon.

The Asian monsoon is really the migration of an area of disturbed weather called the "intertropical convergence zone" as it moves north and south according to the seasons. This zone is where the trade winds collide and is usually rather close to the path of the sun as it migrates between the Tropic of Cancer and the Tropic of Capricorn during the seasonal change. High humidity and rainfall characterize the area. In the Northern Hemisphere summer, this band migrates north and produces the monsoonal rains in India, Bangladesh, and across Southeast Asia.[32] It was this phenomenon that caused the devastating flooding in Thailand in the fall of 2011. The floods submerged the Bangkok airport and parts of its downtown district, caused a 2 percent reduction in Thailand's GDP for the year, killed more than 600 people, and affected more than 13 million others. This event is considered one of the five most expensive disasters in human history.[33]

Asia is plagued by more than just weather issues. Its position on the western edge of the "Ring of Fire" results in geology and plate tectonics creating a wholly different, but yet no less severe, set of frequent natural disasters. Figure 1.6 shows a selected set of earthquakes in the Pacific Basin from 4 February to 1651 Coordinated Universal Time (UTC) on 5 March 2012. Using a Geological Survey tool, the author plotted 6,062 earthquakes with a greater than 0.5 magnitude on the Richter scale during this 30-day period. The color of the plot indicates how recently the earthquake occurred: red is in the past hour, orange denotes the past day, and the various shades of yellow indicate weeks. The size of the square indicates earthquake intensity. The Ring of Fire, delineated by red lines, follows the tectonic plates from the West Coast of North America, around the southern coast of Alaska, down the Japanese archipelago, and then into Indonesia and the Philippines.

While many of these tremors are small, the Asia-Pacific basin frequently experiences catastrophic earthquakes. Since 1 January 2011, 23 major earthquakes of magnitude 7.0 or greater have occurred within the region, including four near Vanuatu, two near Indonesia, one in New Guinea, three just north of New Zealand, one in Fiji, and five on or near the east coast of Honshu Island, Japan, including the catastrophic 9.0-magnitude quake and its first aftershock of magnitude 7.9, both on 11 March 2011.[34]

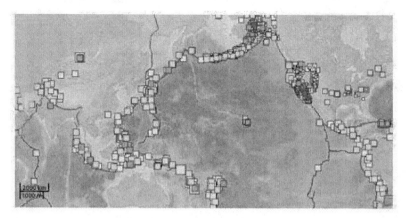

Figure 1.6. Earthquakes in Pacific Basin 4 February–5 March 2012. (Map created by the author using a US Geological Survey tool that allows the display of earthquakes in any region of the world in real time. The tool is available at http://earthquake.usgs.gov/earthquakes /mapping.)

The damage caused by the Japanese earthquake of 2011 was and is creating significant economic challenges both in Japan and in the United States. The earthquake generated tsunami waves measured as high as 38 meters (124.7 feet) in select bays and coves along the Japanese coastline, with many stations reporting surges of 20–50 feet.[35] The tsunami and associated earthquake killed over 15,000 people in Japan, triggering a sequence of events at the Fukushima nuclear power plant that resulted in the evacuation of more than 300,000 people from the vicinity. In addition, the failure of this power plant and others across the country plunged millions into darkness and left 1.5 million households without water.[36] Due to these events and the meltdowns at Fukushima, many manufacturing corporations in Japan had to close operations to save electricity, thus causing parts shortages for automotive and other manufacturers in the United States and the Philippines. As a result, plants closed and workers were laid off. In short, the economic impact was global. In the end, the Japanese stock market plunged 16 percent, and the World Bank estimated total losses at over $230 billion.[37]

This earthquake was the second to equal or surpass magnitude 9 on the Richter scale in the last 10 years. Its predecessor was the 26 December 2004 earthquake just off the coast of Banda Aceh, Indonesia. The Indonesian earthquake also generated massive tsunamis of over 30 meters (100 feet) that washed away homes and businesses and killed over 283,000 people.[38]

The reason that these disasters matter to the United States is two-fold. First, while natural disasters themselves are often unpreventable, proper planning can reduce the amount of damage to infrastructure and to the global economy. An analysis that followed the Japanese earthquake concluded that strategic planning could have prevented many of the issues that led to the loss of electrical power and release of radioactive materials into the Pacific Ocean and atmosphere.[39] A consequence of poor planning at Fukushima was the loss of economic productivity not only for Japan but also for the United States. The United States has a positive economic interest in sharing strategic foresight that enables and enhances planning for these natural disasters. Second, and perhaps more importantly, the US response to these disasters has greatly improved our relations in the region.

When the United States assists nations affected by natural disasters, the people who are helped often develop and retain favorable impressions of the United States and her citizens. In the wake of the earthquake and tsunami in Indonesia, the US government sent $950 million in direct humanitarian assistance to the people of Indonesia, among the top two contributions by any nation.[40] The American response received a great deal of press coverage, particularly as Pres. George W. Bush moved to increase the nation's response from its original $350 million. In addition, charitable donations from the United States were considerable and likely surpassed $1 billion.

The positive press coverage as a result of relief assistance that showed US logos and emblems had a tangible effect on the opinion toward the United States not only in Indonesia but also in places well removed from the disaster in Aceh. For a relatively small investment, the United States reaped great returns in the region.

Popular opinion polling suggests that the relief in the wake of the Indonesian disaster completely shifted the opinions of most Indonesians about the United States in the midst of US operations in the wars both in Afghanistan and Iraq. This is remarkable as much of the population of Indonesia is Muslim, and, as such, the US wars in the Middle East were viewed by some Indonesians as an attack on their faith. The change in opinion was partly driven by the press. Indonesia's weekly news magazine *Tempo* called the giving by Western nations "heartwarming." The goodwill spilled over into negotiations between the government and rebels in the Aceh province, resulting in a peace agreement in 2005.[41] The humanitarian assistance also caused Indonesian public opinion of the United States to change. In 2004, 66 percent of Indonesians had an unfavorable view of the United States. In 2006, for the first time since before the war on terrorism began, a majority of Indonesians viewed the United States favorably.[42] The poll found that 63 percent of Indonesians had changed their views of the United States, with favorable opinions of the United States tripling since the earthquake and tsunami. The full results of the poll are in figure 1.7, below.

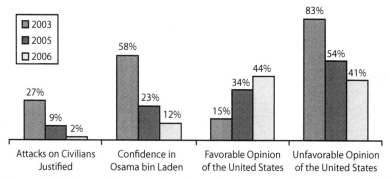

Figure 1.7. Indonesian poll data from before and after tsunami relief efforts. (Reprinted from *One Year Later: Humanitarian Relief Sustains Change in Muslim Public Opinion*, Terror Free Tomorrow Report, 2006, http://www.terrorfreetomorrow.org/upimagestft/INDONESIA%202006 %20Poll%20Report.pdf.)

What is even more interesting is that this same sentiment was replicated in places removed from the disaster. In Pakistan, 78.3 percent of respondents had a more favorable view of the United States because of the relief efforts. The poll also showed that of the respondents, 81.3 percent of Pakistanis felt that American assistance was either very important (40.9 percent) or somewhat important (40.3 percent) in shaping this changed opinion.[43]

Asia is and will always be a region plagued by disasters. Floods, cyclones, earthquakes, tsunamis, and other issues such as illnesses and diseases will remain part of its tapestry. The United States has a vested interest, both economically and diplomatically, in helping the Asia-Pacific region to both better prepare itself to handle these inevitable events and to respond to their occurrence. The American economy is now intertwined with that of the region, so a disaster that affects one will, to some extent, affect all. Further, by being a "good neighbor" and responsibly helping nations recover from nature's fury, the United States gains status as a benevolent power and simultaneously gains respect within the region. As illustrated above, this also translates into respect for America's policy views—a rise in US prestige coincided with a fall in respect for al-Qaeda. As a result—for better and for worse—disasters in Asia matter.

A Military Race . . . but to Where?

Because of the region's economic importance and its frequent interactions caused by trade and disaster relief, security of waterways and even of the Asian landmass has frequently been an issue of concern. Even today, the sovereignty of several areas within the continent and offshore remains unresolved. Disputed territory exists between India and Pakistan in Kashmir; the regions of Aksai Chin and parts of Arunachal Pradesh are disputed between India and China; several Bhutanese enclaves in Tibet are disputed between China and Bhutan; boundary disputes exist between India and Bangladesh; the Hibernia Reef is disputed between Australia and Indonesia; and there are several boundary disputes in the South China Sea that involve China, Vietnam, Brunei, the Philippines, and Malaysia—and this is not an exhaustive list.

Many of these border disputes have little economic importance yet have precipitated conflict. For example, the Aksai Chin dispute is over an inhospitable and ungovernable piece of territory on the border with Tibet. Survey maps as recently as the middle of the last century labeled the region as "area unexplored" and "undemarcated boundary."[44] In one case, previously blank spaces on maps in the mid-1930s were filled in, perhaps merely by creative guesswork since the terrain features added did not match findings in subsequent expeditions.[45] Negotiations in the 1950s between India and China did not resolve the disputes over the territory but eventually did clarify where each nation viewed the boundary to be. The region's inaccessibility makes Askai Chin unimportant both geologically and from a standpoint of resources, yet when Indian forces found Chinese military forces clearly on their side of the disputed boundary, the forces felt compelled to engage their Chinese counterparts—leading to the Sino-Indian war of 1962.

More recently, some of these border disputes have been discovered to have significant economic importance, and their lack of resolution is hampering development of the region. The disputed region encompassing the Spratly Islands is one case in point. Here, within 200 miles of the Philippines, in what the Philippine government views as its exclusive economic zone, oil drilling was to begin in 2012. The government in Manila wants to open new tracts of the seabed off the island of Palawan for exploration, a process to which China has formally objected. China argues that some of the Spratly Islands, many of which are small rocky outcroppings of land visible only at low tide, are humanly habitable and as such seeks to extend its 200-mile exclusive economic zone into the region where Manila wants to drill.[46] As this dispute has not yet been decided under the 1982 United Nations Convention on the Law of the Sea, economic development is impossible.[47]

The Spratly Islands challenge may be the most intractable and contentious in the region. China has published its "nine-dash map" of the South China Sea, where it claims almost the entire sea as its territorial waters. The title comes from the nine dashes in what is a dashed boundary that demarks China's territorial waters from those of other nations, shown on maps used to teach school in China today (figure 1.8). These nine dashes demark a territory that includes the Paracel and Spratly Islands; covers over 80 percent of the South China Sea; and hugs the coast of Malaysia, Brunei, the Philippines, Vietnam, and Indonesia. Within the Chinese claim is Pag-asa Island, one of the largest in the group, on which the Philippines currently maintains a small village. Pag-asa is, incidentally, near where Manila seeks to drill for oil.

While most of these disputes have been quiescent over the past decade, concern over Asia's future appears to be driving increasing investment in military capabilities. For the first time in modern history, Asian defense spending has surpassed that of Europe. China, Japan, India, South Korea, and Australia are the key drivers of defense spending in the region but are not the only ones.[48] Indonesia is increasing defense spending in 2012 by 35 percent in an effort to modernize the military as a deterrent both to terrorism and to overcome "potential military aggression," according to Pres. Susilo Bambang Yudhoyono.[49] This buildup includes a $1.1 billion contract for at least 10 new submarines for the Indonesian navy.[50] Similarly, Singa-

pore's military spending, at 4.5 percent of GDP, is one of the largest—
per capita—in the world. Totaling over $7 billion in 2012, its military
expenditure is larger than that of its neighbors Malaysia ($5 billion)
and Indonesia ($4 billion) but reflects Singapore's realist view of in-
ternational relations and the importance of South Asian geography.[51]

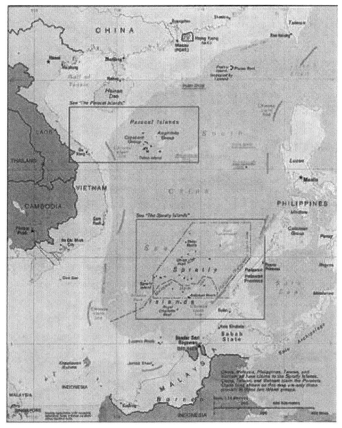

Figure 1.8. Map of the nine-dashed line claim of China. (Map courtesy
of the University of Texas at Austin Perry-Castañeda Library Map Collection, http://www.lib.utexas.edu/maps/asia.html.)

China's defense spending also continues to grow rapidly—a trend
that has been under way for approximately 20 years. In 1993 China's
military spending showed a real decrease of about 2 percent. Since
that time, increases of 9 percent per year in real terms (over 30 percent in 1994) have been consistent.[52] Recent increases in Asian de-

fense spending can be seen in figure 1.9 but indicate that the upward trend continues across the region and on an exponential path.[53]

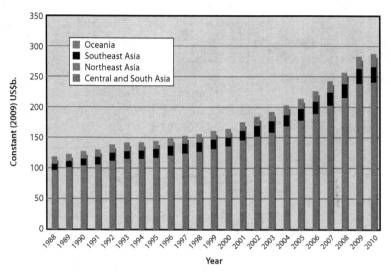

Figure 1.9. Asia military spending by subregion in Asia and Oceania 1988–2010. (*Reprinted from* "Asia and Oceania: Military Expenditure in Asia and Oceania by Subregion, 1988–2010," Stockholm International Peace Institute Database and Graphics Archives, http://www.sipri.org/research/armaments/milex/resultoutput/regional/Milex_asia_ocean.)

Looking outward over the next 10–20 years, no decrease in Asian defense spending is expected. Spending by the major nations across the region should remain on an exponential curve, with China likely becoming the predominant ascendant military power in the region.[54] Indeed, it is possible that in the next 20 years, China may emerge as a peer or near peer to the United States in the region both on the ground and in the air.[55] Meanwhile, India will be investing heavily in procurement to protect its interests in the region, putting perhaps as much as $100 billion in procurement in the next 10 years alone.[56]

This increased spending in Asia does not necessarily mean conflict is inevitable. Indeed, many scenarios have been examined where armed conflict need not occur.[57] Yet the navies, armies, and air forces within the region are receiving large investments as territorial disputes and access to economically lucrative resources may hang in the balance. Asia may be in the midst of its own arms race. If so, while not as fast as that of the Cold War, it is moving apace nonetheless. The question for this race is, A race to where? This is but one of many unanswered questions central to the study of the Asia-Pacific. To that end, the Air Force Research Institute (AFRI) held a global conference on the Asia-Pacific region in December 2011. In support of AFRI's year-long study of the region, a number of the participating scholars contributed the chapters that follow.

These chapters encapsulate some of the most current thinking on the region, with a clear focus on the future. While forecasting economic, military, and political events is fraught with danger, the contributors were asked to look a decade out to provide the US Air Force (USAF) a view of the region that will enable the service to develop a strategic approach best suited to meet the demands of coming years.

As part of that effort, Adam Lowther, in chapter 2, discusses the data collected at the conference held at the Air University on 6–7 December 2011. He presents the results of not only panel discussions in which conference attendees participated in structured focus groups but also a modified Delphi study using the most senior scholars speaking at the conference.[58] In conducting focus groups and a modified Delphi, Lowther captured contemporary thinking on the Asia-Pacific from the perspective of experienced academics, businesspeople, policy practitioners, and military service members.

Chapter 3 offers a broad overview of economic integration in the Asia-Pacific by comparing key economic variables for six of the region's leading economies—Australia, China, India, Japan, Korea, and the United States. According to Brooks Robinson, military conflict over the coming decade is highly unlikely because the countries of the region are well aware of its negative economic impact. Thus, they are actively avoiding the militarization of disputes—instead settling disagreements through peaceful means.

Chad Dacus takes a different tack in exploring economic issues in the region. He suggests in chapter 4 that there is a potential for China to adopt economic policies that not only maximize economic opportunities but minimize real or perceived strategic threats through the use of soft economic warfare. While Dacus does not state that such policies are inevitable, he does suggest how the Chinese government might employ such tactics.

Taking a very different view of Chinese actions, Simon Reich suggests that American realist pessimists are overstating the potential threat China poses to US leadership in the international system.

Rather, chapter 5 explains why power transition theory and hegemonic stability theory are poor theoretical foundations upon which to ground an understanding of Chinese behavior and intentions. Reich believes China's actions—particularly its economic policy—exemplify those of a country bolstering the current international system—not those of a country seeking to alter the status quo.

Justin Logan also focuses on the US-China relationship in chapter 6. He explains how the current policy of "congagement" is shrinking the power gap between the United States and China while also infantilizing America's allies and friends in the region. Logan suggests that the United States alter its policy, placing more responsibility for their own security on the shoulders of Asian nations, while the United States becomes an "offshore balancer."

In chapter 7, Dhirendra Vajpeyi offers a uniquely Indian perspective on the complex relationship that exists among China, India, and the United States. He presents an overview of the motivations and ambitions of each country and the dynamics at work in the bilateral relationships among the three. Vajpeyi concludes by providing recommendations for American leaders as they seek to manage the rise of China.

Analyzing the role of Asian states as China rises, Rajeswari Pillai Rajagopalan argues in chapter 8 that China appears to have veered from its "peaceful development" strategy. As a result, he recommends that the United States, India, Russia, and Japan explore combined partnerships to act as a counterbalance to China in the Asia-Pacific region.

Sanu Kainikara provides a distinctly Australian view of regional security in chapter 9. In a succinct summary of Australian national interests, Kainikara explains what matters most, why, and how Australia will pursue its interests in the years ahead. He also provides a regional view of the Sino-American relationship.

With the potential for conflict in the South China Sea of great concern to many analysts, Sheldon Simon's overview of the various territorial disputes in chapter 10 is instructive. As these waters prove an increasing hot spot for a number of nations, understanding the dynamics of the multiple conflicts is important for American policy makers. In covering the two options for resolving existing disputes (diplomatic and military), Simon advocates the use of diplomacy to deescalate disagreements and reach a final resolution. He also advocates a positive role for the United States in resolving current disputes.

Stephen Cimbala examines the potential for nuclear arms racing in the Asia-Pacific over the coming years in chapter 11. He then employs nuclear stability models that look at the potential for first-strike escalation. Based on the insecurity of nuclear powers in the region, Cimbala sees the real potential for nuclear conflict there—a sobering prospect.

Turning to perhaps the region's longest ongoing strategic challenge, Kimberly Gill and Tom Dolan examine the prospects for reunification on the Korean Peninsula in chapter 12. Contrary to many Korea watchers, Gill and Dolan do not believe that a conflict on the peninsula is likely. Instead, they see the major challenge as finding the most cost-effective and stabilizing method for reunifying the two Koreas. The focus of their paper is an analysis of the available options.

Finally, Adam Lowther narrows his focus in chapter 13 to the USAF's partnership-building efforts. He suggests that it is on its soft-power capabilities that the Air Force is likely to increasingly rely as the nation seeks to shape the region. And, contrary to the views of many Airmen, these soft-power missions are a particular specialty of the USAF.

In the end, what is evident is that a major shift from West to East is under way. Just as the global leadership moved from Europe to North America in the 1900s, so, too, will it migrate across the Pacific to Asia during this century. As it does so, the United States has a strong economic and military interest in shaping this shift in a manner that results in free and unimpeded commerce across the whole of the Asia-Pacific basin—goals that are of mutual benefit to all nations. Further, the tectonic and meteorological instability that causes major disasters provides the United States with opportunities to prove to the region that while America may be a superpower or even a hyperpower, it remains a benevolent one. Thus, while arms spending may increase within the region, the real arms race is not one to preeminence for any one state, but ideally to a point where mutual respect and an end to economic piracy is achieved by all.

Notes

1. Douglas Harper, "Online Etymology Dictionary," s.v. "sterling," http://www.etymonline.com/index.php?allowed_in_frame=0&search= sterling&searchmode=none.

2. John Wilson, "Noctes Ambrosianae No. 42," *Blackwood's Edinburgh Magazine* 25 (April 1829): 527.

3. The British Empire is usually said to have crumbled in the wake of the Suez crisis of 1956. Historian Corelli Barnett discusses this at length in his book *The Collapse of British Power* (London: Morrow, 1972).

4. Henry Luce was the first to use this term. See his article, "The American Century," *Life Magazine* 10, no. 7 (17 February 1941): 61–65.

5. The US gross domestic product (GDP) rose from approximately $200 billion in 1940 to $300 billion in 1950. Christopher Conte and Albert R. Karr, *An Outline of the U.S. Economy* (Washington, DC: US Department of State, 2001). The United States' monopoly on nuclear weapons was short lived, ending in August 1949 with the test of Первая молния, or Pervaya Molniya (First Lightning). See Martin Zuberi, "Stalin and the Bomb," *Strategic Analysis* 23, no. 7 (October 1999): 1133–1153; and Joseph A. Angelo, *The Facts on File Space and Astronomy Handbook* (New York: Infobase, 2008), 243.

6. The original use of the word *hyperpower* appears to come from an interview in 1999 with French foreign minister Hubert Vedrine. Initially quoted in the *International Herald Tribune*, it is also referred to in "To Paris, U.S. Looks Like a 'Hyperpower,'" *New York Times*, 5 February 1999, http://www.nytimes.com/1999/02/05/news/05iht -france.t_0.html.

7. Wilhelm Fucks, *Formeln zur Macht* [*Formulas for Power*] (Stuttgart, West Germany: Deutsche Verlags-Anstalt, 1965).

8. Joseph A. Engelbrecht Jr. et al., *Alternate Futures for 2025: Security Planning to Avoid Surprise* (Maxwell AFB, AL: Air University Press, April 1996), 73, http://www .bibliotecapleyades.net/archivos_pdf/2025_monograms_b.pdf. This colossus was called "King Khan," one of six alternative futures that underpinned the *Air Force 2025* study.

9. International Monetary Fund (IMF), *World Economic Outlook: April 2011: Tensions from the Two-Speed Recovery: Unemployment, Commodities, and Capital Flows*, occasional paper (Washington, DC: IMF, 2011).

10. The term *Asian Millennium* comes from Engelbrecht et al., "Alternate Futures for 2025," 70.

11. The Obama administration described the president's nine-day tour of Asia in late 2011 as a "pivot" in US foreign policy. See David Nakamura and William Wan, "Obama Heads to Asia Focused on China's Power," *Washington Post*, 11 November 2011, http://www.washingtonpost.com/world/obama-heads-to-asia-with-sharp -focus-on-chinas-growing-power/2011/11/10/gIQAOsQkBN_story_1.html.

12. Hong Kong was still a British protectorate during this period. See Robert Garran, *Tigers Tamed: The End of the Asian Miracle* (Honolulu, HI: University of Hawaii Press, 1998), 1–5.

13. Paul Krugman, "The Myth of Asia's Miracle," *Foreign Affairs* 73, no. 6 (November/December 1994): 64.

14. Garran, *Tigers Tamed*, 1–7.

15. Nicola Bullard, Walden Bellow, and Kamal Mallhotra, "Taming the Tigers: The IMF and the Asian Crisis," *Third World Quarterly* 19, no. 3 (1998): 505–56.

16. Ibid.; and Garran, *Tigers Tamed*, 5–21.

17. Statistic comes from the UK organization GeoHive. Its data is published online at http://www.geohive.com/default.aspx.

18. Discussions of several regional economic predictions can be found in John P. Geis II et al., *Discord or "Harmonious Society"?: China in 2030*, Occasional Paper no. 68, Center for Strategy and Technology, Air War College (Maxwell AFB, AL: Air University Press, February 2011), 47–70.

19. Tushar Poddar, chief Indian economist, Global Research Division, Goldman Sachs, "A View from India," February 2012, video, 2:21, http://www.goldmansachs .com/our-thinking/global-economic-outlook/a-view-from-india/index.html.

20. Goldman Sachs Global Economics Group, ed., *BRICs [Brazil, Russia, India, China] and Beyond* (New York: Goldman Sachs, 2007), 149–51. India and the United States share a projected GDP in constant dollars of approximately $38 trillion, with China above $70 trillion. India's growth rate is estimated to be at 5.3 percent and fairly constant vice a 2.5 percent and falling growth rate for China. If such rates and trends were to continue beyond 2050, India would surpass China as the world's largest economy in the 2060–2080 time frame. (Ibid.)

21. Jean-Paul Rodrigue, "Straits, Passages and Chokepoints: A Maritime Geostrategy of Petroleum Distribution," *Les Cahiers de géographie du Québec* 48, no. 135 (December 2004): 357–74.

22. C. S. Kuppuswamy, "Straits of Malacca: Security Implications," Paper no. 1033, South Asia Analysis Group, 18 June 2004, http://www.southasiaanalysis .org/%5Cpapers11%5Cpaper1033.html.

23. "World Oil Transit Chokepoints," 30 December 2011, US Energy Information Administration, http://www.eia.gov/cabs/world_oil_ transit_chokepoints/Full.html.

24. Ibid.

25. Asian Development Bank, *Central Asia Atlas of Natural Resources* (Manila, Philippines: Asian Development Bank, 2010), http://beta.adb.org/sites/default/files /pub/2010/central-asia-atlas.pdf.

26. "Natural Conditions," *China Facts and Figures 2004*, China.org, http://www .china.org.cn/english/en-shuzi2004/zr/zrzy.htm.

27. Fiona Hill, "Siberia: Russia's Economic Heartland and Daunting Dilemma," *Current History*, October 2004, 324–31.

28. Andreas Neef, Tongroj Onchan, and Rainer Schwarzmeier, "Access to Natural Resources in Mainland Southeast Asia and Implications for Sustaining Rural Livelihoods—the Case of Thailand," *Quarterly Journal of International Agriculture* 42, no. 3 (2003): 329–50.

29. "In Myanmar, Loss, Grief and, for Some, Resignation," *New York Times*, 27 May 2008, http://www.nytimes.com/2008/05/27/world/asia/27scene.html?_r=1&ref= cyclonenargis.

30. The Phillippines alone averages nearly 20 typhoons per year. See "Philippines Storm Kills Hundreds in Mindanao Floods," BBC News Asia-Pacific, 17 December 2011, http://www.bbc.co.uk/news/world-asia-pacific-16229394.

31. *India Weather Review 1970, Annual Summary, Part C—Storms and Depressions*, published by the Indian Weather Agency, copy submitted to the National Oceanographic and Atmospheric Administration for archiving in February 2000, http://docs.lib.noaa.gov/rescue/cd024_pdf/005ED281.pdf#page=10.

32. One of the better descriptions of the Asian monsoon for the average person comes from the National Environmental Agency (NEA) of Singapore. See *WEATHER-*

wise Singapore (Meteorological Services Division, NEA, 2009), 9–17, http://app2.nea
.gov.sg/data/cmsresource/20090721544571208250.pdf.

33. The World Bank estimates that as of January 2012, the flooding in Thailand has cost 45.7 billion US dollars. Based on a 2011 report by Accuweather, this would place the Thailand flooding event in fourth place, just below Hurricane Katrina (but above the Northridge earthquake) in the list of most expensive disasters. See Bo Zhang, "Top 5 Most Expensive Natural Disasters in History," Accuweather.com, 30 March 2011, http://www.accuweather.com/en/weather-news/top-5-most-expensive -natural-d/47459. See also The World Bank, "The World Bank Supports Thailand's Post-Floods Recovery Effort," 13 December 2011, http://www.worldbank.org.

34. "2011 Significant Earthquake and News Headlines Archive," United States Geological Survey website, accessed 30 April 2012, http://earthquake.usgs.gov.

35. There are numerous reports from eye witnesses as well as survey teams that wave heights in the Iwate Prefecture reached approximately 38 meters. Among these are the 4 April 2011 editions of the *Japan Times* and the 3 April 2011 edition of the *Kyodo News*.

36. "Millions of Stricken Japanese Lack Water, Food, Heat," National Public Radio (NPR), 14 March 2011. NPR and its wire service news providers estimated 1.5 million households were without water.

37. Victoria Kim, "Japan Damage Could Reach $235 Billion, World Bank Estimates," *Los Angeles Times*, 21 March 2011, http://www.latimes.com/business/la-fgw -japan-quake-world-bank-20110322,0,3799976.story.

38. R. Paris et al., "Costal Sedimentation Associated with the December 26, 2004 Tsunami in Lhok Nga, West Banda Aceh (Sumatra, Indonesia)," *Marine Geology* 238, no. 14 (March 2007): 93–106. See also "Magnitude 9.1 off the West Coast of Northern Sumatra: Sunday, December 26, 2004 at 00:58:53 UTC," US Geological Survey, 15 February 2005, http://neic.usgs.gov/neis/eq_depot/2004/eq_041226/neic_slav_nr.html.

39. Yoichi Funabashi and Kay Kitazawa, "Fukushima in Review: A Complex Disaster, a Disastrous Response," *Bulletin of the Atomic Scientists* 68, no. 2 (March/April 2012): 9–21.

40. By some accounts, Australia may have contributed as much as $1.2 billion (US dollars) of assistance, which would make it the top contributor of disaster aid to the region.

41. Michael Kugelman, *One Year after the Tsunami: Policy and Public Perceptions*, Woodrow Wilson International Center for Scholars Asia Program Special Report, May 2006, http://www.wilsoncenter.org/sites/default/files/FinalAsiaReport_130.pdf.

42. Ibid.; and "2006 Poll: Humanitarian Relief Sustains Change in Muslim Public Opinion," Terror Free Tomorrow, http://www.terrorfreetomorrow.org/articlenav .php?id=82.

43. "2006 Poll," Terror Free Tomorrow.

44. Ron E. Hassner, "The Path to Intractability: Time and the Entrenchment of Territorial Disputes," *International Security* 31, no. 3 (Winter 2006/7): 107–38.

45. Ibid. Hassner refers here to the location of the Yangi Dawan pass, which even on the official map was accompanied by a question mark. In the map of 1990, the only difference is that the question mark was removed, as was the word *pass*.

46. Some of the Spratly Islands are large enough to maintain small settlements. Pag-asa Island is currently controlled by the Philippines. It consists of a small town

and a staff of two officers and is large enough to host a small gravel airstrip. Pag-asa is one of the four largest islands in the Spratly "Archipelago."

47. Robert Beckman, "The China-Philippines Dispute in the South China Sea: Does Beijing Have a Legitimate Claim?," S. Rajaratnam School of International Studies (RSIS) Commentary Paper no. 36/2012, 7 March 2012.

48. James Blitz, "Asia Defence Spending Overtakes Europe," *Financial Times*, 7 March 2012, http://www.ft.com/cms/s/0/0aab435c-6846-11e1-a6cc-00144feabdc0 .html#axzz1oRpN78UZ.

49. Arientha Primanita, Ezra Sihite, and Faisal Baskoro, "Indonesia Pledges to Raise Defense Spending," *Jakarta Globe,* 6 October 2011, http://www.thejakart aglobe.com/news/indonesia-pledges-to-raise-defense-spending/469853.

50. Koh Swee Lean Collin, "Indonesia's Submarine Play," *Diplomat*, 19 January 2012, http://the-diplomat.com/flashpoints-blog/2012/01/19/indonesia%E2%80%99s -submarine-play.

51. Bernard F. W. Loo, "Singapore Defense Spending under Scrutiny," Military Studies at RSIS, 18 February 2011, http://rsismilitarystudies.wordpress.com/2011/02 /18/singapores-defence-spending-under-scrutiny.

52. Keith Crane et al., *Modernizing China's Military: Opportunities and Constraints* (Santa Monica, CA: RAND, 2005), 100–109.

53. "Asia and Oceania: Military Expenditure in Asia and Oceania by Subregion, 1988–2010," Stockholm International Peace Research Institute, military expenditure database, http://www.sipri.org/research/armaments/milex/resultoutput/regional /Milex_asia_ocean.

54. Yong Sup Han, "Changing Security Threats: Future Asian Armies in 2030," in *Imagining Asia in 2030: Trends, Scenarios, and Alternatives*, eds. Ajey Lele and Namrata Goswami (New Delhi, India: The Academic Foundation, 2011), 339–50.

55. John P. Geis, "Asian Air Power in 2030: Capabilities and Technologies Required for Potential Future Scenarios," in *Imagining Asia in 2030,* 351–84.

56. Vijay Sakhuja, "Asian Navies: Trends towards 2030," in *Imagining Asia in 2030*, 386–401.

57. Geis et al., *Discord or "Harmonious Society"?*, 132.

58. The method is named after the ancient oracle at Delphi from which the nomenclature of the participants is derived. The methodology used is from work by Olaf Helmer, Norman Dalkey, and Nicholas Rescher, who all were leaders in refining this method while working at RAND in the 1960s.

Chapter 2

Thinking about the Asia-Pacific

Dr. Adam Lowther
Research Professor, Air Force Research Institute

Introduction

When Secretary of State Hillary Clinton published "America's Pacific Century" in *Foreign Policy* magazine in November 2011, the administration was clearly indicating to domestic and international audiences that the United States is beginning a pivot toward the Asia-Pacific, away from Europe and—to a lesser degree—the Middle East.[1] While the United States will remain a superpower with interests and responsibilities that span the globe, Mrs. Clinton's article serves as a spark for renewed interest in the nation's Asia-Pacific strategy. For those concerned with the region, this is a positive move.

Tasked by the Air Force chief of staff, Gen Norton Schwartz, to offer one take on the elements of a US Air Force strategy for the region, Air Force Research Institute (AFRI) faculty spent fiscal year 2012 examining Asia-Pacific issues. The objective in conducting the research is simple: provide the Air Force with insight into the challenges and opportunities the service may face as it increasingly focuses on the Asia-Pacific. Achieving a viable strategy in the Asia-Pacific requires forward-looking thinking.[2] Toward that end, this chapter provides an analysis of data collected for AFRI's Asia-Pacific strategy development project.

The Delphi Method and Analysis

In support of this effort, AFRI hosted the conference "The Asia-Pacific Century: Overcoming the Strategy Gap" on 6–7 December 2011 at Maxwell Air Force Base, Alabama. Over 150 American and international attendees from academia, industry, think tanks, foreign militaries, US Pacific Command, Headquarters Air Force, and every Air Force major command participated in a series of focus/working groups that examined critical diplomatic, informational, military, and economic variables significant in shaping the Asia-Pacific. Furthermore, the AFRI team invited 16 senior experts to take part in a modified Delphi study exploring important variables affecting the Asia-Pacific; key regional trends; and best, worst, and most likely "alternative paths" in the Asia-Pacific. Data collected from the working groups and the modified Delphi provided a wealth of information, offering an excellent sense of thinking on the region.

Delphi Methodology

Developed by the RAND Corporation in the early 1950s, the Delphi method seeks "to obtain the most reliable consensus of opinion of a group of experts [through] a series of intensive questionnaires interspersed with controlled opinion feedback."[3] In its original design, the Delphi method required a group of experts—also known as oracles—to answer a series of forward-looking questions while physically separate from all other participants. Researchers used anonymity not only to prevent direct confrontation between experts but also to keep participants with the greatest reputation, strongest personality, and most vocal opinion from dominating the discussion. After each round of questioning was completed, the anonymous responses were shared among the experts for further discussion. After group members went through several rounds, the objective was for them to reach a degree of consensus on the future.[4] The Delphi method's underlying purpose is to improve the quality of expert analysis.[5]

The 16 experts employed in this Delphi group are experienced Asia-Pacific specialists from American and Asian universities, think tanks, and militaries. International contributors ensured that an American perspective did not dominate. Experts completed questionnaires and debated responses in a common setting—unlike in a traditional Delphi. The lack of anonymity as well as more interaction and unstructured discussion deviate from the original design of the Delphi method. Thus, the data collection method used here falls within the category of a modified, versus the classic, Delphi method.[6] Experts were asked to complete a 32-question survey on a wide range of variables, trends, and futures currently or potentially affecting the Asia-Pacific. Questions were scored on a five-point Likert scale with "strongly disagree" and "strongly agree" representing opposite ends of the scale. Group members then openly debated the variables after individually completing each questionnaire. The results were then tabulated and reported to the participants for further discussion.

Delphi Analysis

The results of the Delphi group responses are divided into three categories: variables, trends, and alternative paths.

Variables. Participants did not generally agree about the likely impact of many variables between 2012 and 2020. This lack of consensus serves to highlight the need for further work on Asia-Pacific strategy and for a better understanding of the who, what, when, where, why, and how of change in the region.

Of prime concern to many is the stability of the relationship between the People's Republic of China (PRC) and the Republic of China (ROC), or Taiwan. Some experts agree that stability is likely to depend on the leaders of each country. For example, should a leader who insists upon reunification ascend to power in Mainland China, the probability of conflict increases. Similarly, should either of the main political parties in Taiwan take a strong pro-independence position or move toward independence, the likelihood of conflict also increases. Beyond this point, the group did not concur about the future of the China-Taiwan relationship.

Participants are also uncertain regarding the stability of the current regime in North Korea. Reaching consensus on the prospects for regime collapse within the next decade proved difficult. The group was almost evenly split between those who think collapse was likely and those who think it unlikely. Those who believe the regime would remain in power did not believe that the PRC would allow the Kim regime to fail.

The regional presence of violent Islamic fundamentalists and other terrorist groups as a strategic concern for the United States is a third variable where consensus proved difficult. Some experts view the terror threat as a declining concern. Those who think terrorism would remain a strategic risk for the United States see the Arab Spring and the potential for a number of Islamist governments to take power in the Middle East as a reason for renewed apprehension in Asia's Muslim countries.

Whether major powers in the region would employ surrogates in irregular conflict as a means of avoiding direct confrontation with one another is a final variable about which experts dissent. While a majority thinks that this is unlikely, some agree that irregular warfare may persist across the region. Such conflicts are, however, unlikely to reflect those of the Cold War, where the United States and Soviet

Union used proxies. Instead, local grievances are likely to drive future irregular conflicts. Most of the experts believe that conflict in the Asia-Pacific will remain intrastate.

One variable where experts reached consensus involves the probability of US bilateral and multilateral relations playing a critical role in supporting—although not guaranteeing—stability and prosperity across the Asia-Pacific region. Many in this group agree that including China, India, and Russia in multilateral efforts is central to any US engagement strategy. Given the power and proximity of each country, the United States' decisions must be weighed with clear consideration of how each is likely to perceive American action.

Experts unanimously agree that US trade with Asia-Pacific nations will expand over the next decade. There was some disagreement, however, as to whether this constitutes a vital national interest. Some suggest that the vast majority of this growth may be focused narrowly on just a few of the region's 49 countries, such as China and India.

One final area of concurrence deserves mention. Participants agree that the United States is likely to find itself engaged in a major humanitarian assistance operation in the Asia-Pacific within the next decade. This effort will be an operation of choice and may be the result of environment change or the region's seismic instability. Whatever the cause, there was some dispute as to whether the United States will have the capabilities required to provide the needed assistance.

While there are certainly many more variables affecting the region, those mentioned above were central to the discussion among experts. A second area of discussion was a series of trends occurring across the region and their relative importance in shaping the Asia-Pacific. As with the discussion of variables, experts hold divergent opinions.

Trends. The discussion of trends begins with a look at areas of dissention among group members. Delphi group members disagree with the popular perception that global influence (economic and military) will continue to shift from West to East. While a majority hold this view, others believe that the West will play a larger role than its relative economic and demographic size would indicate. Some experts believe that growth in the Asia-Pacific may be overstated, as are expected growth rates over the next decade. If true, this circumstance could mitigate the eastward movement of influence.

Related to the previous trend, group members disagree about the continued movement of the region's poorest citizens out of poverty. Rather, some believe that the income gap will increase. With population growth at its highest in the poorest countries, economic growth will be unable to keep up with population growth. Similarly, no consensus was reached about the role technological access will have in the region—with the exception of China. Thus, technological access and economic growth are seen as tools of limited utility in alleviating mass poverty.

For trends related to defense and national security, participant views do not coincide on either the shifting strategic balance or the future of interstate conflict. In the case of defense, experts diverge concerning the true scope of the challenge to US military power. While low-end capabilities are expected to proliferate, those that pose a risk to American dominance are viewed as far less likely to exist in numbers sufficient to threaten US military superiority before 2020. In the case of national security, experts believe that competition over natural resources in the South China Sea and a border dispute between India and China present an interstate conflict risk, while the risk of intrastate conflict remains because of poverty, illiberal regimes, and related factors.

Finally, with globalization firmly rooted in the Asia-Pacific, the experts consider the effects of the move to just-in-time supply chain management should a local supply chain disruption occur. Many do not see a growing dependence on the just-in-time approach as a threat to the global economy for two reasons. First, alternative suppliers are often available. Second, with countries such as China, India, and Japan principally producing consumer goods (with noted exceptions), experts think that consumers would find alternative products or wait out delays. Thus, little consensus was reached concerning potential threats resulting from the interconnectedness of the modern global economy.

Experts did, however, reach a consensus on a number of trends. They widely agree that integration within the Asia-Pacific will continue but will be accompanied by increased competition among nations. Similarly, they agree that capital flows to and across the region will grow, depending on a country's economic stability and prospects.

Three trends stand out in the defense and national security arena. First, experts agree that the United States will remain the greatest power in the region but can expect to face continued economic, military, and political challenges from Asia-Pacific countries pursuing their own interests. If countries choose to bandwagon with the United States, American power will appear greater for a longer period of time.

In their desire to supplant the United States, future adversaries will acquire and/or develop increasingly complex technologies that diminish American capabilities. This task will grow easier as barriers to access and price decline. Reverse engineering, espionage, and domestic development are all playing a role in the technological empowerment of potential adversaries.

Consensus on two final trends deserves mention. First, countries such as China and India are experiencing a rapid economic growth enabling some of their citizens to move out of poverty. Second, and related, this growth creates an acute demand for food and clean water, which governments must find ways to provide or risk creating internal instability.

Alternative Paths. For the final area of the modified Delphi, AFRI researchers provided group members with best, worst, and most likely case scenarios—alternative paths—for analysis.[7] Experts revised these scenarios through the Delphi method's iterative process, arriving at three alternative paths with the following distinctive characteristics.

In a best-case alternative path, nations operate within international norms, abiding by international treaties and following established international law. Also, multinational organizations—such as the World Trade Organization (WTO), Association of South East Asian Nations (ASEAN), and Asia-Pacific Economic Cooperation (APEC) forum—play a central role in providing an institutional framework for economic and political cooperation, thus mitigating potential conflict. While each nation's interests will vary, economic, resource, and other forms of competition will not devolve into military conflict but be resolved in ways that are amicable, if imperfect. In a best case, a regionwide focus on economic growth, social progress, cultural development, and environmental concerns will serve as a check on conflict while the United States plays an important role as a facilitator and—if necessary—guarantor of stability.

In a worst-case alternative path, the regional state of affairs is the opposite. Rather than Asia-Pacific nations—particularly the region's most powerful—working within a multilateral framework where international rules and norms constrain the aggressive pursuit of national interests, the region is rife with conflict. Whether it is the quest for natural resources in the South China Sea, a border dispute between India and China, or any of a long list of old antagonisms, the peaceful resolution of disputes fails. In such a case, economic growth falters across the region, making competition more intense and explosive. With the stakes seemingly higher, nations are willing to go to greater lengths to defend their interests.

The most likely alternative path is—in many ways—somewhere in between. The rapid economic growth fueling dramatic transformation in the Asia-Pacific will continue over the next decade but may slow. For example, China may see its economic growth move from 9 or 10 percent annually to 7 or 8 percent—well above that of the United States. Growing economic and military powers such as China and India will periodically seek to assert themselves through show-of-force operations while avoiding conflict. Although countries across the region are likely to modernize their militaries—often in response to a growing and confident China—an Asian arms race is unlikely. For some countries, drawing closer to the United States will prove attractive, while others will take a neutral position in great-power politics as they pursue their own economic and security interests. Although the possibility for conflicts between states exists, they are likely to remain intrastate.

In each of the three alternative paths, experts were unwilling to speculate on characteristics or events that were highly improbable but of potentially great consequence—the proverbial black swan. Instead, they walked down each path focused on the impact a potential change would have on the region. Thus, the three cases do not include more dramatic or unusual possibilities. They are, however, potentially closer to a likely regional outlook that the United States can effectively plan to face.

Focus Group Analysis

While the modified Delphi provides valuable information, the use of focus groups further enriches the breadth and depth of the data collected. Over 150 attendees from around the globe and across the military, academia, and industry participated in a series of focus/working groups where they discussed a number of questions addressing economic, military, and political issues facing the region.

Conference attendees were organized into about a dozen focus groups of approximately 10 each, with careful attention paid to dispersing them evenly based on their professional demographics—including skills and experience.[8] Air University faculty members received facilitator training in the days prior to the event and led the groups. Each group also had a recorder responsible for documenting the discussion using a standardized spreadsheet.[9] At the beginning of each of the four focus group sessions, facilitators gave participants 15 minutes to answer short surveys of four to five questions. They then spent one hour in a discussion of the questions and were then given time at the end of the session to modify their initial answers.[10] Data collected across the focus groups provides insight into the thinking of a broad group of experienced professionals, often working on Asia-Pacific issues at the operational and strategic levels. Several themes emerged.[11]

Strategic Challenges: Session One

Session one asked panelists to address four questions:

1. How is the balance of power shifting in the Asia-Pacific?
2. What is the potential for another cold war in the region?
3. What is the probability that the rise of regional powers will promote stability?
4. What transnational threats will the region face?

Unlike with the Delphi method, there was no purposeful effort to reach consensus in the focus groups. However, clear themes appear in examining responses to these questions.

For question one, more than two-thirds of respondents focus on the impact of China—as a rising power—in reshaping the balance of power over the next decade. Many see the United States as a power in decline and one that could play the role of balancer in a competitive region where China and India dominate. A minority suggest that Japan will remain an important player in the region and is a country that can't be forgotten. Arguably, Japan is, and will remain, the most technologically advanced nation in the world.

Almost one-third of participants are concerned with the role North Korea will play in the region given its erratic behavior and nuclear weapons. The role of smaller countries, such as Vietnam, Australia, and Singapore, was also a point of discussion. For many, the United States and Australia will play a central role in building alliances or partnerships with Asia-Pacific nations seeking to balance against China. India, the region's other great power, is largely seen as friendly toward—but not as an ally with—the United States and benign in regional affairs. In short, a perceptible shift in the balance of power is expected, but the degree to which the United States' influence may decline is uncertain.

Question two generated near universal agreement that a future Asia-Pacific cold war is unlikely, with some participants even rejecting such a scenario as an irrelevant concept of a previous era. The reasons behind this view are straightforward. First, economic interdependence makes it more difficult to effectively engage in a cold war. Second, there are no clearly opposing ideologies that pit great powers against one another. Third, the relationship between China and the United States is built on mutual economic interests, which is fundamentally different than the relationship between the United States and Soviet Union. A minority of participants believe that a real possibility for interstate conflict in the region exists, even if a cold war is highly unlikely. The potential for an arms race is also seen by some participants as an area of significant concern over the next decade.

While a majority of responses to question three suggest that the rise of regional powers in the Asia-Pacific will promote stability, a large minority take the opposite view. For those who think that regional stability is probable, China plays a central role in stabilizing the region. A number of conditions or characteristics of the region's strategic environment are also critical to stability. For one, multilateral institutions such as ASEAN and APEC must play an active role in the region if the great powers are to be constrained in their pursuit of national interests. Such institutions give a disproportionate say to smaller states that must cooperate to mediate the ambitions of larger states—principally China. While the PRC has benefitted greatly from stability, continued prosperity will depend on the willingness of Chinese leaders to compromise. Some who view continued stability as likely suggest that equality among the great powers (China, India, and the United States) would further act to stabilize the region.

Participants who see future stability as unlikely express a distinct concern that resource competition would drive arms racing, thus leading to interstate conflict. Others believe that the principal driver of regional discord is likely to be domestic instability within China. Should the Chinese Communist Party's leadership find itself under intense pressure from the Chinese people, a crisis may be manufactured as a means of redirecting discontent. Several participants also see great-power politics among several rising states as reason to believe that the Asia-Pacific will prove unstable over the coming decade.

The fourth and final question of the strategic challenges focus group session has the greatest consensus across all groups. An overwhelming majority of participants describe one or more of the following transnational threats as ones the region will face over the next decade. Most frequently mentioned are environmental challenges and natural disasters such as sea-level rise, food and water shortages, pollution, floods, and earthquakes. The Mekong River, for example, is a major water source for China, Myanmar, Laos, Thailand, Cambodia, and Vietnam. With China planning to build multiple hydroelectric dams on the river and with water demand increasing, water is becoming a transnational challenge.[12]

International criminal organizations are also posing a transnational threat across the region. They are often responsible for drug trafficking, illicit goods smuggling, piracy of intellectual property, cyber attacks, and human trafficking. Some participants view these organizations, which states could use as surrogates, as a growing threat.

Additionally, piracy in the Gulf of Aden and Straits of Malacca, disruptive cyber attacks, violent Islamic fundamentalists, weapons of mass destruction proliferation, state failure in North Korea and Myanmar, and pandemic disease are also seen as transnational threats to order in the region. While few of these threats pose an existential threat to governments, they can impede economic growth and degrade stability.

Economic Interests: Session Two

Focus group session two was devoted to an examination of economic interests and their influence on the Asia-Pacific. During this session, participants were asked to respond to five questions:

1. How will economic interdependence influence conflict in the Asia-Pacific?

2. How long can the Asia-Pacific sustain economic growth?

3. How are economic trends in the Asia-Pacific altering the global balance of power?

4. What effect would an economic crisis in the Asia-Pacific have on the global economy?

5. How can US air capabilities support regional economic stability?

As with the previous session, participants provide a wide range of responses that show a breadth of perspectives in some areas and continuity in others.

With few exceptions, regarding the first question, the role of economic interdependence in the region is seen as positive. In fact, there was almost universal agreement that expanding interdependence will lead to a decrease in the probability of conflict. One participant describes the relationship created by economic interdependence as "mutually assured economic destruction." Some argue that collaboration and cooperation are encouraged and therefore act as moderating factors. In the case of Taiwan and China, it was suggested that growing cross-straits trade, investment, and travel are responsible for reducing tensions between the two. Further, should such economic interdependence continue to grow, a conflict can be avoided and peaceful reunification achieved.

Two points of concern were raised. First, with economic interdependence playing an important role in boosting economic growth and improving living standards for millions across the Asia-Pacific, resultant resource competition could lead to interstate conflict. Second, the balance of economic influence is shifting toward China—the largest trading partner of most Asia-Pacific nations—making it more difficult for the United States to influence countries across the region. While this is a positive shift from the Chinese perspective, American participants view it as a negative trend. Underscoring this point, participants from Asia-Pacific nations indicate that their countries are finding it increasingly difficult to balance their economic ties to China with their ideological and military ties to the United States.

Regarding the second question, participants generally agree that continued growth across the Asia-Pacific is likely. However, they also expect high growth rates in China, in particular, to slow over the coming decade. India and South Korea are also countries where sustained growth is anticipated. North Korea, on the other hand, is a country where poor economic conditions are seen as a destabilizing variable. The degree to which the region continues to grow—in the view of many—will depend on the ability of policy makers to implement the required banking, currency, intellectual property, and other reforms necessary to continue developing regional economies. Because China and India, for example, must maintain high (8 to 10 percent) economic growth rates to keep up with a rising population's demand for energy, water, and other public goods—necessary for domestic stability—reform will continue and economic growth rates will remain well above those in the West.

However, a minority of participants expect economic growth rates to come down substantially in the years ahead—particularly in China. A lack of transparent banking practices, currency manipulation, overproduction of infrastructure (make-work projects), and an inefficient and corrupt public sector are expected to have a negative impact on the Chinese economy in the near future. China is also experiencing significant wage inflation, making China less competitive in the manufacture of goods. This too may slow growth. And, should China experience a relative decline in economic growth, the region will likewise suffer. One final issue drew considerable concern—resource scarcity. Should critical resources such as water, fossil fuels, rare earth minerals, or other natural resources experience significant price increases due to demand outstripping supply, economic growth across the region could decline dramatically.

Any discussion of a shift in the global balance of power—question three—invariably centers on the rise of China and the absolute or relative decline of the United States and Europe. Such was the case among participants. While most concede that economic power is shifting to the Asia-Pacific, several specific points made by panelists are worth mentioning. First, a shift in military power is lagging behind the shift in economic power. However, military power will eventually shift as well. Second, China's economic strength and role as primary lender to the US government is effectively deterring the United States from challenging Chinese efforts to alter the status quo. Finally, China's growth is enabling its leaders to reshape international rules and norms in ways harmful to the United States, which is unable to circumvent them.

In responding to the fourth question, a majority of the group members contend that an economic crisis in the Asia-Pacific would negatively affect the global economy. However, others subscribe to the idea that some positive outcomes for the United States could ensue as well. Three conditions in evaluating the effects of an economic crisis in the region were considered. First, the length of any Asia-Pacific economic crisis would play a central role in its global effect. Second, the effect of an Asia-Pacific economic crisis would depend on the economies involved. As one participant notes, "When China sneezes, Asia catches a cold." If, however, smaller economies were involved instead, the effect would be significantly less. Third, as the 1997 Asian economic situation, the 2008 US housing bubble, and the present turmoil in Europe illustrate, the reasons for an economic crisis are key to understanding its short- and long-term results.

Of principal concern to participants is the impact of an Asia-Pacific economic crisis on trade and global finance. Another fear is the effect of a decline in American exports to the region and subsequent effects on industry and the trade deficit. So, too, is a likely weakening of investments in the United States from the region. Should China face a significant economic downturn, the United States may find financing federal debt difficult and, because of a capital shortage, face higher borrowing costs.

On the positive side, one participant comments that an Asia-Pacific economic crisis could delay or forestall a continued shift in the balance of power. For the United States, an economic crisis in the region would strengthen the dollar as investors looked for a stable currency. And, as two participants point out, the United States and the global economy weathered Japan's "lost decade" and the 1997 Asian economic crisis well. Thus, a minority of participants see opportunity for the United States should Asia-Pacific economies begin to falter.

With Air Force officers the single largest group among participants, question five solicited the most detailed responses. The overarching theme of discussion centers on the US role in promoting stability across the region. By keeping the lines of commerce and communication (LOCC) open, promoting economic and political stability, ensuring freedom of the skies, and providing safe navigation through the global positioning satellite network, the US Air Force can play a central role in the region. As one participant observes, there is a role for airpower in any Asia-Pacific strategy.

Some of the US Air Force's capabilities will play a critical role in providing stability. Surveillance and reconnaissance will indicate threats to LOCCs. Airlift will provide critical assistance during humanitarian relief operations. Airmen will work with their regional counterparts as part of the USAF's building partnership activities—providing assistance, training, aircraft, and more. The service's long-range strike capabilities (conventional and nuclear) will also deter aggression throughout the region. In all, the Air Force is likely to play an active role across the region in the years ahead.

American Interests: Session Three

Panel three moved from a regional focus to one devoted to the interests of the United States in the Asia-Pacific. Participants were asked to answer and discuss five questions:

1. How can long-term stability in the region be achieved?

2. What changes would threaten US strategic interests in the region?

3. Through what means can the United States maintain influence and facilitate cooperation across the region?

4. What are catalysts for change across the Asia-Pacific?

5. How can the United States and the USAF promote stability in the region?

As with the previous panels, participants provide a range of opinions.

Responses to the first question are best organized according to the diplomatic, information, military, and economic (DIME) model. Interestingly, the Air Force lieutenant colonels and colonels who were the single largest demographic within the focus groups largely gravitate toward diplomatic solutions to promoting stability. Their proposed options include formal alliances built on shared interests, public diplomacy efforts designed to improve the US image in the region and targeted at youths, a policy of transparency and consistency, a focus on peaceful conflict resolution and norm building, and multilateral efforts that do not require that the United States lead. Related to diplomacy, informational efforts should be geared toward informing citizens across the Asia-Pacific region of the United States' positive role in the region and toward promoting a pro-American view.

Militarily, the United States should pursue a "layered presence" based on existing presence, regional base access, and the ability to deploy rapidly across the region. Achieving this goal will require a strong effort toward building partnerships, the expansion of joint exercises and operations, and the informed use of military power. Economically, continued growth may be the single best means for promoting continued stability. Economic interdependence will also play a central role in stabilizing the region.

Responses to question two include a number of potential conflicts and challenges within the strategic environment as threats to American interests were discussed. Among the conflicts that participants frequently mention are war on the Korean peninsula; open conflict on the Indo-Chinese border; large-scale Islamist insurgencies in the Philippines, Thailand, and Indonesia; conflict in the South China Sea; and a Chinese invasion of Taiwan. All would pose a threat to US interests in the region. Negative conditions include a regional arms race (conventional and nuclear), a shift in Chinese foreign policy toward expansionism, a significant reduction in economic growth in China, internal instability in China, closure of the LOCCs to American access, economic decline in the United States, and a move toward isolationist policies in the United States or the Asia-Pacific. Should one or more of these occur, the United States' principal interests in the region—stability and economic growth—would suffer.

As previously, participants focus their answers to question three on familiar themes. In an effort to maintain US influence and facilitate cooperation, US participation in bilateral and multilateral organizations such as ASEAN, APEC, and the WTO is seen as essential. Diplomatic, economic, and military cooperation through the US Agency for International Development, the Peace Corps, foreign military sales, military officer exchanges, and other options are suggested as tools the United States can employ in a broad soft-power strategy. Participants also offer some striking criticism of the American approach to foreign policy.

A small number of responses suggest that the United States could benefit from strengthening its linguistic and cultural understanding of the region. Others advise that American policy makers change their approach to the region by talking less, listening more, and reducing the pressure on Asia-Pacific nations to conform to American ideals and practices. Too great a level of pressure may force some countries into the open arms of China. In short, trade, presence, and engagement are the central means for maintaining influence and facilitating cooperation.

Over the next decade, catalysts for change in the Asia-Pacific are surprisingly bereft of those that are inherently military, according to the opinions of participants regarding question four. Responses often lean toward economic issues. For example, economic growth is seen as the single most important change agent. A broad middle class could have a distinct pacifying effect (more to lose), but the growing demand for manufactured goods and commodities could also surpass the ability of governments to provide food, clean water, fuel, and the other wants that accompany a higher standard of living. A large middle class could also place greater pressure on illiberal regimes to reform—perhaps leading to a "Jasmine Revolution" or an Asian Arab Spring. Greater access to the Internet and to international media, through satellite television, is increasing the demand for reform in some countries. A growth in individual wealth may also be accompanied by environmental degradation, which could also serve as impetus for change. The Chinese and Japanese populations are also aging. How these countries deal with the "graying of society" will prove central to their success.

A global wild card is cyber. With technology developing so rapidly and in often unexpected ways, participants saw cyber as a force that could level the playing field between states and nonstate actors, serve as a weapon of mass destruction, and play a critical role in promoting civil unrest. Whatever the case may be, cyber is likely to play a leading role in future change.

Responses of panelists to question five regarding methods the United States/USAF can employ to promote stability in the region generally parallel points previously made. Presence and engagement are most often mentioned as key tools. As one participant points out, "Virtual presence is actual absence." Two issues discussed, however, are worth noting. First, basing is likely to play a central role in any USAF effort to promote stability in the region. "Resilient basing," where the United States can rapidly expand its presence, may serve as a viable alternative to bases with large footprints. Second, building a "global community of airmen" across the Asia-Pacific can serve as a stabilizing concept that brings military officers and leaders together. Professional air forces, staffed and led by airmen with ties to their foreign counterparts, have the potential to serve as a voice for cooperation. A collaborative environment would promote a setting in which political leaders would seek alternative solutions to conflict.

Regional Perspectives: Session Four

Whereas previous sessions looked at the region largely from an American perspective, the goal for participants in the final session was to view the cultural, economic, military, and political challenges of the Asia-Pacific through Chinese, Japanese, Thai, or other regional eyes. The approach was intended to solicit responses with a markedly different frame of reference—eliminating the mirror-imaging that all too often occurs when Americans attempt to make sense of the world and how it works. (As was previously noted, many participants have had significant experience in the region and are working Asia-Pacific issues.) Participants were asked five questions:

1. What role do regional actors desire the United States to play?

2. As China rises, will its neighbors bandwagon or balance?

3. How do regional elites and average citizens view the United States?

4. From an international perspective, how can/should nations in the region partner with the United States?

5. How are Asia-Pacific nations hedging their bets on the future?

While it is difficult to step outside one's own context, participants provide some insightful responses.

Answers to question one often reference the role of the United States as a stabilizer in the region. With each of the Asia-Pacific's 49 countries having distinct languages, culture, history, interests, and strategic concerns, participants suggest that American policy makers cannot apply a one-size-fits-all approach to stability. They add that the desired US role will expand or shrink based on the actions of China—the country many in the region fear. While few countries will seek formal alliances with the United States, the desire to work with the United States is growing (the Philippines, Indonesia, Vietnam, etc.). However, in collaborating with the United States diplomatically and militarily, countries do not want to be seen as taking sides against China—the largest trading partner for many Asia-Pacific nations. For countries having formal alliances with the United States, a credible security commitment is needed. Such assurance is particularly crucial in regard to extended deterrence.

Anticipating whether Asia-Pacific nations will bandwagon with China or balance against it is a difficult task, but it is the focus of question two. With a firm understanding of the often long-held animosities between China and many of its neighbors, most participants strongly believe that Asia-Pacific nations would strengthen their ties to the United States in an effort to diplomatically and militarily balance against a rising China. However, countries throughout the region understand that their relationship with China is critical to their long-term economic prosperity. Thus, they are not seeking to balance China in a way that harms that relationship.

India is one state that is unlikely to move decidedly toward the United States given its precarious geographic position and border dispute with China and China's growing partner, Pakistan. Like other countries of the region, India will pursue its interests—sometimes siding with and sometimes against the United States. Participants did, however, warn that should the United States reduce its presence in the region, countries may see their best option as bandwagoning with China. Myanmar, North Korea, and Pakistan, for example, have been expanding their defense ties to China.

Shaping the views of elites and average citizens across the region will play a major role in the success of the United States over the next decade—question three. Currently, the opinions of both elite and average citizens concerning the United States vary widely across the region. Countries where the United States maintains long-standing ties (Japan, South Korea, and Thailand) support the United States in positive ways, according to participants. Support is weakest in the Asia-Pacific's Muslim countries, largely as a result of the conflicts in Afghanistan and Iraq. A positive disposition toward the United States is often found within the region's militaries, which often have regular and sustained interaction with American forces and whose members may have spent time in the United States.

While the United States is a place many citizens of Asia-Pacific nations would like to live or visit, participants suggest that elites and average citizens have starkly different opinions toward it. Elites better understand the role of the United States as a global power and as a critical market. Average citizens are more concerned by real or perceived hypocrisy within American foreign policy. However, both groups are thought to respect American power.

If the United States' objective is to better partner with countries in the Asia-Pacific—question four—American leaders will need to determine shared interests that benefit the region and individual countries. With economic development the principal concern of many Asia-Pacific nations, expansion of trade opportunities may be the single best opportunity to strengthen relations. The United States can also engage in confidence building activities that span the diplomatic and military spectrum. If the United States treats other countries as peers, an oft-repeated point, elites and average citizens will see it as a more attractive partner. With so many states across the region poorly equipped to handle cyber crime and terrorism, these two challenges are a good place to start.

Countries across the Asia-Pacific may, however, hedge against a regionally dominant China or United States in a number of ways—question five. Panelists are already seeing a number of countries undertake concerted efforts to diversify their economies—making them less dependent on China and the United States. Countries are also seeking to constrain the two potential adversaries by increasingly working through multilateral organizations such as APEC and ASEAN. Smaller countries are making a concerted attempt to increase their own military capabilities while also strengthening relationships with one another. However, the stakes that each of the region's countries have in their relationships with China and the United States will ensure that most walk a fine line between the two great powers as they attempt to pursue their own interests.

Conclusion

As the United States shifts its strategic focus from Europe and the Middle East to the Asia-Pacific, strategists will need to make strides in understanding the region, its challenges, and how the United States can best play a constructive role in promoting stability. The task is certain to prove tricky since the nature of strategy requires a forward-looking approach that calls for action—often in the absence of needed information. The analysis presented here is designed to assist in the broader effort to develop a USAF strategy for the Asia-Pacific. Bringing together senior experts and a range of academics and practitioners from industry, the military, and think tanks contributes to developing an appreciation of the challenges and opportunities the region presents. While incomplete, these perspectives further expand the knowledge base from which strategists can operate.

Notes

1. Hillary Clinton, "America's Pacific Century," *Foreign Policy*, November 2011, http://www.foreignpolicy.com/articles/2011/10/11/americas_pacific_century.

2. Jack D. Kem, "Military Transformation: Ends, Ways, and Means," *Air and Space Power Journal* 20, no. 3 (Fall 2006): 85–93, http://www.airpower.au.af.mil /airchronicles/apj/apj06/fal06/kem.html.

3. Norman Dalkey and Olaf Helmer, *An Experimental Application of the Delphi Method to the Use of Experts* (Santa Monica, CA: RAND Corporation, 1962), 1.

4. Olaf Helmer, *Analysis of the Future: The Delphi Method* (Santa Monica, CA: RAND Corporation, 1967), 6–9.

5. N. Dalkey, B. Brown, and S. Cochran, *The Delphi Method, IV: Effect of Percentile Feedback and Feed-in of Relevant Facts* (Santa Monica, CA: RAND Corporation, 1970); and Gregory Skulmoski, Francis Hartman, and Jennifer Krahn, "The Delphi Method for Graduate Research," *Journal of Information Technology Education* 6 (2007): 2–5.

6. See Francis Hartman and Andrew Baldwin, "Using Technology to Improve Delphi Method," *Journal of Computing in Civil Engineering* 9, no. 4 (Winter 1995): 244–49; and Kenji Kobayashi et al., "Development of Consensus Statements for the Diagnosis and Management of Intestinal Behçet's Disease Using a Modified Delphi Approach," *Journal of Gastroenterology* 42, no. 9 (2007): 737–45. In addition to the modifications to the classical Delphi method described in these articles, a number of studies make varying modifications to the Delphi method.

7. In 1953 Pres. Dwight Eisenhower authorized Project Solarium as a high-level strategic planning effort. One aspect of Project Solarium was its creation of best, worst, and most likely alternative paths. It was on this effort that much of the Eisenhower administration's foreign and national security grand strategy was based. See Michèle Flournoy and Shawn Brimley, *Strategic Planning for U.S. National Security: A Project Solarium for the 21st Century* (Princeton, NJ: The Princeton Project on National Security, 2006), 6–9.

8. Russell Schutt, *Investigating the Social World: The Process and Practice of Research* (Thousand Oaks, CA: SAGE/Pine Forge Press, 2009), 345–46.

9. John Creswell, *Qualitative Inquiry and Research Design* (Thousand Oaks, CA: SAGE/Pine Forge Press, 2007), 135.

10. John Creswell and Vicki Plano Clark, *Designing and Conducting Mixed Methods Research* (Thousand Oaks, CA: Sage Publications, Inc., 2011), 71–72.

11. William Gibson and Andrew Brown, *Working with Qualitative Data* (Los Angeles: SAGE, 2009), chap. 8.

12. Michael Richardson, "Dams in China Turn the Mekong into a River of Discord," *Yale Global Online*, 16 July 2009, http://yaleglobal.yale.edu/content/dams-china-turn-mekong-river-discord.

Chapter 3

Top Five Asia-Pacific Economies

Integration, Conflict, Vulnerability, and Crisis, 2010–2020

Dr. Brooks B. Robinson
Economic Advisor, US Pacific Command

Abstract

Second only to the undulating financial crisis and lethargy that characterize much of the global economy today, the most important questions facing policy makers around the globe are how Asia will evolve over the next decade and how military conflict can be avoided there. This chapter provides an analysis of these two questions by focusing on the real economy for the top five Asian economies using key statistics. Our analysis reveals that the largest Asian economies are expected to become increasingly integrated as we move through the decade. While the literature on economic integration (EI) and military conflict is divided as to whether EI reduces prospects for military conflict, an extensive game that accounts for economic development and symbiotic economic relationships causes us to conclude that military conflict is likely to be avoided. We also employ statistical analyses to assess economic vulnerability in the region. Forecasts of future regional growth in output and trade enable us to determine that an Asian economic crisis, should one materialize, would appreciably affect the global economy. Generally, our findings lead us to the view that the current state of the world serves as an important backdrop for convincing world leaders of a cooperative and collaborative approach as best for addressing regional and global economic issues. Reason suggests that a similar approach is applicable for military issues.

Introduction

The twists and turns of a seemingly endless financial crisis that now clouds Europe's and the world's future are an important concern for world policy makers. However, if one is concerned about the distant future, a key policy quandary is how the Asia-Pacific region will evolve economically. Because of existing tension in the region—particularly over South China Sea territorial claims—and because regional players have called on the United States to serve as a counterbalance to China, we also ask the question, Can military conflict be avoided in Asia?[1] At this early juncture of the twenty-first century, these two concerns should reasonably occupy center stage. Consequently, the recent Asia-Pacific conference, organized by the Air Force Research Institute, is timely and valuable. We hope that this contribution to this volume, produced as a result of the conference, will provide a few transparent insights on EI in the region, military conflict, economic vulnerability among regional players, and the effect of a regional crisis on the global economy.

This chapter provides perspectives on the two key questions by focusing on the top five Asian economies (Australia, China, India, Japan, and South Korea), their interrelations, and their relationships with the United States and by concentrating on statistical analysis of the real economy.[2] We focus on the top five economies to keep analyses tractable and because, at least for 2010, the output (gross domestic product [GDP]) of these economies accounted for about 84 percent of the economies in the United States Pacific Command's (USPACOM) area of responsibility (AOR).[3] In addition, exports of these economies comprised about 64 percent of exports of AOR economies. We use successive sections to (1) examine the extent to which the largest economies in the Asia-Pacific region experience EI, (2) consider the literature on EI and an extensive game-theoretic framework to ascertain prospects for military conflict between the large economies in Asia and between Asian economies and the United States, (3) assess economic vulnerabilities among key regional players, (4) evaluate the potential impact of an Asian economic crisis on the global economy, and (5) develop final conclusions concerning our two starting-point questions. Throughout the analysis, we consider the period 2010 to 2020.

Bottom Line Up Front

Our analysis reveals that the leading Asian economies are likely to become increasingly integrated over the next decade—even to the extent of seeming economic dependence on China. With minor excep-

tions, these economies promise to be generally robust and characterized by little volatility in growth, good sectoral balance, and
manageable debt burdens. By 2020 the top five Asian economies will
comprise about 30 percent of not only the world's output but also its
imports. We conclude that increasing EI with its many benefits, along
with continued development of defense deterrents, will serve as a
hedge against military conflict.

Economic Integration

Several economic variables might serve as reasonable symmetrical
measures of EI between economies. The first that comes to mind is
trade—preferably total bilateral trade.[4] In this section, we provide
statistics on the symmetrical total bilateral merchandise trade shares
between the top five Asian economies and the United States. A second statistic that conveys a sense of integration is correlation; it reflects how two time series co-vary through time. In this case, we develop correlation statistics using GDP growth rates for the top five
Asian and US economies.[5]

Table 3.1 provides symmetrical total bilateral merchandise trade
shares for 2010, while table 3.2 provides these statistics based on forecasts out to 2020.[6] (The columns are the starting point for reading the
tables. For example, in table 3.1, column 1, the value 22.5 percent
represents China's share of Australia's bilateral trade.)

Table 3.1. Pair-wise total bilateral trade shares, 2010

	Australia	China	India	Japan	Korea	US
Australia		2.9%	2.4%	4.2%	3.0%	0.9%
China	22.5%		10.1%	20.7%	21.1%	14.2%
India	4.1%	2.1%		1.0%	1.9%	1.5%
Japan	14.1%	10.0%	2.3%		10.4%	5.7%
Korea	6.3%	7.0%	2.4%	6.2%		2.8%
US	7.7%	13.0%	7.4%	13.0%	10.2%	

Developed from CEIC Data Company Ltd. database, a product of Internet Securities, Inc.
Emerging Markets, accessed October/November 2011, http://www.ceicdata.com; and Bureau
of Economic Analysis, "Table 12, U.S. International Transactions, by Area," accessed 7 November 2011, www.bea.gov.

Table 3.2. Pair-wise total bilateral trade shares, 2020

	Australia	China	India	Japan	Korea	US
Australia		4.1%	3.2%	5.5%	3.4%	0.9%
China	48.7%		27.8%	33.3%	36.3%	25.5%
India	9.8%	4.9%		1.4%	3.7%	2.5%
Japan	12.8%	6.8%	1.6%		7.9%	3.9%
Korea	6.8%	6.8%	3.3%	6.4%		2.4%
US	4.9%	11.4%	5.1%	8.5%	6.6%	

Developed from CEIC Data Company Ltd. database, a product of Internet Securities, Inc. Emerging Markets, accessed October/ November 2011, http://www.ceicdata.com; and Bureau of Economic Analysis, "Table 12, U.S. International Transactions, by Area," accessed 7 November 2011, www.bea.gov.

In table 3.1, trade shares that exceed 20 percent are highlighted in yellow. Derek Scissors argues that shares exceeding 30 percent signal trade dependence.[7] In table 3.2, shares that exceed 30 percent are highlighted in pink. In other words, by 2020, it is possible that three of the top five Asian economies will be "dependent" upon China with respect to total bilateral trade. Notably, China has managed its trading relationships such that its trade shares with the remaining countries represented in the table do not exceed 13.0 percent. Generally, we can conclude from these data that Asian economies are likely to be increasingly integrated as we move through the decade. Notably, China's share of total US trade by 2020 nears the 30 percent dependency mark.

Figure 3.1 provides a matrix that presents the Pearson correlation coefficients for the economies under study. They are prepared using real GDP growth rates from the International Monetary Fund's (IMF) September 2011 *World Economic Outlook* for 1996–2016.[8] Again, these statistics are designed to indicate the extent to which the economies vary together across time. Correlation coefficients near or above 0.70 are assumed to convey a significant degree of correlation.[9] In figure 3.1, the three cells highlighted in pink represent correlation coefficients of greater than 0.66. The highest correlation is between Australia and the United States (0.70). Notably, whether small or large, most correlation coefficients are positive, indicating that the economies grow and contract simultaneously. The point here is that from 1996 to 2016, three cross-correlation statistics (Australia–United States, China-India, and Japan–United States) reflect a meaningful level of correlation, implying significant EI.

	Australia	China	India	Japan	Korea	US
1 Australia	1					
2 China	-0.026	1				
3 India	-0.121	0.662	1			
4 Japan	0.339	0.353	0.375	1		
5 Korea	0.056	0.078	0.071	0.530	1	
6 US	0.700	-0.103	0.079	0.662	0.322	1

Figure 3.1. Correlation matrix: real GDP growth, 1996–2016. (*Adapted from* IMF, *World Economic Outlook: Slowing Growth, Rising Risks* [Washington, DC: IMF, September 2011], http://www.imf.org/external /pubs/ft/weo/2011/02/weodata/index.aspx; and USPACOM computations.)

We conclude that, based on statistical analysis alone, the top five Asian economies are likely to reflect a significant degree of EI as they proceed through the current decade. This projection is depicted more forcefully in the bilateral merchandise trade data presented in tables 3.1 and 3.2 than in the correlation of real GDP growth rates presented in figure 3.1. Next, we will recall these outcomes as we consider the relationship between EI and conflict.

Economic Integration and Military Conflict

So-called commercial liberals have a long-standing claim that EI reduces prospects for military conflict. Opponents of commercial liberals, on the other hand, say that EI creates opportunities for conflict—especially low-level conflict. Others argue that trade is not tightly correlated with military conflict.[10] As a case in point, from 2001 (when China joined the World Trade Organization [WTO]) through 2010, US-China total two-way trade in goods and services expanded from $130.9 billion to $490.2 billion—a 17.9 percent average annual growth rate.[11] Over this same period, the United States and China, on a combined basis, according to the *Financial Times*, have filed over 25 trade disputes with the WTO.[12] While this period produced only one case of US-China military conflict, it certainly produced many complaints, assertions, and threats that can be defined as nonmilitary conflict, which could serve as precursors to military conflict or war.[13]

Although John Oneal et al. find that trade inhibited military disputes from 1950 to 1985, Katherine Barbieri finds that higher levels of commerce increased hostilities from 1870 to 1938. For more recent periods on which we should probably direct our attention, Edward Mansfield and Jon Pevehouse contend that regional preferential trading institutions originating due to trade play a critical role in reducing military hostilities. Therefore, we can surmise that trade and the related prospect for military conflict must be considered through a temporal lens (the more recent period witnessing less conflict) and a lens of institutional arrangements (the existence of such institutions helping to reduce conflict). Extending the importance of institutional arrangements, Barbieri finds that dyads reflecting a common democratic political system are less likely to engage in military conflict. Geographic contiguity is another factor that facilitates or deters potential military conflict in light of EI. That is, states that share borders may reflect a greater proclivity to engage in military conflict than states that are distant.[14]

Given these insights we should ask, How does a dyad that enjoys a high level of EI make a strategic decision to engage or not to engage in military conflict? Next, we establish a range of assumptions, develop a crisis point, and then walk through the moves of a multiplay extensive strategic game to identify critical escalating factors in that strategic decision-making process.

Economic Integration in a Game-Theoretic Framework

Imagine a noncontiguous dyad with a high degree of EI. In fact, the states are economically dependent (as defined by Scissors) with respect to trade. The states are members of the WTO and a regional trade organization. They enjoy comparable militaries in terms of capacity and capability (budgets, size, and weaponry). The two nations are engaged in an island-chain territorial dispute, with both nations claiming jurisdiction over the island chain and the surrounding waters. Geological and geophysical studies show oil and gas beneath the territorial waters surrounding the island chain. Both nations have urged the other not to attempt to develop oil or gas wells in the disputed territory, with the threat of reprisal. The nations have discussed joint development of the oil and gas resources but have not reached agreement. Leading up to the crisis, nation "A" has stated an intent to develop the oil and gas resources by drilling wells. Both states "A" and "B" depend heavily on oil and gas imports from the Middle East, with nation "A" being more dependent.

General scientific findings indicate that no major breakthrough in any form of alternative (sustainable) energy will occur for at least 10 years. Simultaneously, experts determine that a key Arab nation in the Middle East has developed nuclear capabilities, raising the prospect for conflict and a disturbance in the smooth flow of oil from the Middle East on which nations "A" and "B" depend. Under these conditions, nation "A" makes an offer to jointly develop with nation "B" the oil and gas in the waters around the disputed island chain under a 70 (nation "A") to 30 (nation "B") sharing arrangement. Nation "B" categorically refuses the offer.

After the Arab nation with newly found nuclear capabilities threatens Israel with a two-state solution requirement (creating conditions under which the flow of oil might be disrupted), nation "A" decides to go it alone and drill for oil and gas in waters surrounding the island chain. Global GDP growth is high, and oil markets are tight. It is late fall, with winter approaching. In these circumstances, the people of nation "A" could suffer severe hardship, while nation "B" could probably survive the winter using its strategic petroleum reserves (SPR). With winter expected to be severe worldwide, other nations hesitate to provide oil from their SPR to assist nation "A" in case of an energy crisis. Nation "A" has been told by its top oil company that it can open a well in time to supply the nation with the oil it needs from a well near the disputed island chain. Nation "B" is interested in negotiating the terms of the drilling arrangement. What should nation "B" do?

The following extensive game with perfect information unfolds (fig. 2):

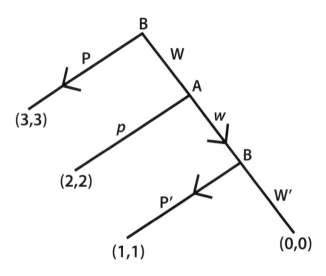

Figure 3.2. Extensive game with perfect information

Figure 3.2 presents successive plays in an extensive game by nations "B" and "A," with payoffs in parentheses (the first entry is for nation "B" and the second for nation "A"). Given that nation "A" has already decided to drill, nation "B" begins the game and chooses to attack nation "A" (W), or, not attacking, calls for a halt to the drilling and requests negotiations on the oil/gas sharing rights (P, payoff [3,3]). After the nation "B" play, nation "A" chooses to return the attack and continue drilling but agrees to negotiate the oil/gas sharing arrangement (w) or stops drilling and negotiates (p, payoff [2,2]). In the final play, nation "B," in response to the play of nation "A," chooses to accelerate the attack (W', payoff [0,0]) or halt the attack and negotiate a mutually acceptable oil/gas sharing arrangement (P', payoff [1,1]).

For simplicity and using a backwards-induction equilibrium approach that Levent Kockesen describes, we conclude that the optimal strategy is (PP', w).[15] That is, the optimal strategy is for nation "B" to not attack nation "A" and to negotiate the oil/gas sharing arrangement. Why is this reasonable? Because by doing so, the two nations could possibly come to an agreement and both benefit from access to the oil/gas during the winter, not suffer the vagaries of war, and continue receiving unimpeded benefits of trade. If nation "B" attacks nation "A," then an entire trove of bad results could occur. In the case of (W, w), nation "A" would have incurred possible loss of lives and property, damage to the dyad's important trading relationship, plus the uncertainty engendered by the knowledge that nation "B" is willing to attack. In the other case (W, p), even though nation "A" stops the drilling and opens the door to negotiation, the damage from nation "B's" attack has already been done. Moving down the game tree to (WW', w), an escalation of nation "B's" attack on nation "A" can only lead to a "race to the bottom," where both nations suffer from loss of lives and property, injury to the important trading relationship, and development of animosity for an extended period. If we consider (WP', w), then the nations may come to terms on the oil/gas sharing rights and may mutually benefit; however, only after both nations have been substantially injured by attacks on one another will this occur. The backwards-induction outcome is (PP', w).

This hypothetical extensive game with complete information reveals that nations fitting the descriptions and conditions of nations "A" and "B" are likely to avoid military conflict. Their high-level EI should serve as an influential factor in helping them to make strategic choices that lead to avoidance of military conflict. Of course, there are always special cases. However, as Oneal emphasizes, economies that reflect a high level of EI tend to avoid military conflict—particularly during recent times. Furthermore, as Mansfield and Pevehouse point out, preferential trading organizations to which most nations are attached appear to play a major role in mitigating military conflict—with or without high levels of EI.[16] Therefore, we conclude that, given our current place in history and the types of institutional arrangements in the Asia-Pacific region, the higher the level of EI between nations, the greater the probability that those nations are likely to avoid military conflict.

Economic Vulnerability

Finally, we assess the impact of an Asian economic crisis on the global economy. Before tackling that objective, it seems reasonable to inquire, How vulnerable are Asia's top five economies to an economic crisis? To answer this question, we consider three real economy statistics: (1) volatility in economic growth, (2) sectoral balance, and (3) debt-to-GDP ratios.

Volatility

Using historical IMF (2011) data on GDP growth for the top five Asian economies over the concluding 20 years that are in the database (1996–2016), we prepared estimates of variance (see table 3.3).

Table 3.3. Variance of the top five Asian and US economies, real GDP growth, 1996–2016

	Australia	China	India	Japan	Korea	US
Variance	0.81	2.28	3.05	4.90	10.40	3.43

Developed from IMF, *World Economic Outlook: Slowing Growth, Rising Risks* (Washington, DC: IMF, September 2011), http://www.imf.org/ external/pubs/ft/weo/2011/02/weodata/index.aspx; and USPACOM computations.

Table 3.3 reveals that South Korea reflects the highest variability in real GDP growth of the six nations under consideration, with a variance of 10.40. Japan is second in the hierarchy with a variance of 4.90. The United States is third with a variance of 3.43. If variability signals instability in growth, then the leading Asian economies do not appear to have a problem in this regard.

Sectoral Balance

For sectoral balance, we highlight the long-held opinion that well-developed and balanced economies reflect relatively high levels of consumption and moderate levels of investment.[17] For example, in a 9 November 2011 statement that was part of the Asia-Pacific Economic Cooperation Meetings in Honolulu, Hawaii, the president of the Asian Development Bank, Haruhiko Kuroda, said that the realignment of Asian economies towards more domestic demand was an important challenge. He added that such action "will help keep the region's economies strong."[18] Are the top five Asian economies aligned appropriately in terms of domestic demand? To answer this question, we parsed the output of the leading Asian economies into three well-known components (consumption, investment, and net exports) and compared average shares for 2000–2010 with share values for the US economy (table 3.4).

Table 3.4. Sectoral balance: average GDP sector shares, 2000–2010

	Australia	China	India	Japan	Korea	US
Consumption	74.6%	55.9%	73.4%	74.6%	67.2%	84.6%
Investment	26.4%	40.8%	28.9%	24.2%	30.2%	19.1%
Net Exports	-1.0%	3.3%	2.4%	1.2%	2.6%	-3.7%

Developed from CEIC Data Company Ltd. database, a product of Internet Securities, Inc. Emerging Markets, accessed October/November 2011, http://www.ceicdata.com. US data is from Bureau of Economic Analysis, "National Income and Product Account Table 1.5.5.— Gross Domestic Product, Expanded Detail," accessed 7 November 2011, www.bea.gov.

At one end of the spectrum, the United States reflects the highest consumption and lowest investment shares among the nations covered. Notably, the United States reflects the largest trade deficit as a share of GDP. At the other end of the spectrum, China reflects the lowest consumption and highest investment shares. China has the largest trade surplus as a share of GDP. The best fit is probably somewhere in between. Remaining economies under consideration fall between the US and China extremes. A common-sense approach to identifying an ideal point would be to produce a consumption share in the 70 percent range, an investment share in the upper 20 percent range, and a small positive net export share.

If we were to assess the sectoral balances presented in table 3.4 as indicators of instability, then we would single out the China and US configurations as the least stable/sustainable. Otherwise, we would conclude that the remaining leading Asian economies reflect sectoral balances that appear to be stable and sustainable.

Debt-to-GDP Ratios

As a final real-economy statistic that can signal instability and the onset of a crisis, we consider the debt-to-GDP ratios for the top five Asian economies and the United States (table 3.5).

Table 3.5. Debt-to-GDP ratios, 2010

	Australia	China	India	Japan	Korea	US
Debt-to-GDP Ratio	20.5%	33.8%	64.1%	220.0%	33.4%	94.4%

Developed from IMF, *World Economic Outlook: Slowing Growth, Rising Risks* (Washington, DC: IMF, September 2011), http://www.imf.org//external/pubs/ft/weo/2011/02/weodata/index.aspx.

With the exception of Japan, which has an exceptionally high debt-to-GDP ratio, the remaining leading Asian economies reflect subdued debt-to-GDP ratios—much lower than the ratios of the faltering economies in the eurozone now on the brink of default—usually over 100 percent. Japan's debt-to-GDP ratio is misleading because Japanese citizens own about 95 percent of the debt.[19] Obviously, the US debt-to-GDP ratio is bordering on problematic, as evidenced by credit rating agencies lowering the US sovereign debt rating from AAA to AA+ in August 2011.

Generally, table 3.5's statistics do not signal problems on the debt front for Asia's leading economies going forward, although it would be favorable for Japan to lower its debt despite most of it being owned domestically. Moreover, India must take care to prevent its debt from rising dramatically.

Therefore, whether we assess volatility, sectoral balances, or debt-to-GDP ratios, we surmise that Asia's top five economies appear to be generally stable and sustainable. We should caveat this conclusion with the fact that these economies are well integrated with the global economy and that problems (slowdowns or downturns) in the global economy could have significant impacts on the Asian economies. We will keep this latter point in mind as we consider next how an Asian economic crisis might affect the economy worldwide.

Impact of an Asian Crisis on the Global Economy

Given the ongoing financial crisis in Europe, the current global economic concern is that Europe will fall into a second recession. Add in the slow growth of the US economy, and one concludes that only the world's emerging markets and developing economies—including those in Asia—are holding up world GDP growth. But the story does not end there. Slow growth among Western economies adversely impacts growth in emerging market economies that rely on the West to absorb their exports. Without sufficient Western demand, growth among Asia's emerging market economies, Japan, and Australia stands to suffer. In fact, it is this scenario—at least in the short run—that is likely to considerably slow economic growth in Asia. In turn, slowing Asian growth will reverberate back and further inhibit growth in Western economies.

However, consider that later in the decade some factor leads to an economic crisis in Asia. To what extent would such a crisis among Asia's top five economies affect the global economy? We seek to answer this question by considering two real-economy statistics: (1) top five Asian economies' output as a share of world GDP; and (2) top five Asian economies' imports as a share of world imports.

First, figure 3.3 shows the trend of the output of the top five Asian economies as a share of world GDP over the years 2000–2020.[20] Notably, the output of these economies increases around 25 percent from 2010 to 2020. By 2020 the output of the top Asian economies is forecasted to be just over 30 percent of world GDP. If it turns out that Western economies are even weaker than anticipated, then this ratio could rise even higher. Consequently, an economic crisis among the leading Asian economies would be reflected in 30 percent of global GDP growth—a significant outcome.

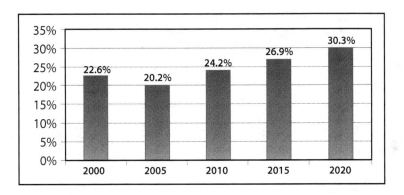

Figure 3.3. Top five Asian economies' GDP as a share of world GDP. (*Developed from* IMF, *World Economic Outlook: Slowing Growth, Rising Risks* [Washington, DC: IMF, September 2011], http://www.imf.org/external/pubs/ft/weo/2011/02/weodata/index.aspx; and USPACOM forecasts.)

Second, figure 3.4 provides estimates and forecasts of the imports of the top five Asian economies as a share of global, US, and European Union (EU) exports over the years 2000 to 2020.[21] The figure shows that imports of the top five Asian economies as a share of global imports are expected to grow by over 50 percent from 2010 to 2020. Similarly, imports of the top five Asian economies as a share of US and

EU exports are expected to grow by 40 percent and 47 percent, respectively, over the next decade. By 2020 the imports of the top five Asian economies will comprise 30 percent of global imports, 18.2 percent of US exports, and 15.4 percent of EU exports. Again, this is significant.

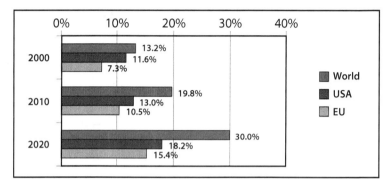

Figure 3.4. Top five Asian economies' import shares. (*Developed from* CEIC Data Company Ltd. database, a product of Internet Securities, Inc. Emerging Markets, accessed October/November 2011, http://www.ceic data.com; Bureau of Economic Analysis, "Table 12, U.S. International Transactions, by Area," accessed 7 November 2011, www.bea.gov; WTO database, www.wto.org; and USPACOM forecasts.)

Therefore, it is reasonable to conclude that the top five Asian economies will grow in significance relative to the global economy out to 2020. Additionally, an economic crisis among the top five Asian economies is forecasted to have a considerable impact on the global economy based both on output (~30%) and on imports from global trading partners (~30%).

Conclusion

Imbedded in the question, How will Asian economies evolve? are the questions, How will Asian economies grow? and How will Asian economies impact the global economy? To answer these questions, we have analyzed key real-economy statistics for the top five Asian economies. We surmise that these economies are likely to become increasingly integrated over the next decade—even to the point of developing near-trade dependence with China. With Korea and—to a much lesser extent—Japan as exceptions, economic growth among the leading Asian economies is not volatile. Except for China, Asia's leading economies reflect good sectoral balance. None of these economies project heavy debt positions dependent on massive foreign borrowing. When we look out to 2020, we forecast that the output of the top five Asian economies will comprise over 30 percent of the global GDP and account for over 30 percent of global imports. Consequently, economic turbulence among these economies is expected to have a major impact on the global economy. On the other hand, an economic boon to these economies will buoy the global economy.

We searched the literature and operationalized an extensive game with perfect information to address apprehensions about military conflict—particularly among nations that reflect high levels of EI. Our conclusion is that greater EI serves as a main factor in reducing the probability of military conflict, particularly when dyads are not contiguous, do not share democratic policies, and are parties to preferential trade agreements. There is evidence that greater EI can provide more opportunities for conflict but that it is likely to be of a nonmilitary nature. We do not contend that this inference is a tautology. Factors may enter the equation that cause our finding to be stood on its head. However, the greater the EI and its benefits, the greater the prospect that nations will find ways to negotiate their way out of military conflicts and preserve those benefits.

Coming to this conclusion and expecting it to hold without further action or intentional inaction are insufficient. For example, we should ask whether a competing trans-Pacific partnership would create conditions for military conflict with other preferential trade groups in Asia. At the same time, we should appreciate the importance of noneconomic factors in helping prevent military conflict. Uppermost, military posture and presence can serve as a deterrent to military conflict. Hence, it is wise for both the Asian countries under study and for the United States to use their economic prowess to continue building and posturing their militaries to ensure that economic and defense strategies can help prevent military conflict.

Notes

1. The distinction between *conflict* and *military conflict* is important. While *conflict* could entail a range of actions, such as complaints, assertions, and verbal threats

between dyads, *military conflict* is the active and antagonistic engagement of military forces.

2. The current global preoccupation with the European financial crisis and recent memories of the 2008–9 global economic crisis, which was set off by a financial crisis, may lead readers to believe that we will miss important factors by focusing on the real economy. The reality is that financial concerns are either precursors to or extensions of the real economy. Therefore, study of the real economy is sufficient to capture the impact of financial transactions on the economy, either as a cause or as a result. In addition, our analysis of financial factors is restricted by country-by-country data availability, comparability, and quality issues.

3. Each of the five economies reflects GDP at market prices of greater than $1.0 trillion, with China ranking as the second largest economy in the world and Japan as third largest—both with GDPs that exceed $5 trillion. The United States had the largest GDP in 2010 at $14.5 trillion.

4. Trade is a flawed metric for assessing EI, mainly because supply chains permit products to be developed in multiple nations or economies. For an accurate assessment of EI, one must fully comprehend what is produced in a nation/economy, that is, value-added production. A value-added analysis must occur in an input-output framework. See Andreas Maurer and Christophe Degain, "Globalization and Trade Flows: What You See Is Not What You Get!," World Trade Organization, June 2010, http://www.wto.org/english/res_e/reser_e/ersd201012_e.pdf.

5. As noted above, we are not highlighting analysis of financial variables in this study. However, financial variables that would signal EI would include symmetrical share estimates of bilateral foreign direct investment between economies. Similar measures of portfolio investment would also suffice as indicators of EI. In addition, cross-correlations in the movements (percent change) of foreign exchange rates can also indicate the extent to which economies are interlinked.

6. We adopted a simplified method for developing forecasts of total bilateral trade out to 2020. First, we estimated average growth rates for bilateral trade for 2000–2010 for each economy. Second, we extrapolated the 2010 value out to 2015 using 75 percent of the 2000–2010 average growth rates. Finally, we extrapolated the 2015 value out to 2020 using 50 percent of the 2000–2010 average growth rates. This moderation of growth rates across time is in keeping with growing and expanding economies but at an increasingly slower pace.

7. Derek Scissors, *Free Market and National Defense: U.S. Import Dependence on China* (Washington, DC: Heritage Foundation, September 2010), 21, http://www .heritage.org/research/reports/2010/09/free-markets-and-national-defense-us -import-dependence-on-china.

8. IMF, *World Economic Outlook: Slowing Growth, Rising Risks* (Washington, DC: IMF, September 2011), http://www.imf.org/external/pubs/ft/weo/2011/02/weodata /index.aspx. The IMF includes forecasts out to 2016 in this database.

9. We should take caution in drawing a direct line between significant correlation (as signaled by correlation statistics) and significant EI. Anscombe produced a "quartet," proving that a particular correlation statistic can emerge from a variety of configurations of the same data—not all indicating a smooth linear relationship. See F. J. Anscombe, "Graphs in Statistical Analysis," *The American Statistician* 27, no. 1 (1973): 17–21.

10. James Morrow, Randolph Siverson, and Tressa Taberes, "The Political Determinants of International Trade: The Major Powers, 1907–1990," *American Political Science Review* 92, no. 3 (1998): 649–61.

11. The data on total trade in goods and services are from the US Department of Commerce, Bureau of Economic Analysis, "Table 12, U.S. International Transactions, by Area," 2011, www.bea.gov.

12. Justin Lau, "Major Trade Disputes between China and the US," *Financial Times*, 18 May 2010, http://www.ft.com/intl/cms/s/ b585524e-b3ea-11de-98ec-00144 feab49a,dwp_uuid=abb716b0-2f7a-11da-8b51-00000e2511c8,print=yes.html.

13. The lone incident of a military conflict between the United States and China during the period was the USNS *Impeccable* incident. See Demetri Sevastopulo and Kathryn Hille, "Beijing's Naval Harassment Rouses US," *Financial Times*, 25 March 2009, http://www.ft.com/intl/cms/s/0/38043386-196b-11de-9d34-0000779fd2ac.html #axzz1djv3Dp dq.

14. John Oneal et al., "The Liberal Peace: Interdependence, Democracy, and International Conflict, 1950–85," *Journal of Peace Research* 33, no. 1 (1996): 11–28; Katherine Barbieri, "Economic Interdependence: A Path to Peace or a Source of Interstate Conflict?," *Journal of Peace Research* 33, no. 1 (1996): 29–49; and Edward Mansfield and Jon Pevehouse, "Trade Blocs, Trade Flows, and International Conflict," *International Organization* 54, no. 4 (2000): 775–808.

15. Levent Kockesen, "Extensive Form Games with Perfect Information," lecture notes from a class taught at Koc University, 1999, http://home.ku.edu.tr/~lkockesen /teaching/uggame/lectnotes/uglect5.pdf.

16. Oneal et al., "Liberal Peace," 11–28; and Mansfield and Pevehouse, "Trade Blocks," 775–808.

17. For example, it is common knowledge that the United States and the wider Western community of nations have urged China to reduce its investment and to expand domestic consumption. The argument is that high levels of investment result in the development of excess infrastructure, which can ultimately induce slowdowns or downturns in the business cycle. More generally, the West has urged China to reduce investment and its reliance on export-led growth in exchange for growth that is stimulated by significantly higher levels of domestic consumption.

18. East-West Center, "ADB President: Domestic Demand Is Greatest Growth Challenge for Asia's Developing Countries," 10 November 2011, http://us1.campaign -archive1.com/?u=044cc59d69d5fff92f2ab7675&id=43b89c7c9b&fblike=true&e=1 60c7b1da8.

19. Michael Schuman, "A Hard Look at Japan's Debt Problem," *Time*, 6 April 2011, http://curiouscapitalist.blogs.time.com/2011/04/06/a-hard-look-at-japans-debt -problem.

20. Data for 2000 to 2010 are actual. The IMF prepared forecasts for 2011 to 2016. Forecasts for 2017–2020 are the author's extrapolation using a growth rate that is 50 percent of the average growth rate from 2000 to 2010.

21. The data for 2000 to 2010 are actual from the CEIC and WTO databases. Forecasts for 2011–15 are extrapolations based on 75 percent of the growth rate from 2000 to 2010. Forecasts for 2016–2020 are extrapolations based on 50 percent of the growth rate for 2000–2010.

Chapter 4

Chinese Soft Economic Warfare

Dr. Chad Dacus
Defense Analyst/Economist, Air Force Research Institute

Introduction

Of the world's largest economies, China boasts the lowest ratio of debt to gross domestic product (GDP) and has accumulated the most extensive currency reserves. Indeed, the People's Republic of China (PRC) holds more US treasury notes than any other country.[1] Furthermore, China's economic growth rates during the last decade have dwarfed those of its rivals. These factors permit China to flex its muscles on the international stage and enable Chinese leaders to choose from a wide variety of economic policies. This chapter explores how the PRC might exploit its economic power in the coming years. That is, will the PRC adopt policies that will embrace the international community and maximize opportunity, or will it seek to minimize threats through forming strategic partnerships and attempting to isolate and weaken its most worrisome competitor, the United States?

China's future economic policy options can be characterized as one of three possible states: peace and prosperity, soft economic warfare, and hedging between these two extremes. While it is useful to sketch out the spectrum of possibilities, it is highly improbable that China will adopt a pure strategy at either end of the spectrum and more probable that it will instead seek hybrid solutions to achieve national goals. Wise leaders will hedge their bets with a combination of elements from each strategy, and the question becomes which pure strategy the chosen hybrid strategy will most resemble. This research effort focuses on the likelihood and the ultimate results of Chinese leaders choosing a peace and prosperity strategy. The elements of such a strategy are similar to many countries' current practice and do not require exposition. Meanwhile, selected elements of the soft-economic-warfare strategy are examined in some detail. No attempt is made to present a complete soft-economic-warfare strategy, but it is hoped that enough of the strategy's flavor will be conveyed to allow the reader to mentally fill in the gaps.

Chinese leaders envision a "harmonious society in a harmonious world" and profess they value internal stability and economic growth above military conquest.[2] Moreover, relations with Taiwan have thawed recently, so prospects for a militarily aggressive China over the next decade seem remote. Therefore, it is more likely China will seek economic means to mitigate the risks posed by the military might of the United States.

Peace and Prosperity

China's economy has experienced remarkable economic growth over the past 20 years. According to the Organization for Economic Cooperation and Development's statistics, China's GDP growth rates averaged 9.8 percent in the 1990s and 10 percent between 1990 and 2008.[3] An unprecedented number of people were elevated out of poverty during this miraculous transformation of the Chinese economy. In 2010 the PRC surpassed Japan as the world's second-largest economy, and some predict that China could overtake the United States as the world's largest economy as early as 2020. With such breathtaking growth and a bright future, China's most likely economic strategy will most closely resemble what could best be labeled a "peace and prosperity" strategy. In effect, the country's leaders could conclude that the best way to protect the country's national interests is by attempting to outgrow its principal rivals, the United States and Japan, while continuing to liberalize trade policies—thus enhancing the perception of China as an asset in the international community. With China having already eclipsed Japan's economic might and rapidly closing on the United States, this strategy is certainly the most intuitively appealing.

China has signaled such a strategy might be in the cards through its 2010 China national defense white paper. In this document, Chinese leaders describe their national security policy as "defensive in nature" and proclaim that "China will never seek hegemony, nor will it adopt the approach of military expansion now or in the future, no matter how its economy develops."[4] These words project the unmistakable self-confidence a rapidly burgeoning economy with accompanying military might can justify.

To evaluate the likelihood of Chinese leaders continuing to implement policies consistent with this mind-set over the coming decades, the amount of time it will take China to approach outpacing all other countries in defense spending is quite informative. If the country's leaders believe the United States can be surpassed over a relatively short time horizon, then the need to neutralize America economically dissipates because biding the time until the PRC reaches economic and military supremacy will not require Herculean patience. This subject can best be examined by comparing future Chinese defense spending with the projected expenditures of the world's current leader in military capability, the United States. This comparison extends to 2025 and involves generating a range of possible expenditures for both countries. As China is a developing country, the primary emphasis is estimating highly unpredictable economic growth rates. For the United States, the closest scrutiny will concern uncertainty in future political decisions.

China's Defense Expenditure

To project upper bounds for the PRC's defense expenditures in 2025, the following process was followed: The nation's economic output sets an upper limit on defense spending, and then policy makers decide what percentage of this output will be dedicated to defense. These components can be forecast by estimating future economic growth and by assuming Chinese leaders' decisions involving defense reflect the future threat environment. Unfortunately, China's exchange rate regime complicates estimation of the country's GDP. Since the renminbi's exchange rate is soft-pegged to the dollar, choosing either the purchasing power parity (PPP) or market exchange rate works well for some goods and services but not for others. RAND researchers resolved this problem by using a combination of the two measures depending on the type of spending involved.[5] Currency and force-composition issues prevent a discussion of the relative capabilities purchased with the defense budgets of the two countries. For example, China spends an estimated 34 percent of its defense budget on personnel, while the United States allocated 22.5 percent of defense appropriations to personnel in 2009.[6] Evaluating relative capabilities is beyond the scope of this report.

China's impressive economic growth over the past 30 years has astounded the world. Although some analysts believe this trend will continue unabated, a slowdown in growth is more consistent with history. Barry Eichengreen, Donghyun Park, and Kwanho Shin examine the point at which fast-growing economies' growth has slowed since 1957.[7] They found that, on average, fast-growing economies slow down by 3.5 percent at a GDP per capita of almost $17,000 in 2005 international dollars. Depending on China's rate of growth in the next few years, China should eclipse this level of prosperity between 2017 and 2021.[8] Therefore, unless mitigating factors indicate that a deceleration is less likely in China, a slowdown is likely in the next five to 10 years.

According to these analysts, five of China's prominent economic characteristics increase the probability of an imminent deceleration of economic growth, while only two aspects of China's economic policy lower the probability of a slowdown. China's unusually fast pre-slowdown growth, undervalued currency, and exceptionally low ratio of consumption to GDP are powerful predictors of weakened growth. In Eichengreen, Park, and Shin's models, these variables are the most highly statistically significant, and China has relatively extreme values compared to the countries in the sample. Meanwhile, China's trade openness and high investment as a percentage of GDP slightly decrease the economy's high probability of diminishing growth, but these variables are not as statistically significant in explaining the probability of a slowdown. The authors conclude that China's probability of experiencing a significant slowdown in growth is over 70 percent. Finally, they examine the effects of a few policy variables on the timing of the weakening growth rate. An undervalued currency and high and rising inflation were found to accelerate the weakening of growth in terms of GDP per capita. While China's undervalued currency has been discussed, its inflation rate has been highly variable, so this result is not particularly informative.[9] The available evidence supports the conclusion that China is quite likely to have a significant slowdown in the next five to 10 years, with the highest likelihood of diminished growth clustered closer to five years than to 10.

These empirical results will serve as the foundation for projections of China's GDP over the next 20 years. Although a bit of a leap of faith is still required, the gap between the historical record and future expectations is much easier to traverse with strong empirical support. The International Monetary Fund (IMF) expects China's GDP to grow by an average of 8.5 percent in 2012 and 2013.[10] If this rate of growth is maintained through the slowdown point, China's GDP by PPP surpasses that of the United States in 2017.[11] Beyond 2017 China's economic growth rate is assumed to decrease permanently by 5 percent yearly. This diminished growth rate is consistent with the average slowdown of countries in the Eichengreen, Park, and Shin sample, with pre-slowdown growth rates of between 8 and 9 percent.

These empirical results can be explained using theoretical arguments. Economist Jack Goldstone takes a more theoretical approach and discusses factors that have contributed to China's startling growth but that will play a lesser role in its expansion in the next 20 years.[12] First, converting agricultural labor to more productive manufacturing and service employment has played a key role in the Chinese economic miracle. According to the United Nations, the rate of urban growth for 2015–20 will drop by 47 percent compared to 2000–2005.[13] Second, commodity costs will continue to rise and cause prices to rise in this increasingly import-dependent country. Finally, the dramatic aging of Asian countries, including the PRC, will shrink both the domestic labor markets and regional export markets. According to Gladstone, the confluence of these negative trends will grind China's growth rate down to a practical maximum of 5 percent. This research uses this figure to establish the pessimistic growth projection. According to Morgan Stanley's historical data, this growth scenario is more likely than the optimistic scenario.[14] Analysts who believe China's economic growth has been consistently overstated may also prefer this growth scenario. Economists have argued that growth rates are unsustainable because smaller gains will result from further increasing investments from government-owned enterprises and exports.[15]

Two prominent issues arise when estimating defense expenditures based on a percentage of Chinese GDP. First, should defense expenditure be quantified using PPP spending, through market currency valuation, or by a weighted average of the two approaches? RAND researchers deal with this issue in *Modernizing China's Military: Opportunities and Constraints.*[16] Because China must import much of its military technology, PPP is inappropriate. That is, prices are very low in China and do not realistically represent how much future defense procurement is likely to cost. In any event, the renminbi's value is likely to rise over the coming years. For this reason, projected market exchange rates are intuitively appealing for military procurement. Meanwhile, goods and services not appropriate for international trade, such as wages for personnel, are best quantified through the PPP rate. Therefore, shares of future Chinese military expenditure in these spending categories will be weighted with these thoughts in mind. The other question that comes to mind is what percentage of GDP will China devote to defense spending in 2025? RAND estimates that the PRC's actual military spending as a percentage of GDP is between 40 and 70 percent higher than reported rates and thus constitutes between 2.3 and 2.8 percent of GDP. Since it is difficult to anticipate how threatened China will perceive itself to be in 2025, this analysis will remain consistent and assume China spends 2.5 percent of its future GDP on defense. Adapting these approaches and assumptions to 2011 data, Chinese defense spending in 2025 is projected to be around $650B in 2011 dollars.

US Defense Spending

To analyze federal budgets, the Congressional Budget Office (CBO) routinely forecasts economic growth. Between 2011 and 2025, the CBO expects real GDP to grow at an average rate of 2.67 percent.[17] Theoretically, increasing real growth rates allows real defense expenditures to rise without consuming a higher percentage of GDP. However, Congress ultimately decides how to allocate federal tax dollars. Although the CBO expects total US government expenditure to rise as a percentage of GDP through 2025, discretionary spending as a percentage of GDP will almost certainly fall. Under its more optimistic scenario, the CBO expects defense spending to fall from 4.7 percent of GDP in 2011 to about 3.6 percent of GDP in 2021.[18] For the purposes of this analysis, defense expenditures will be budgeted at 3.5 percent of GDP for the baseline scenario and at 3 percent of GDP for a more budget-constrained scenario. Although predicting political decisions is often particularly challenging, the United States could well face borrowing constraints that will limit the generosity of the federal coffers and, therefore, the errors associated with these predictions. Under the baseline scenario, China's defense expenditures reach 88 percent of US defense spending by 2025. Meanwhile, in the more pessimistic scenario, China's defense outlays eclipse US expenditures by about 2 percent of total spending.

Implications

The defense spending gap between the United States and China will narrow appreciably over the next 15 years and will probably reverse direction thereafter. Although parity in spending will not necessarily mean comparable *capability* by 2025, China will be on the precipice of becoming a true peer competitor. China's defense spending will almost certainly be at a level that strongly deters the United States from military intervention in Chinese affairs.

In light of these projections, setting cooperative and transparent economic policies is seemingly the most rational mind-set for Chinese policy makers. However, Chinese leaders may have a more risk-averse, pessimistic, or impatient outlook and choose to adopt a less harmonious strategy. Taking these actions would almost certainly be suboptimal economically and cause the Chinese to forgo some gains from trade. Nevertheless, history provides many examples of countries choosing to act in ways that minimize risk while sacrificing economic gain.[19] Even the author of *The Wealth of Nations*, Adam Smith, declared that "defense is much more important than opulence."[20] China's military buildup indicates that the country's leaders are not immune from worrying about external threats—by far the biggest of which is the US military.

Soft Economic Warfare

Although engaging in foreign trade without caveats will almost certainly maximize China's future economic growth and, therefore, military strength, the country's leaders may reason that a more constrained approach minimizes risk more effectively. It is abundantly clear that China considers the United States to be its primary rival and only real existential threat. Additionally, the 1979 Taiwan Relations Act requires the United States to "provide Taiwan with arms of a defensive character" and to "maintain the capacity of the United States to resist any resort to force or other forms that would jeopardize the security, or the social or the economic system, of the people on Taiwan."[21] Indeed, in 2010 the United States sold Taiwan $6B in arms. Not surprisingly, the PRC considers this "an unwarranted intrusion by the United States into the internal affairs of China."[22] Although the United States and China are unlikely to go to war over Taiwan, each arms sale again raises the ire of the PRC. Chinese leaders may desire a less provocative means of neutralizing the US threat; this can be partially achieved through economic means.

To provide motivation for the soft economic warfare strategy from a decision-theoretic perspective, one can imagine that the economic utility function that most international policy makers would favor for developing economies would be to maximize economic growth subject to pollution and government budget constraints. If China's leaders are considered risk neutral, this seems to be a reasonable way to specify their constrained maximization problem. If the Chinese begin focusing more on hampering their principal rival, the United States, then their objective function transforms into maximizing the difference between PRC and US economic growth rates. The constraints could be considered identical to those for the risk-neutral problem specification. It is clear that conventional warfare would not maximize the policy makers' utility in either case, but under the second, more risk-averse utility function, Chinese leaders may desire a less provocative means of decreasing the threat posed by the United States. The strategy implied by this worldview can be carried out, in part, by accelerating liquidation of China's long position in US Treasury bonds, by limiting US access to certain commodities and lines of communication, and by seeking exclusive partnerships with European Union (EU) countries and Japan in high-tech industries.

The concept of soft economic warfare is somewhat analogous to the microeconomic strategy of raising rivals' costs.[23] The usual scenario for the application of this strategy involves a firm acquiring a supplier that wields considerable market power in the good it produces. The firm then raises the price of the input good in sales to its competitors in the production of the final good. Its competitors then become high-cost producers—improving the profits of the acquiring firm and seriously damaging its competition. A classic example is when a South African steel producer bought a major iron ore producer. The underlying logic is that a firm with higher costs will decrease output, and the same general reasoning applies to an entire country's economy. Production, or economic growth, will be lower than it would have been absent the deleterious economic policies of the Chinese. The analogy breaks down a bit because the Chinese economy itself does not benefit from most of these strategies, such as the vertically integrating firm. However, enough of the stratagem's spirit applies to serve as intuitive support for soft economic warfare.

Many have been calling for the end of the dollar's reign as the de facto world currency for some time now.[24] The difference between word and deed is particularly stark, however, because no practical alternative to the dollar currently exists. Though China does not publish the currency composition of its official foreign reserves, it is widely believed that China has been steadily diversifying its reserve holdings and decreasing its exposure to the risk of a precipitous decline in the dollar's value.[25] Because the PRC pegs the value of its renminbi to the dollar and runs huge trade surpluses with the United States, it is difficult for the nation to distance itself from the dollar. In addition, dumping dollars at an accelerated pace would cause the currency's foreign exchange value to dive and substantially decrease the value of China's reserve holdings. Some have referred to a decisive Chinese move against the dollar as "economic mutual assured destruction."[26] The United States has far more to lose from such a move, however, because the cost of financing its already tremendously burdensome debt would rise.

The consequences of a precipitous decline in demand for American treasury securities are potentially dire. The most obvious repercussion would be an increase in the cost of servicing the national debt due to an interest rate spike. The CBO states that a 4-percentage point across-the-board increase in interest rates would cause a jump in federal interest payments of about $100 billion for fiscal year 2011 alone. In future years, the impact of this rate increase would be much more pronounced, with an estimated $460 billion in increased expenditure in 2015.[27] Such pressure on already strained budgets could not be sustained, and a fiscal crisis would likely ensue with debt restructuring or inflationary monetary policy becoming essentially obligatory. If the PRC is intent on neutralizing the United States, moving away from the dollar and causing it to lose its status as the world's default reserve currency would undoubtedly do the most damage.

Control of strategic minerals is another tool that China may use to exercise economic leverage over its competitors. The International Union of Pure and Applied Chemistry defines rare earth elements (REE) as members of the family of lanthanoid metals, scandium, and yttrium.[28] The heavy rare earths are used in high-technology applications such as lasers, magnetic resonance imaging, and fiber optics. Although REEs can be found throughout the world in the earth's crust, locations where it is economically feasible to mine for them are much less common. Currently, China controls approximately 97 percent of the world's REE market and boasts 58 percent of world reserves.[29] China has instituted export controls of rare earth minerals, and some experts envision scarcity of some REEs by 2015.[30] The PRC has a near-stranglehold on the market, and the country is devoting substantial resources to discovering industrial and military uses for these metals.[31]

The United States controls 9 percent of the world's REE reserves and is beginning to realize its vulnerable position.[32] California's Mountain Pass rare earth mine once supplied the majority of the world's rare earth minerals and is undergoing modernization efforts that should bring it back up to full production by the end of 2012. This mine was reopened so that China and Japan could not corner the market and expose the United States to significant national security risk with an export moratorium. It might be able to fulfill the United States' future needs if demand does not skyrocket due to a scientific breakthrough, but other developed nations could well be entirely dependent on China's exports. While substitutes exist for some of the REEs, they are generally less effective and could compromise military superiority.[33]

Clearly, China's REE monopoly could be a powerful tool for the PRC in forming economic and, eventually, perhaps in some cases, military alliances with Japan and other strategically important nations. Barring a larger commitment to revitalizing rare earth mining in the United States, the country is highly unlikely to possess sufficient productive capacity to export in substantial amounts. If a future technological advance requires the exploitation of REEs, the United States would likely exhaust the Mountain Pass mine's capacity and be 10 to 15 years away from augmenting current production through another mine. The potentially stark implications for national security are obvious.

China can also interfere with American lines of communication (LOC). Closing selected sea and air LOCs to some of America's commercial traffic would have negative consequences such as starting a trade war, sacrificing trade revenue, and losing goodwill among other allies. Taking this action would be unnecessarily provocative and would arguably end up damaging Beijing much more than Washington. Interference with cyber LOCs is a more intriguing possibility. Cyber attacks aimed at commercial targets offer the possibility for furthering the objectives of soft economic warfare because attribution is difficult. A lone hacker sitting at a keyboard in a remote location cannot necessarily be connected to the Chinese government. Furthermore, if estimated economic damage from past computer viruses is even remotely accurate, commercial virus production and hacking may play a crucial part in the soft economic warfare strategy.[34]

The decision of whether to implement a more structured commercial cyber operation reduces to a relatively straightforward cost-benefit analysis that will illuminate important aspects of the stratagem. The benefits associated with corporate hacking—lowering of US GDP— are relatively straightforward. However, as Martin Libicki observes, cyber attacks are self-depleting.[35] To simplify the term and put it into economic language, computer hacking exhibits diminishing returns to labor. Some of the costs involved in producing commercial hacking are less tangible than the benefits. The opportunity costs of the labor and expenses for the computer equipment and infrastructure are relatively simple to estimate. Estimating loss of goodwill associated with suspicion of government participation is more problematic, but losses are likely to increase rapidly as the size of the operation expands. China's utility function for commercial hacking could therefore be expressed as the economic damage inflicted on the United States minus direct costs, economic damage inflicted indirectly on China, and total loss of international goodwill. Since the marginal economic damage inflicted by the next hacker is almost certainly decreasing, direct costs are at best linear in labor, and marginal loss of international goodwill is likely to be increasing. As the number of hackers goes up, the PRC should devote a relatively small, highly trained rotating group to this effort. The staff should rotate to ensure that fresh ideas are infused periodically into the operation.

Another area in which the PRC might be able to undermine the United States' hegemony is through its international trade policy. China is the number one exporter in the world, and exports account for about 25 percent of Chinese GDP. However, China's reliance on the US consumer market for economic growth could easily be overstated. In "China's Embrace of Globalization," the authors state that it is untrue that exports were the primary driver of Chinese growth in recent decades.[36] During the period 2002–7, increases in net exports accounted for only 15 percent of total real GDP growth.[37] Nevertheless, it would still be catastrophic for the Chinese to lose access to any considerable portion of the US consumer market. Therefore, the primary goal of the Chinese would be to retain access to as much of the US consumer market as possible while distancing itself from the United States in other areas. China would want to err on the side of caution and refrain from coming close to forfeiting strong trade relations with the United States, but the PRC could still implement policies to advance its interests at America's expense.

Strengthening economic partnerships with the EU countries and Japan would diversify sources of demand for Chinese producers and thus decrease dependence on the US market. Partnerships excluding the United States in key high-technology sectors with potentially substantial military value would characterize this aspect of the PRC's soft economic warfare policy. China is already the top exporting nation to both the EU and Japan.[38] However, among the larger EU economies, China is the largest exporter only to Germany, so much more can arguably be accomplished through increased outreach. This objective may have motivated Vice Premier Li Keqiang's trip to Europe in early 2011.[39]

Since the EU still has an arms embargo on China dating from the Tiananmen Square massacre, the PRC has its work cut out for it in reaching trade agreements with EU countries on advanced technologies with possible military applications. China's ability to bankroll the EU countries' debts could provide the necessary leverage for substantial influence with EU leaders, and its transition to the world's largest economy will certainly attract potential trade partners to the table for trade agreements with neither the need nor the concern for American participation.[40] The PRC's tremendous economic leverage is likely to motivate European countries to transfer and share technological advances to China for economic benefits in other areas without regard for how this will affect US national security interests. That is, the Europeans could find that their concerns for international security and human rights become subordinate to economic necessity. The long-rumored end of the North Atlantic Treaty Organization (NATO) would smooth the path to cozier relations with China.[41] Although European countries will not necessarily intend to damage US national security, their actions could result in serious damage to American interests. This implicit collusion by the EU in advancing Chinese national security objectives could cause the United States to lose some of its technological edge over the PRC.

Japan's potential future role in implicitly undermining US national security through warmer relations with China could prove decisive over the coming decades. Using the PPP valuation of GDP, the combined economies of China and Japan are roughly comparable to that of the United States. A coalition led by these states would be incredibly powerful and eventually far outstrip the United States in economic might. Japan leads the world in patent applications, and China ranks third.[42] Moreover, a Sino-Japanese alliance could create a scientific juggernaut of 1.5 billion people.

The question of whether this alliance becomes a fait accompli yields mixed results. When the Democratic Party of Japan (DPJ) became Japan's majority party, the nascent government began to make overtures toward Beijing.[43] Meanwhile, Japan and the United States were engaged in a heated dispute over the relocation of Marine Corps Air Station Futenma, so the long-term trajectory of Sino-Japanese and US-Japanese relations looked very much in doubt. However, a century of ill will between China and Japan will not fade away quickly, and the United States is the only nation that can act as a counterbalance to the PRC's power. A series of Sino-Japanese naval incidents have reignited historic mistrusts and heightened the contemporary rivalry. The US-Japanese alliance has benefited from the increased tension, but this state of affairs could be only a temporary pause along the path to a Sino-Japanese alliance.

China led the list of Japan's trading partners in 2010, and the United States lagged behind with a distant second-place finish.[44] The gap between the countries will undoubtedly widen as China's economic growth continues to outpace that of America's. In addition, Japan relies on China to fulfill more than 90 percent of its demand for REEs.[45] While Japan's very public perception of China as a military threat may seem to undermine the prospects of a close relationship, such an alliance is arguably inevitable.[46] To risk understatement, economic ties between the countries are substantial and strengthening quickly as China grows. The large disparity in defense expenditures between the nations may convince Japan that prolonged resistance is futile and that the United States will eventually be powerless to help. A cozy economic relationship between the two powers coupled with somewhat intensified protectionism toward the United States would deal a substantial blow to American economic interests.

The US Response

Since the US government's budget is more constrained than that of the PRC's, Washington's strategy space is more confining. If the Chinese choose to pursue destructive economic policies, the United States can do surprisingly little to lessen the effectiveness of the PRC's approach. However, the United States can take preventative steps to attempt to discourage China from pursuing this path.

Most importantly, the United States must reform its social welfare programs so that it is perceived as more fiscally sound. If the United States returns to fiscal rectitude, the PRC may perceive America as being less vulnerable to soft-economic-warfare policies. America's leaders must realize that the nation's burdensome deficits and debt are truly a national security threat. In a different context, as chairman of the Joint Chiefs of Staff, Adm Michael Mullen identified the national debt as the nation's single biggest national security threat, but it is unclear that the nation's lawmakers grasp the connection between the country's fiscal health and its long-term security.[47]

The United States should intensify its efforts to produce higher quantities of rare earth elements and fund applied research to find substitutes and manufacturing approaches that do not require REEs. Although the resurrection of California's Mountain Pass mine is a promising start, much more should be done. Industry sources have identified rare earth deposits in the United States, Canada, Australia, and South Africa that could theoretically be mined by 2014.[48] Since preparation for mining can take a decade, the United States must quickly seize economically feasible mining opportunities.

Deterring China from commercial hacking could prove quite challenging. Since China's most important costs associated with soft cyber warfare are likely to be loss of international goodwill, shaming the PRC could provide a productive avenue for deterrence. That is, magnifying the costs associated with loss of international goodwill is arguably the most effective tactic to use against a country vying to build its credibility. The Chinese Olympic doping scandal serves as a useful exemplar of this approach—when the international community condemned China for cheating, the Chinese responded by cracking down on doping.[49]

Finally, the United States should choose whether it will adopt an inclusive or more combative international trade policy. The inclusive policy would involve advancing the cause of free trade and engaging in international dialogue to promote the breaking down of barriers to trade. The US history of selective protectionism could discourage allies and lead them to overlook China's human rights violations to find alternate suppliers. For example, France's Nicolas Sarkozy has scolded the United States for protectionism in the refueling tanker bidding process.[50] Even though this perception could well be undeserved, the circuitous process through which Northrop Grumman and the European Aeronautic Defense and Space (EADS) Company lost the contract leads to the appearance of protectionism. Under this approach, the United States should jettison its "stealth" protectionist image.

The United States has already threatened trade sanctions against China for currency manipulation—even taking the step of passing a bill in the House of Representatives.[51] It has also imposed sanctions on the Chinese steel industry because of its dumping practices. Trade sanctions that target multiple industries would serve as a powerful deterrent to the Chinese but could result in a trade war. Research has shown that trade sanctions are relatively ineffective in achieving their expressed goal but are often useful for other reasons, such as demonstrating national resolve.[52] Conversely, trade liberalization has exerted a robust, positive effect on economic growth.[53] It is highly unlikely that moving in the opposite direction would be beneficial to either country's economy. Considering the sheer volume of trade between the two nations, the effects of strong sanctions could prove to be economically devastating.

If the United States takes on its fiscal issues in a credible manner and demonstrates transparency and fairness in its international dealings, China is unlikely to consider America a serious threat or soft target and will probably refrain from these destructive policies. Responding to Chinese policies with threats and retaliation could be risky and counterproductive since the Chinese help fund our debt and supply US consumers with cheap imports. The best policy options are to develop internal US capabilities where possible and necessary for national security and to cultivate existing international relationships and alliances.

Notes

1. Department of the Treasury/Federal Reserve Board, "Major Foreign Holders of Treasury Securities," 16 April 2012, http://www.treasury.gov/resource-center /data-chart-center/tic/Documents/mfh.txt.

2. Hu Jintao, "Hold High the Great Banner of Socialism with Chinese Characteristics and Strive for New Victories in Building a Moderately Prosperous Society in All," report to the 17th National Congress of the Communist Party of China, Beijing, China, 15 October 2007. The "harmonious society" theme was stressed throughout the address.

3. Organisation for Economic Co-operation and Development, Statistical Extracts, "Gross Domestic Product (Annual)" (select China and referenced years), http://stats.oecd.org/index.aspx. Author's calculations are based on website's raw data.

4. Information Office of the State Council of the PRC, *China's National Defense in 2010* (Beijing: People's Republic of China, Information Office of the State Council, March 2011), sec. 2, "National Defense Policy," 5.

5. Keith Crane et al., *Modernizing China's Military, Opportunities and Constraints*, RAND Report MG-260 (Santa Monica, CA: RAND, 2005), 230–31.

6. Information Office of the State Council of the PRC, *China's National Defense in 2010*, sec. 8, "National Defense."

7. Barry Eichengreen, Donghyun Park, and Kwanho Shin, "When Fast Growing Economies Slow Down: International Evidence and Implications for China" (Working Paper 16919, National Bureau of Economic Research, Cambridge, MA, March 2011).

8. Author's calculation based on 7 to 10 percent growth per annum.

9. World Bank, *World Development Indicators* (Washington, DC: The World Bank, updated 17 September 2012), http://data.worldbank.org/indicator/NY.GDP.DEFL.KD.ZG.

10. International Monetary Fund, "IMF Marks Down Global Forecast, Sees Risk on the Rise," IMF survey online, 24 January 2012, http://www.imf.org/external/pubs/ft/survey/so/2012/NEW012412A.htm.

11. International Monetary Fund, *World Economic Outlook* (Washington, DC: International Monetary Fund, 21 September 2011), statistical appendix, http://www.imf.org/external/pubs/ft/weo/2011/02/weodata/index.aspx, and author's calculation.

12. Jack Goldstone, "What If China's Economic Expansion Is about to Slow?," *Washington Post*, 14 April 2011.

13. United Nations, Department of Economic and Social Affairs, Population Division, "Average Annual Rate of Change of the Urban Population, 1950–2050" (selecting China and then referenced time periods, author calculated percentage change), http://esa.un.org/unpd/wup/CD-ROM/Urban-Rural-Population.htm.

14. Qing Wang, Steven Zhang, and Ernest Ho, *The China Files: Chinese Economy through 2020*, Morgan Stanley Blue Paper (New York: Morgan Stanley, 8 November 2010), 5. In the decade following the realization of a GDP per capita of $7,000, 11 of the 40 countries experienced less than half of their preinflection growth rate.

15. Bob Davis, "Beijing to Slow Growth," *Wall Street Journal*, 28 February 2011.

16. Crane et al., *Modernizing China's Military*, 2005, 231.

17. CBO, *The Budget and Economic Outlook: Fiscal Years 2010 to 2020* (Washington, DC: CBO, January 2010), 123 (and assumptions consistent with historical policy).

18. Ibid., 54.

19. John J. Mearsheimer discusses a particularly egregious example, England's 1651 Navigation Act. This law was clearly enacted to damage Holland's commercial interests. See Mearsheimer, *The Tragedy of Great Power Politics* (New York: W. W. Norton & Co., Inc., 2001), 48.

20. Adam Smith, *An Inquiry into the Nature and Causes of the Wealth of Nations*, ed. Edwin Cannan (Chicago: University of Chicago Press, 1976), vol. 1, 487.

21. Taiwan Relations Act, Public Law 96-8, HR 2479, 96th Cong., 1st sess., 10 April 1979, sec. 4.

22. Embassy of the People's Republic of China in the United States of America, "China Opposes US Congress Resolution on Taiwan," press release, 19 July 2004, http://www.china-embassy.org/eng/xw/t143465.htm.

23. Steven C. Salop and David T. Scheffman, "Raising Rivals' Costs," *American Economic Review* 73, no. 2 (May 1983): 267–71, http://academico.direito-rio.fgv.br /ccmw/images/9/96/Salop_e_Scheffman_-_Raising_Rival's_Costs.pdf.

24. International Monetary Fund, *Enhancing International Monetary Stability— A Role for the SDR [Special Drawing Right]?* (Washington, DC: IMF, 7 January 2011).

25. Wang Xiaotian, "China Starts Diversifying Forex Reserves," *China Daily*, 18 August 2010.

26. Ambrose Evans-Pritchard, "Concerns Grow over China's Sale of US Bonds," *Telegraph*, 23 February 2010.

27. Jonathan Huntley, *Federal Debt and the Risk of a Fiscal Crisis*, Economic and Budget Issue Brief (Washington, DC: CBO, 27 July 2010), 7.

28. International Union of Pure and Applied Chemistry (IUPAC), *Nomenclature of Inorganic Chemistry: IUPAC Recommendations 2005* (Cambridge, UK: RSC Publishing, 2005), 51, http://old.iupac.org/publications/books/rbook/Red_Book_2005 .pdf.

29. Cindy Hurst, *China's Rare Earth Elements Industry: What Can the West Learn?* (Leavenworth, KS: Institute for the Analysis of Global Security, March 2010), 3, http://www.iags.org/rareearth0310hurst.pdf.

30. Robin Bromby, "Caution, Rare Earths Ahead," *Australian*, 26 April 2010.

31. Hurst, *China's Rare Earth Elements Industry*, 7.

32. Ibid., 14.

33. US Geological Survey, "Rare Earths," *Mineral Commodity Summaries* (Washington, DC: US Department of the Interior, January 2009), 131.

34. For instance, Computer Economics estimates economic damage from malicious code at $13.2B in the year 2001 alone. See "Malicious Code Attacks Had $13.2 Billion Economic Impact in 2001," September 2002, http://www.computer economics .com/article.cfm?id=133.

35. Martin Libicki, "Cyberwar as a Confidence Game," *Strategic Studies Quarterly* 5, no. 1 (Spring 2011): 133.

36. Lee Branstetter and Nicholas Lardy, "China's Embrace of Globalization" (Working Paper 12373, National Bureau of Economic Research, Cambridge, MA, July 2006), 14.

37. Pranab Bardhan, *Awakening Giants, Feet of Clay* (Princeton, NJ: Princeton University Press, 2010), 24.

38. European Commission, Eurostat statistical database, "Leading Client and Supplier Countries of the EU27 in Merchandise Trade," 2011, http://trade.ec.europa .eu/doclib/docs/2006/september/tradoc_122529.pdf; and Ministry of Finance, Trade Statistics of Japan (using 2011 cumulative total for 227 displayed cases), http://www .customs.go.jp/toukei/srch/indexe.htm?M=23&P=1.

39. Banning Garrett, "Is China Trying to Divide U.S. and Europe?," CNN Opinion, 20 January 2011, http://articles.cnn.com/2011-01-20/opinion/garrett.china.europe.us_1 _vice-premier-li-keqiang-chinese-president-hu-jintao-china?_s=PM:OPINION.

40. Nerys Avery, "Greater China Daybook: China May Buy More Europe Bonds; Chalco Profit Drop," *Bloomberg News*, 21 April 2011, http://www.bloomberg.com /news/2011-04-21/greater-china-daybook-china-may-buy-more-europe-bonds -chalco-profit-drop.html.

41. In 2002 the *New York Times*'s Thomas Friedman sounded the alarm in his article "The End of NATO?," 3 February 2002. In 2011 the Libyan uprising signaled the end of NATO to some. See Steven Metz, "Is Libya the End of NATO?," *New Republic*, 15 April 2011.

42. World Intellectual Property Organization (WIPO), *World Intellectual Property Indicators, 2011* (Geneva, Switzerland: WIPO, 2011), table P.1, 126.

43. For example, see Julian Ryall and Malcolm Moore, "China and Japan Begin Talks on Building Alliance," *Telegraph*, 22 April 2011, http://www.telegraph.co.uk/news/worldnews/asia/japan/6258990/China-and-Japan-begin-talks-on-building-alliance.html; and Lev Navrozov, "China and Japan Develop 'Strategic Relationship,'" Newsmax.com, 15 April 2010.

44. Japan External Trade Organization, "Japanese Trade and Investment Statistics," February 2011, http://www.jetro.go.jp/en/reports/statistics.

45. Takashi Nakamishi, "Japan METI [Ministry of Economy, Trade, and Industry] Unveils Steps to Cut Reliance on China Rare Earth by a Third," Fox Business, 25 February 2011.

46. Japan Ministry of Defense, *National Defense Program Guidelines for FY 2001 and Beyond*, 17 December 2010, 4, http://www.mod.go.jp/e/d_act/d_policy/pdf/guidelinesFY2011.pdf.

47. Adm Michael Mullen, chairman of the Joint Chiefs of Staff (address, Detroit Economic Club, Detroit, MI, 26 August 2010).

48. Government Accountability Office (GAO), *Rare Earth Minerals in the Defense Supply Chain*, GAO-10-617R, briefing for congressional committees (Washington, DC: US GAO, 14 April 2010), 17.

49. Juliette Macur, "China Redoubles Effort to Avoid Doping Shame," *New York Times*, 8 August 2004.

50. Daniel Stone, "Sarkozy Has the Meeting He Needed with Obama," *Newsweek*, 30 March 2010.

51. "House Overwhelmingly Passes Trade Sanctions Bill Targeted at China," *Huffington Post*, updated 25 May 2011, http://www.huffingtonpost.com/2010/09/29/house-china-trade-sanctions-bill-passed_n_744688.html.

52. GAO, *Economic Sanctions: Effectiveness as Tools of Foreign Policy*, GAO/NSAID-92-106 (Washington, DC: US GAO, February 1992).

53. Romain Wacziang and Karen Horn, "Trade Liberalization and Growth: New Evidence," *World Bank Economic Review* 22, no. 2 (June 2008): 187–231.

Chapter 5

Steaming up the Hudson

China, the United States, and the Problem of Misperception

Dr. Simon Reich
Professor, Rutgers, Newark University

Introduction

> The Pentagon has been long aware of Chinese ambitions to build not just one, but multiple aircraft carriers as part of an effort to modernize its military force, a spokesperson for the U.S. Department of Defense said today. The U.S. will "maintain the military capabilities necessary to protect our interests, defend our allies, and deter potential adversaries from acts of aggression and intimidation," the spokesperson said.

> "All of the great nations in the world own aircraft carriers—they are symbols of a great nation," Chen's assistant chief, Lt. Gen. Qi Jianguo, assistant chief of the general staff, told the *Hong Kong Commercial Daily*. But Jianguo also emphasized that after the carrier was deployed it would "definitely not sail to other countries' territorial waters."[1]

The news that China is to develop its first aircraft carrier, a reconditioned Ukrainian ship, elicited much concern and consternation among American policy makers and pundits—although the United States is so far ahead in its program that it struck its first purpose-built aircraft carrier in 1946 and retired its first one, built over 50 years ago, soon after China's announcement.[2] Since the carrier is traditionally regarded as the conduit for extended power projection, some American analysts expressed concern that this development marked a watershed in China's shift from a continental to a regional military power, given Chinese claims of sovereignty over the South China Sea. What was less justifiable was the suggestion that this marked China's transition from a regional to an intercontinental power, one that would soon overtly challenge the United States for global military supremacy. Ignoring both America's inordinate military capability and expenditures, critics of China reached back into the pantheon of Cold War rhetoric in portraying an image of China's imminent rise to superpower status and challenging America's military supremacy. Implicitly, they painted a picture of this aircraft carrier, or one like it, "steaming up the Hudson" as the Chinese invaded New York.[3]

President Obama has employed a rhetoric far more conservative than the shrill tone of American commentators outside of government. Yet his administration has internalized at least part of that message, evident in its new focus on sea- and air-based capability in Asia. The announcement of a renewed attention to Asia after at least a decade of neglect, epitomized by the creation of a new base in northern Australia, appears part of a buildup that risks the appearance of an encirclement strategy to the Chinese.[4] These recent developments beg the questions: Why has the United States embarked on such a potentially incendiary policy? Is it justified? And what are the implications? I explore these questions in the following discussion.

Why Do Americans Fear China's Growth into a Great Power?

The answer to the first question is, perhaps surprisingly, deeply embedded in American scholarship, recalling John Maynard Keynes's famous quote that "practical men, who believe themselves to be quite exempt from any intellectual influences, are usually the slaves of some defunct economist. Madmen in authority, who hear voices in the air, are distilling their frenzy from some academic scribbler of a few years back."[5] Dating back to the seminal work of A. F. K. Organski in the late 1950s, American academics and policy makers have wrestled with the question of the effects of power distributions on the propensity for war. Organski's answer highlighted the importance of a unipolar distribution of power, where one country dominates, in curtailing the prospect of a "great power war."[6] Organski's work set in train at least two relevant research programs, the first centered on "power transition theory" that focused largely on military capabilities. The second, best represented by the influential work of Robert Gilpin, initiated "hegemonic stability theory."[7] Gilpin moved beyond a security focus to link economic and military development to military capabilities, stressing the importance of growth rates and technological innovation in fueling the rise of prospective challengers and resulting in hegemonic wars. Aaron Friedberg summarizes what has been translated into one popular, indeed currently dominant, policy position in the United States in regard to China with the comment that "realist pessimists note that, throughout history, rising powers have tended to be troublemakers, at least insofar as their more established counterparts in the international system are concerned."[8] At the risk of oversimplifying a rich literature for the sake of brevity, what the advocates of power transition theory and hegemonic stability theory implicitly share is a view of how to deter or combat rising powers that threaten American preeminence. Both employ rational choice models assuming that a nation's interests can be objectively defined, that leaders make comparable calculations based on a given distribution of power, and that a preponderance of power in the hands of one country is more stable in avoiding great-power wars. They also largely deny the significance of domestic factors, notably cultural influences, on decision making about conflict.

Subsequent criticism of this body of work has brought into question the empirical validity of the most noteworthy of these claims. Richard Ned Lebow and Benjamin Valentino are among the most vocal and effective of these critics. They suggest, for example, that no country has been able to dominate the global system, as these theories suggest, for over 350 years. A. F. K. Organski wrote his original work, for example, at the zenith of US power, but that has been in relative decline since the 1960s. Furthermore, Lebow and Valentino claim that the purported "power transition" wars described in this work occur only *after* a redistribution of power has taken place—and not between a dominant power and a rising challenger. One important implication of their work is that the notion of relying on deterrent strategies as the major thrust of policy in restraining rising powers is therefore misplaced. Such strategies are more likely to lead to miscommunication and misperception—and thus heighten the risk that a war will become a self-fulfilling prophecy.[9]

Gilpin's work is particularly relevant to our discussion precisely because it shifted attention away from the Soviet Union, whose military prowess was not matched by an economic capability, to a focus on the importance of the linkage between economic development and national security—thus turning the attention of policy makers to a whole new set of potential challengers. The decline of Soviet power therefore did little to alleviate America's concern with potential or existent threats in some quarters. Certainly, the end of the Cold War did herald a sense of triumphalism among some commentators, reflected in Francis Fukuyama's premature declaration of the "end of history" and the subsequent emergence of an optimistic "liberal peace" literature proclaiming that a world of liberal democracies would be free of interstate war.[10] But, perhaps predictably, this view was matched by an expression of fatalism among others, represented in the kind of work that effectively applied Gilpin's argument to an emergent Japan. Notable among this populist literature was that of George Friedman and Meredith Lebard, who claimed that an economically weakened America faced a "coming war with Japan," as an aspiring hegemonic power, within two decades.[11] The logic was simple: according to an eccentric form of calculation, the Japanese economy would outgrow that of the United States within a relatively short time frame. At that point, Japan would pursue a more aggressive posture, demanding a series of changes in the international system that posed a challenge to America's dominant position. The refusal of the United States to concede its global leadership would result in conflict and, eventually, great-power war.

Although this claim seems quaintly absurd in retrospect—given the subsequent implosion of the Japanese economy—many of the same kinds of claims are now being recycled, with the substitution of China for Japan. Dating back to the turn of the century, noted scholar John Mearsheimer suggested that an emergent China posed such a challenge for the United States.[12] A series of academic pieces by American realists has developed and reinforced that claim.[13] Their work relies heavily on two sources addressing when the size of the Chinese economy will be comparable to that of the United States. The first is a comprehensive Organization for Economic Cooperation and Development (OECD) study first published in 1998 by Angus Maddison that relies largely on macroeconomic estimates. The second is a series of Global Trends reports published by the US government's National Intelligence Council, effectively a research arm of the Central Intelligence Agency. Both Maddison's study and the Global Trends reports are largely comparative in nature—big-picture studies that downplay the challenge domestic factors could pose to such linear projections. The Global Trends reports (targeting 2010, 2015, 2020, and, most recently, 2025) are particularly interesting because of their successive revision of estimated dates for when the Chinese economy will approach/exceed that of the United States. They now indicate that parity could be reached as soon as this decade, compared to the original projection of 2050. Thus—albeit possibly inadvertently—the reports have helped fuel the speculation that a great-power war between the United States and China, as a challenger, is moving ever closer.[14]

In tandem, the Maddison and Global Trends studies have formed the baseline that many American realist scholars use in moving up the date for when China's gross national product (GNP) will surpass the United States' GNP. Doing so has given them the license to generate a sense of urgency in addressing what they regard as the challenge posed by China, both economically and militarily. Aaron Friedberg reflects this approach:

> For realist pessimists, the single most important feature of the PRC today is its rising power. Everything else, including the likely character of the U.S.-China relationship, follows from this fact. . . . As was true of the United States in the late nineteenth and early twentieth centuries, so too is China's rapidly growing economy bringing expanding military capabilities in its train. The rising levels of productivity, per capita incomes, and technological competence that accompany economic growth should also translate into an increasing ability both to absorb sophisticated weapons imported from foreign suppliers and eventually to develop such systems indigenously. Although the picture is mixed, and the PRC continues to lag in many areas, these expectations too are borne out by the general pattern of Chinese military development over the last several decades. There are good reasons to expect that China will be able to build and deploy more increasingly capable military systems in the years ahead.[15]

Such prognostications have therefore contributed to generating an environment characterized by distrust and recrimination—one in which cooperatively engaging with China and striving for the best has taken a backseat to preparing for the worst.

Is This Sense of Alarm Justified?

Inevitably, in preparing for the worst, we risk the onset of a vicious circle—a spiral in which the search for security by both sides creates the danger of a costly and potentially damaging military conflict. American policy makers focus on what they regard as bellicose Chinese claims asserting their sovereignty over the South China Sea and Taiwan. They also point to the growth in China's defense budget during the first decade of the century. The Stockholm International Peace Research Institute (SIPRI) estimates that China's budget sharply increased by an average of 12.5 percent a year to a total of $119 billion by 2010, constituting 7.3 percent of global expenditure.[16]

These figures, of course, pale in comparison to the United States' absolute expenditure and percentage of global expenditure on defense in 2010, amounting to $698 billion and 43 percent, respectively. By 2011 the US defense budget had reached $739 billion, 4.91 percent of the GNP.[17] Nonetheless, China's consistent growth in defense expenditure, coupled with official Chinese government estimates for 2012 that project a further 11.2 percent growth, has been the source of concern in Washington, where there is general skepticism about China's habit of underreporting figures on defense expenditures.[18] The aforementioned creation of an aircraft carrier program, evidence of China's attempts to build its own Stealth fighter, its development of a missile program targeting satellites, and claims that it engages in cyber warfare all give substance to the concerns about these aggregate figures.

The unfolding evidence suggests that America's political leadership has concluded that the appropriate response is the military encirclement of China in Asia through the formation or strengthening of a series of alliances, together with the judicious distribution of a network of military bases reliant on a new air-sea strategy. Complementing this military strategy is an economic strategy designed to cajole the Chinese into abandoning residual protectionist trade practices, reforming its currency, and upholding intellectual property rights in China.

Yet questions remain about China's priorities, its intent, and whether its current force posture warrants the kind of concerns expressed in Washington. Although such comparisons are not warranted given its far greater openness, like the old studies that "Sovietologists" conducted during the Cold War, analysts currently attempt to demystify debates among China's leadership through practices such as studying who is attending the Communist Party's annual meetings, observing where people are standing in photographs, reporting scandals about which they have precious little information, and seizing on any supposed snippets of information that may emerge about the growth in China's military budget. Realists use this material as confirmations of the country's general approach, although the link between the two is not always self-evident and is often tenuous. What may be more relevant is evidence about the linkage between what China's key representatives say and what China does.

Joshua Cooper Ramo, noted China watcher, succinctly captures the general principles upon which Chinese foreign policy is based.

They are distinctly different from the dominant American view of China's foreign policy goals. He remarks that "the country's so-called New Security Concept [NSC], introduced in 1997 at an ASEAN [Association of Southeast Asian Nations] meeting and refined in 2002, formalizes this Sino-U.S. difference. Chu Shulong calls the heart of the NSC, which was endorsed publicly by Hu Jintao in April of 2004, 'the Four No's,' which read like a manifesto for multi-polarity: No hegemonism, no power politics, no alliances and no arms races. It's like a Chinese Monroe Doctrine."[19]

Tangibly, prominent Chinese academic Zheng Bijian suggests that China could experience a "peaceful rise to great power status" through what he calls "the developmental path to a peaceful rise." Indeed, in specifically addressing the concerns of American realist scholars about a possible great-power war, Zheng declares that "China will not follow the path of Germany leading up to World War I or those of Germany and Japan leading up to World War II, when these countries violently plundered resources and pursued hegemony. Neither will China follow the path of the great powers vying for global domination during the Cold War. Instead, China will transcend ideological differences to strive for peace, development, and cooperation with all the countries of the world."[20] Others among China's leadership reinforce this view. Notably, Chinese foreign minister Yang Jiechi suggested in a statement to the National People's Congress in 2008 that China accept more international responsibility in ways that serve its interests and that it can help define.[21]

Achieving these goals requires a tricky combination for China's leaders: establishing asymmetric forms of power that deter any foreign threat, maintaining unprecedented growth rates, and yet ensuring diplomatic engagement. They recognize, and often state, that the size of China's economy doesn't carry the importance that American realists attribute to it. With hundreds of millions of people still deeply mired in poverty, their primary goal is to reduce the numbers living below two dollars a day, quell demands for autonomy among ethnic minorities, and thus enhance domestic political stability.

This precarious balancing act requires consistency and predictability in some areas of policy combined with exploration and dynamism in others. It entails fundamentally addressing, if not erasing, one of China's most dominant collective memories for the last 150 years—its utter humiliation at the hands of the West—and replacing it with a sense of respect abroad, particularly from its regional neighbors and the United States and Europe. To achieve these goals requires that the United States aim its policies toward engagement and reassurance based on mutual interest rather than encirclement and containment.[22] In effect, to project America's own ambitions for sustained primacy onto the Chinese is errant. The Chinese seek eminence, respect, accommodation, and broad global influence in the context of the current rules of the global system, not preeminence and domination under a new set of rules of their making, as hegemonic stability theory would anticipate from a new challenger.

Some American scholars reject the realist position and accept this alternative view. They characterize China as a "status quo" power rather than one that seeks to radically change the rules of global engagement to better suit itself.[23] While American realists have focused on what China might do if it sustains its current growth levels, the evidence regarding both its military and economic policies supports this alternative interpretation of China's goals.

China's force structure, for example, remains heavily skewed toward positioning itself as a continental power with a massive army reliant on battle tanks and infantry fighting vehicles. It has less than 25 percent of the United States' fourth-generation tactical aircraft, 15 percent of its ICBMs, and just under 10 percent of its nuclear submarines. Unlike the United States, the Chinese navy has no capacity to fight a global conflict that requires transporting hundreds of thousands of troops across the globe and manning extended supply lines, with only 13 destroyers (compared to the United States' 83), 57 heavy/medium transport aircraft (the United States has 847), and now one aircraft carrier (versus the United States' 11).[24] In sum, even this cursory examination suggests that China's forces are built to fight a continental war with a regional capacity. Even allowing for new programs, at least a generation of production is required to shift to a compellence posture—and little evidence exists that the Chinese seek to do so.

In contrast to its regional military focus, China has worked assiduously to position itself globally as a key economic actor. In the aftermath of the 2008 global crisis, China has embedded itself globally and extended its influence in international aid, trade, and finance. It has sought to implement domestic reforms designed to redress global current account imbalances that are a major source of global financial instability by reducing its historically unprecedented private and corporate savings rates and increasing domestic private and public consumption rates.

Aid figures are notoriously unreliable when looking at figures for countries that are not members of the OECD. But the most reliable data suggests that China, awash with huge currency reserves, spent more money on aid loans and grants than the World Bank and has become so important to global aid expenditures that the World Bank now seeks to coordinate its policies with the Chinese government. The Chinese have distributed their aid across the Global South, spending heavily in Africa and Latin America.

These practices are the subject of criticism. Some American realists suggest that they are predatory, focused more on ensuring access to raw materials for China's economy than cultivating local economies. In some countries, Chinese firms working on infrastructure projects have been accused of unfair trade practices toward local firms and of treating local laborers poorly. Yet the aggregate result has been that the Chinese have served as an indispensible source of capital during the credit crunch in the G-7 countries of the last five years. One effect of their aid has been to increase global trade among southern states, as many countries have been able to boost their exports as a result of Chinese aid and investment. Africa, for example, received 14 percent of Chinese investment in 2010.[25] This pattern has heavily contributed towards the continent increasing the size of its exports to China, which had been negligible a decade before, to over $120 billion a year.[26]

This is not the only area where Chinese cash has proved critical. Critics could argue that China is in the process of attempting to position itself as independent of the United States and Europe by investing outside the OECD, had it not also tied itself so heavily to the fortunes of the US and Europe. Indeed, China is now the largest foreign holder of US public debt. Official figures estimate that China holds $3.2 trillion in US treasury bonds, although that figure undoubtedly underestimates the total because of the Chinese practice of also buying debt at auctions through third parties. Likewise, the Chinese have proven to be reliable investors in European government bonds in the case of the ongoing Eurozone crisis, repeatedly meeting with Europe's major leaders and investing heavily in bonds in the most "at risk" countries—notably Greece, Ireland, and Portugal—in an attempt to ward off a global financial crisis.

These patterns of trade, aid, and investment are significant in supporting my general argument. Despite the criticisms about the effects of China's investment on local producers and labor, the slowness of its currency reform, its calls for the reduced importance of the dollar as a global currency, or its predatory trade practices, the evidence suggests that it is seeking to uphold the current system from which it is the greatest beneficiary, not to change the rules—as American realists, reliant on the assumptions of hegemonic stability theory, would anticipate. Indeed, China is becoming more embedded in, and reliant upon, the existing global economic and political system. It is not an advocate of an alternative one.

What Are the Consequences of the Current Trend in US-Chinese Relations?

The composite picture I have painted is of an emergent US policy that relies heavily on the alarmist warnings of American academics and commentators. It is a policy predicated on two elegant but problematic theories supposing that the United States still dominates that system, that the Chinese want to usurp that position, and that this can best be avoided by a combination of military containment and economic confrontation over a variety of issues spanning from intellectual property rights to access to rare earth commodities mined in China. This approach ignores not only China's articulated goals but also evidence of its increasing investment in sustaining global economic stability and of its force posture focus on addressing domestic instability and deterring a continental challenge to its sovereignty.

While, inevitably, China's rise has led to areas of friction with the United States, it is how that friction is addressed that is most critical. The alternative view—that accommodation based on mutual interest is most likely to serve the US interest—is being drowned out by claims about China's predatory practices and its military goals. While some evidence may support the former, little evidence supports the latter. Feeding that particular fire will serve only to reinforce the most robust, nationalist voices in China striving to recapture the country's self-respect and to enhance mutual suspicion—potentially bringing about strategic miscalculations.

Notes

1. Clarissa Ward and Lee Ferran, "First Chinese Aircraft Carrier Revealed," ABCNews.com, 9 June 2011, http://abcnews.go.com/Blotter/chinese-aircraft-carrier -revealed/story?id=13800990#.T1x_Zcxo CPE.

2. "Storied US Aircraft Carrier Makes Final Deployment," Associated Press, 11 March 2012.

3. See Steven W. Mosher, *Hegemon: China's Plan to Dominate Asia and the World* (San Francisco: Encounter Books, 2000). Stefan Halper offers a more sober, and sobering, form of the argument in *The Beijing Consensus: How China's Authoritarian Model Will Dominate the Twenty-First Century* (New York: Basic Books, 2010).

4. See, for instance, Charles Glaser, "Will China's Rise Lead to War? Why Realism Does Not Mean Pessimism," *Foreign Affairs* 90, no. 2 (March/April 2011): 80–91, http://www.foreignaffairs.com/articles/67479/charles-glaser/will-chinas-rise-lead -to-war.

5. John Maynard Keynes, *The General Theory of Employment, Interest and Money* (New York: Harcourt, Brace, 1935), 379, http://www.scribd.com/doc/11392072/The -General-Theory-of-Employment-Interest-and-Money.

6. A. F. K. Organski, *World Politics* (New York: Alfred A. Knopf, 1958).

7. See Robert Gilpin, *War and Change in World Politics* (New York: Cambridge University Press, 1987). See also A. F. K. Organski and Jacek Kugler, *The War Ledger* (Chicago: University of Chicago Press, 1981). This voluminous literature is too long to cite here. But for an empirical evaluation of the latter, see Indra De Soysa, John R. Oneal, and Yong-Hee Park, "Testing Power-Transition Theory Using Alternative Measures of National Capabilities," *Journal of Conflict Resolution* 41, no. 4 (August 1997): 509–28.

8. Aaron L. Friedberg, "The Future of U.S.-China Relations: Is Conflict Inevitable?," *International Security* 30, no. 2 (Fall 2005): 18.

9. Richard Ned Lebow and Benjamin Valentino, "Lost in Transition: A Critical Analysis of Power Transition Theory," *International Relations* 23, no. 3 (2009): 19–20.

10. Francis Fukuyama, *The End of History and the Last Man* (New York: Free Press, 1992). For remarkable examples of postwar triumphalism, see Mortimer Zuckerman, "A Second American Century," *Foreign Affairs* 77, no. 3 (May–June 1998): 18–31; and Charles Krauthammer's, "The Unipolar Moment," *Foreign Affairs* 70, no.1 (Winter 1990/91): 23–33. The theoretical basis for the liberal peace argument is found in Michael Doyle, "Liberalism and World Politics," *American Political Science Review* 80, no. 4 (December 1986): 1151–1169.

11. George Friedman and Meredith Lebard, *The Coming War with Japan* (New York: St. Martin's Press, 1991). A famous counterpart from the Japanese perspective is provided in Shintaro Ishihara, *The Japan That Can Say No: Why Japan Will Be First among Equals* (New York: Simon & Schuster, 1991).

12. John J. Mearsheimer, *The Tragedy of Great Power Politics* (New York: Norton, 2001), 400.

13. Friedberg, "Future of U.S.-China Relations?," 18; and Christopher Layne, "The Waning of U.S. Hegemony—Myth or Reality?," *International Security* 34, no. 1 (Summer 2009): 147–72.

14. Angus Maddison, *Chinese Economic Performance in the Long Run* (Paris: Development Center of the Organization for Economic Cooperation and Development, 1998), 95–99. A revised edition was published in 2007. For the most recent Global Trends report, see National Intelligence Council (NIC), *Global Trends 2025: A Transformed World* (Washington, DC: NIC, November 2008), http://www.dni.gov/nic /PDF_2025/2025_Global_Trends_Final_Report.pdf.

15. Friedberg, "Future of U.S.-China Relations?," 18–19.

16. SIPRI, *SIPRI Yearbook 2011: Armaments, Disarmament and International Security* (New York: Oxford University Press USA, 2011), 159, 9, respectively.

17. International Institute for Strategic Studies (IISS), *The Military Balance 2012* (London: IISS, 2012), 31.

18. "China Military Budget Tops $100bn," BBCNews.com, 4 March 2012, http://www.bbc.co.uk/news/world-asia-china-17249476.

19. Joshua Cooper Ramo, *The Beijing Consensus: Notes on the New Physics of Chinese Power* (London: The Foreign Policy Centre 2004), 41.

20. Zheng Bijian, "China's 'Peaceful Rise' to Great-Power Status," *Foreign Affairs* 84, no. 5 (September/October 2005): 20, 22.

21. Minxin Pei, "Out into the World: China Is Ready to Become a Good Citizen—but on Its Own Terms," *Newsweek*, supplemental edition, 31 December 2008.

22. For a discussion of this problem, see Glaser, "Will China's Rise Lead to War?," 80–91.

23. See, as examples, M. Taylor Fravel, "International Relations Theory and China's Rise: Assessing China's Potential for Territorial Expansion," *International Studies Review* 12, no. 4 (December 2010): 505–32; Alastair Iain Johnston, "Is China a Status Quo Power?," *International Security* 27, no. 4 (Spring 2003): 5–56; and David C. Kang, *China Rising: Peace, Power, and Order in East Asia* (New York: Columbia University Press, 2007).

24. IISS, *The Military Balance 2012*, 34; and "Military Balance: The US and Other Key Countries," BBCNews.com, 5 January 2012, http://www.bbc.co.uk/news/world-us-canada-16428133.

25. "Trying to Pull Together," *The Economist*, 20 April 2011, http://www.economist.com/node/18586448.

26. "Chinese in Africa: The Chinese Are Coming . . . to Africa," *The Economist*, 22 April 2011, http://www.economist.com/blogs/dailychart/ 2011/04/chinese_africa.

Chapter 6

The Contradictions of US China Policy

Implications for the US Air Force

Justin Logan
Director, Foreign Policy Studies, Cato Institute

Abstract

The United States has a bipartisan China policy. Despite rhetorical differences, both parties support a two-pronged policy of "congagement" and reassuring America's regional allies. Congagement combines military containment with economic engagement. Reassurance attempts to convince American allies in the region that America will act as the ultimate guarantor of those states' security.

These two policies pose problems for the country and, by extension, the US Air Force. The economic engagement policy has helped China narrow the relative power gap with the United States, thereby fueling Beijing's regional ambitions. As Beijing's relative power grows, China will become harder to contain militarily. Meanwhile, the policy of reassurance infantilizes America's allies, encouraging them to shirk their responsibility to provide the majority of their own defense. The incoherence of the policy—and the effects it has had on US partners—should lead to a shift in strategy. A more prudent American policy would change US force posture to that of a genuinely offshore balancer, forcing Asian nations to do more for their own defense.

Introduction

The Pentagon's January 2012 defense strategic guidance states its intention to "rebalance toward the Asia-Pacific region."[1] As it does so, the defense budget is likely to grow at a much slower rate than it did during the last decade. With this rebalancing taking place in the con-

This chapter is adapted from the author's Cato Institute Policy Analysis no. 717, *China, America, and the Pivot to Asia*, 8 January 2013. The author thanks Charles Zakaib for editorial assistance.

text of relatively constrained budgets, increasing focus on Asia may force the Pentagon to accept a zero-sum tradeoff toward conventional capabilities and away from counterinsurgency and nation-building projects like those in Iraq and Afghanistan. One symbol of that shift is the ongoing promotion of Air-Sea Battle, a concept emphasizing rapid and integrated power projection that can penetrate anti-access/area-denial threats.[2] Its emphasis on distant platforms with the ability to attack in-depth, including the new long-range bomber, will assign much of the responsibility for producing security in the region to the US Navy and Air Force.

More importantly, however, the changes in strategy and battle concepts signal a fundamental acknowledgment that the main potential threat to US national security is a potential peer competitor. After a decade of chasing terrorists and insurgents, US policy makers have chosen rightly to focus on the growing economic and military strength in Asian states, particularly China. States remain the most important actors in international politics. Neither transnational economic, religious, or identity-political forces nor international organizations can compete with powerful states in the realm of international security affairs. To produce security—and to cause much trouble in international politics—you need a state.[3]

Looking into the twenty-first century, it seems increasingly possible that America will be eclipsed in national economic—and possibly military—terms by China. China is likely to overtake the United States in gross domestic product (GDP) at market exchange rates in 2018. To give a sense of China's staggering growth, its GDP was one-eighth that of America's in 2000 at market exchange rates, and by 2010 it was one-half.[4] Given the potential impact of US-China competition on both US security and domestic politics, getting Sino-American relations right is the most important challenge for US foreign policy makers.

Beyond China, India is undergoing rapid economic development, possesses a favorable demographic profile, and is likely to play an increasingly prominent role in both regional and international politics. Japan, despite demographic and fiscal problems, remains an important player. In short, no other region on earth is likely to see its share of global power grow as much as the Asia-Pacific region in the decades ahead. To the extent that the concentration of power in the international system shifts toward East Asia, American strategists should focus on that region.

First among US concerns in Asia is the US-China security relationship. China has been at the center of American thought on East Asia for more than two decades. This chapter is not an effort to provide a net assessment or a projection of the future military balance between the United States and China. Similarly, it is not a recap of the past few decades or even years of US-China diplomacy. Rather, it scrutinizes the way US policy makers think about China and the consequences of any shortcomings. Getting the United States' China policy right will have profound significance for America generally and for the US Air Force in particular.

US Policy toward China

Washington's China policy is a mix of elements taken from both the liberal and realist schools of international relations. Liberal elements include efforts to promote democracy, including by furthering economic development in China. In a mechanism reminiscent of modernization theory, which came into vogue during the Vietnam War, economic growth produces a growing middle class that tends to demand greater political rights. In turn, these demands generate more democratic politics.[5] These increasingly democratic politics then are supposed to plug into a crude version of democratic peace theory, in which the domestic institutions of democratic countries prevent them from going to war (or presumably, in this case, even engaging in serious security competition) with other democracies.[6]

The other liberal aspect of US policy includes attempts to constrain China in a web of international institutions that would allow it to rise into the existing international order—shaped by the institutions created under American leadership after World War II—thereby preventing it from transforming the rules that govern the order.[7] This logic holds that while "the United States cannot thwart China's rise, it can help ensure that China's power is exercised within the rules and institutions that the United States and its partners have crafted over the last century, rules and institutions that can protect the interests of all states in the more crowded world of the future."[8]

The realist element of US China policy is the effort to prevent China from gaining a dominant military position in the Asia-Pacific region. American military planners have developed a posture in Asia designed with the explicit purpose of putting China's energy supplies at risk. As longtime Asia correspondent Richard Halloran recently wrote in the official journal of the US Air Force Association, Washington "has begun positioning forces which could threaten China's supply lines through the South China Sea. The oil and raw materials transported through those shipping lanes are crucial to a surging Chinese economy—an economy paying for Beijing's swiftly expanding military power."[9]

Halloran then cites the work of an active-duty Air Force major explicitly likening China's predicament to that of Japan's in the 1930s and 40s, arguing that Washington should "exploit a critical vulnerability—China's dependence on sea lines of communication [SLOC]."[10] Former US Pacific Command commander Dennis Blair and China analyst Kenneth Lieberthal write that "the United States has employed and will likely in the future continue to use naval blockades when necessary," including specific reference to China, but then wave off the idea that other nations should be concerned: "US naval hegemony, however, need not be unsettling to other countries."[11] The slightest effort to look at things from Beijing's perspective shows that Washington's military posture in the Asia-Pacific is perfectly tailored to amplify China's worst fears about Washington's intentions.

This combination of liberal and realist policies toward China has produced incoherent strategy. This incoherent policy has a name: *congagement*—part military containment, part economic engagement.[12] Congagement, for all intents and purposes, has been America's China policy since at least the end of the Cold War.

Beyond congagement, the other aspect of Washington's bipartisan China policy is the effort to reassure America's allies about Washington's commitment to provide their security. Instead of forcing states like Japan, South Korea, Vietnam, and India to carry the bulk of the burden of hedging against China while watching how the balance of power plays out from across the Pacific, the bipartisan establishment favors reassuring these allies that Washington's commitment is unshakeable. In a recent address to the Australian Parliament, President Obama referred respectively to an "unbreakable alliance" with Australia, a "commitment to the security of the Republic of Korea" that will "never waver," and a "larger and long-term role in the region" for the United States. He added that the "United States is a Pacific power, and we are here to stay."[13]

To summarize, the foreign-policy establishment favors a China policy with three major components: economic engagement; military containment; and efforts to depress the autonomous military exertions of US allies, including through forward US deployments, diplomatic reassurance about American security guarantees, and Washington's own military spending.

The Problems with US Policy

US policy toward China suffers from two fatal errors of internal logic and is unlikely to produce the desired ends of policy makers. First, congagement, the combination of economic engagement and military containment, relies on a hopeless contradiction: it makes China more relatively powerful while seeking to ensure it acts as though it is weak. Second, reassuring US allies guarantees that the American taxpayer will continue funding the defense of states rich enough to defend themselves, forcing the United States to bear the burden as the balancer of first resort.

While Washington is trying to contain Chinese power, its policy of economic engagement is helping China to narrow the relative power gap. Unless one assumes that China is a historical and theoretical aberration—that it is entirely at peace with foreign military domination of its region—China is going to seek a larger politico-military role as it grows wealthier, and that growing wealth will make it harder to contain. It becomes even more difficult to believe that China is at peace with US military dominance in Asia when former high-ranking US officials state openly that "stripped of diplomatic niceties, the ultimate aim of American strategy is to hasten a revolution, albeit a peaceful one, that will sweep away China's one-party authoritarian state."[14] It truly would be bizarre if the men at the helm of China's one-party authoritarian state felt comfortable leaving China's security in Washington's hands.

At bottom, congagement relies on extraordinary faith in the idea that economic engagement and pleas for reform will transform China's political system and/or that the existence of international institutions will limit its international ambitions. If the congagement advocates have the courage of their convictions, they should explain why they believe both that (a) economic growth will necessarily lead to democratization, and (b) democratization will necessarily lead either to a China that is at peace with American military hegemony in Asia or a China whose security interests will become identical with

Washington's. Otherwise, the whole argument hangs on the constraints posed by international institutions, and it is far from clear that institutions will limit China's desire to develop greater control of its own security.

Beyond the dubious logic of congagement, the second problem with American strategy is that the policy of continually reassuring America's allies has ensured that a disproportionate share of the cost of hedging against China will need to be borne by the American taxpayers and their creditors. Instead of urging states in China's region to defend themselves, Washington reassures these states that America is committed to act as the balancer of first resort. This generates free riding and increases the costs to the United States. As University of Chicago professor John Mearsheimer points out, geography and distribution of power are crucial factors that determine when states should balance against a potential threat or pass the buck to states closer to trouble.[15] In the current context, both geography and the distribution of power should allow Washington to pass the buck for balancing against China to other countries in the region.

But America's Asian allies do not carry even a proportional share of the burden of constraining China's ambition. While repeatedly stating their concerns about China's power and behavior, America's allies' military spending as a share of alliance spending has continually dropped. Japan spends only 1 percent of its GDP on defense, and Taiwan and South Korea spend less than 3 percent, despite their much closer proximity to both China and North Korea. While it is true that Japan, with a large economy, gets a lot out of that 1 percent—including a powerful navy—absent a formal US security commitment, Japan would likely be doing more.[16]

The United States, with the benefit of geographic isolation and a massive nuclear arsenal, spends nearly 5 percent of national income on its military. Despite this fact, the Beltway foreign-policy establishment claims that Americans should carry the bulk of the cost of securing Asia. As Georgetown's Victor Cha has written, that policy is based on Washington's long-standing desire to "exert maximum control over [its] smaller ally's actions" and "amplify US control and minimize any collusion among its alliance partners."[17] Thus, despite constant admonitions from American officials that allies—both in Asia and the North Atlantic Treaty Organization (NATO)—should do more, there has been considerable desire in Washington that allies not do more for fear that more powerful allies would be more autonomous allies, reducing America's leverage over their security policies.[18]

While such a rationale was dubious during the Cold War, it makes even less sense today. By constantly rushing to "reassure" US allies of the firmness of America's military commitment every time there is a diplomatic or security flare-up in Asia, Washington risks creating a dynamic similar to the one it created in NATO: demilitarizing US allies to the point where they appear unable or unwilling to defend themselves without help from America.

This subsequently raises the question, under what sort of circumstances would Washington seriously consider war with China over a given ally or partner? Moreover, exactly how sure are US partners of the solidity of America's alliance commitments and other assurances? If recent history is any indication, US analysts outside the Pentagon have given few considerations to actually fighting China.[19] Accordingly, US allies should probably think long and hard about the validity of US commitments.

As mentioned above, Taiwan's military spending is entirely inadequate to the potential military task it faces, suggesting strongly that it believes it has some commitment of US support in the event of Chinese bullying or coercion.[20] When confronted with arguments that America's commitment to Taiwan is a wasting asset, Taiwanese foreign-policy thinkers protest that "if Taiwan were to fall, the United States would suffer a geostrategic disaster," possibly including "a Chinese nuclear attack on the US homeland."[21] Significantly less time has been dedicated to getting Taiwan's own house in order by reversing the trends in Taiwanese domestic politics that allow most Taiwanese to look away from the growing threat posed by the People's Republic of China (PRC) than has been spent pleading for a broad interpretation of the 1979 Taiwan Relations Act.[22]

To illustrate Taiwan's domestic political obstacles to defense, a recent survey reveals that a significant plurality of 12–17 year olds state they would not be willing to fight or have a family member fight to defend Taiwan from China. A former Taiwanese defense minister admitted, "It goes without saying that the number of Taiwanese willing to fight has come down significantly in recent years. I'm even surprised that the number of pro-defense people [in the survey] is so high."[23]

At the same time, there have been quiet indications that Washington would not fight China over Taiwan. For example, in a video posted on the website of *Foreign Policy* magazine in 2007, an American scholar mentioned a conversation he had had with former US secretary of state Hillary Clinton, then a presidential candidate. In that conversation, Clinton remarked that it is absurd to think the American people would support a war with China over Taiwan. Although the video was quickly edited to remove the discussion of this remark, it calls into question the strength of the US commitment to Taiwan.[24]

Finally, and most importantly, no one has detailed precisely how even a much more powerful China would threaten the national security of the United States, with "security" defined narrowly and traditionally, to include America's political autonomy, the safety of its citizens, and its ability to secure its economic well-being. At the bottom of realist theories of international relations is the prospect of being conquered or otherwise losing political sovereignty. Just as it is terrifically difficult to envision the United States conquering China today, it is similarly difficult to imagine China conquering the United States, given the Pacific Ocean and the massive American nuclear arsenal.

Of course, a number of intermediate problems are more likely. China is unlikely to be happy leaving its maritime security to the whims of American policy makers forever. A much more powerful China could attempt to use its navy to exclude the United States from engaging in commerce with states in Asia. If it could overwhelm neighboring states with so much power as to render them helpless, China could hold hostage the SLOCs in Asia to extract concessions from other states in the region. But it bears asking how likely those scenarios are, especially considering the considerable costs China would bear to achieve such results.

Problematically, US officials seem to think that Chinese policy makers should entrust the United States with China's security. For example, Michael Schiffer, deputy assistant secretary of defense for East Asia, has stated that Washington welcomes a "strong, responsible, and prosperous China" that will take on a "constructive" role in regional and global institutions.[25] In this formulation, however, "responsible" and "constructive" are doing a lot of work. What these words mean, in practice, is that Washington would like to see Beijing step up as a junior partner working under Washington's leadership to help America pursue its policy goals. In practice, however, there is little evidence that Washington wishes to include Chinese prerogatives in its definition of "responsible" policies or "constructive" roles. Indeed, as discussed above, the United States has sought to control the policy even of its allies.

Nevertheless, hawkish Washington policy makers act mystified by the idea that China would seek a more capable military. As former secretary of defense Donald Rumsfeld famously mused, "Since no nation threatens China, one must wonder: Why this growing investment [in its military]? Why these continuing large and expanding arms purchases? Why these continuing robust deployments?"[26]

But the answer is obvious: China's military modernization—particularly that of the People's Liberation Army Navy (PLAN)—is designed to bring control of China's national security into the hands of the Chinese government. As the Heritage Foundation's Dean Cheng sensibly observes, "With its growing dependence on sea lanes, China almost inevitably will need to expand the PLA's [People's Liberation Army] naval capabilities, both to protect the country's access to resources and markets and to deny opponents the ability to endanger that access."[27]

Changes for US China Policy

A prudent American policy would urge Japan, South Korea, India, Indonesia, the Philippines, Vietnam, Australia, and other nations in Asia with concerns about China's ambition to provide for their own defense while carefully watching Chinese military developments and behavior. Existing US policy creates a de facto agreement between Washington and its Asian allies in which we agree to defend them and they agree to let us.[28] As one report puts it, the deal is that allies "provide bases and ports for the US military and contribute generously to supporting their presence," and "in return, America provides deterrence and defense."[29]

Were the United States to create distance between itself and its Asian allies and clients, however, several things would likely happen. First, those states would probably increase their own efforts to balance against China's growing power. Indeed, in the 1970s when the Soviet Union was increasing its military buildup in East Asia and the United States was not keeping pace, Japan began boosting its own military efforts.[30] News reports in recent months indicate these countries have a considerable amount of anxiety about Chinese behavior, reflected in their diplomacy. However, the resources these countries have dedicated to defending themselves from potential Chinese coercion do not reflect this concern.

For wealthy and technologically advanced Asian states with ballooning retired populations and shrinking workforces, such as Japan, doing more to secure themselves would create powerful pressures to pursue nuclear weapons programs. Although in the wake of the Fukushima nuclear disaster such a discussion would be fraught with domestic as well as international political perils in Japan, the powerful logic of substituting capital for labor and securing its territory with the ultimate deterrent would likely weigh heavily on the minds of Japanese—and possibly South Korean and Taiwanese—policy makers.

Washington policy makers have historically viewed such developments as anywhere from extremely undesirable to apocalyptically bad. However, willfully plunging headlong into security competition with China—while our economic policies help to narrow the relative power gap between the two countries—is even more unappetizing. Moreover, the longer Washington infantilizes its Asian allies and other countries with frontline concerns about China's growing power, the more difficult it will be to get them off the dole and to convince them to devote a larger share of their national resources and attention to the potential challenges posed by China.

In terms of policy, Washington should stop intervening at every diplomatic flare-up in Asia. It should not seek to cultivate anti-China paranoia but should instead sow doubts about exactly where the American military would be committed. Such measures should include private conversations with longtime allies like Japan and South Korea as well as countries that have grown close to Washington more recently, like India and Vietnam. Washington should encourage closer coordination between these countries without the United States even being present, let alone leading the discussions. Such measures would raise questions about America's commitment to the region, minimizing the free riding that American policies have heretofore encouraged.

The most difficult dilemma posed by this policy would be sowing doubt and uncertainty among US allies without indicating to China that Washington does not care about Chinese aggression. Washington should make clear to China that while Washington is not encouraging South Korean or Japanese nuclear proliferation, a more distant United States coupled with Chinese provocations toward Taiwan or other neighbors could conceivably have the result of producing such proliferation, an outcome the PRC strongly wants to avoid.

Relatedly, Washington should undertake a review of its basing arrangements in the region. In particular, it should put the bases in South Korea at the top of the list for potential closure. Moreover, Washington should indulge the Japanese political impulse that allows them to free ride on the US military commitment while various Japanese political factions complain endlessly about the US presence in the country. If Japanese public opinion really is opposed to allowing America to pay for Japan's defense, Washington should use that reality to remove its troops from Japan. Washington should not want to defend Japan more than Japan wants to be defended.

Potential Objections to the Alternative Strategy

There are three main objections to the approach described above. First, one could argue that while US allies in the region would attempt to balance Chinese power, they simply could not keep up; the growth in Chinese economic and military power is too much for them to match. Second, one could object that if the United States were to create distance from its allies, they would not balance against Chinese power but would instead bandwagon with China.[31] Finally, one could argue that Asian countries can and would balance against Chinese power, but that this would create dangerous arms races that threaten to result in war. I deal with these objections below, showing that Asian countries could place significant obstacles in the way of Chinese hegemony in the region, that they would likely do so, and that the risk of war under that scenario is not grave.

Objection One: Other Countries Cannot Effectively Balance against China

The first objection to a more restrained US security policy in Asia is that America's Asian allies are too weak to balance against China effectively. This argument relies on a number of ideas, mainly about economics, demographics, and military power. Military power depends on economics and demographics, so the argument usually runs that because of economic and demographic constraints, even relatively wealthy countries in Asia would have difficulty converting their wealth into military power to hedge against Chinese adventurism. Accordingly, dealing with this objection involves examining the economic, demographic, and military realities in Asia.

Economic indicators. While accurately predicting economic output is notoriously difficult, basic assumptions about future economic trends are required to formulate policy. Economic forecasts for Asia vary wildly, but there is general agreement that Asia—and particularly China and India—will continue to grow in economic clout in the coming decades. The table below shows the projections of one recent report from Goldman Sachs:

Table 6.1. GDP estimates (constant $2010 billions)

Country	2010	2030	Percent Growth
China	5,633	31,731	563%
United States	14,614	22,920	157%
India	1,594	7,972	500%
Japan	4,773	5,852	123%
Russia	1,689	4,730	280%
Indonesia	692	2,446	353%
South Korea	1,014	2,112	208%
Australia	1,191	1,802	151%
Thailand	302	904	299%
Malaysia	235	889	378%
Philippines	186	793	426%

Adapted from Timothy Moe, Caesar Maasry, and Richard Tang, *EM [Emerging Market] Equity in Two Decades: A Changing Landscape*, Goldman Sachs Global Economics Paper no. 204 (New York: Goldman Sachs & Co., 8 September 2010), 13.

It is worth reiterating that making these sorts of forecasts well is exceedingly difficult, if not impossible, but the projection above is far from an outlier.

Still, the same report estimates that although China is likely to possess approximately 23 percent of world GDP in 2030, the other countries in Asia will constitute 22 percent of world GDP, with the United States possessing 17 percent.[32] This should allow a significant amount of burden shifting, given the geography of Asia and China's own demographic, economic, and domestic political problems.

Economic growth in the countries of Asia will provide merely the foundations on which these nations can develop national power. Economic growth is determined by gains in productivity (which are extraordinarily difficult to predict) as well as demographics (much easier to predict). And economic power is relevant in large part because it can be used to develop military power. Below I examine demographic and military spending trends in Asia.

Demographic trends. Demographics have played a central role in international politics for centuries. The interaction between the size and composition of national populations with geography, economic output, and military power has helped to make the modern world. Today, most developed countries have seen advances in medical technology combine with shifting cultural mores to produce increased life expectancy and fewer babies—the productive workers of tomorrow.[33] This trend has posed important problems for fiscal programs instituted under earlier, different demographic distributions. Countries have dealt with this issue in different ways, from attempting to provide financial incentives for families to have children, to allowing for increased immigration to import workers in order to prop up welfare states.

Individual nations in Asia face different demographic challenges. Russia, for example, confronts remarkably low life expectancy, net decrease in population, and a generally bleak demographic picture overall. As Nicholas Eberstadt points out, Russia's population has shrunk by more than 7 million people since 1992, and the life expectancy of a Russian boy born today is lower than it was in the 1950s.[34] In stark contrast, countries like Japan and South Korea have populations that are living exceptionally long by world standards, with smaller percentages of their overall populations comprised of working-age citizens.[35] Japan, especially, faces a challenging situation. By 2040, 14 percent of the Japanese population is projected to be 80 years of age or older, and its working-age population will drop 30 percent, placing significant stress on its economy and its pension and health systems.[36] Similarly, South Korea's entire working-age population will be barely larger than its over-60 population by 2050.[37] Figure 6.1 indicates the shifting percentages and numbers of working-age populations from 2010 through 2040.

In China the net effect of Beijing's "one-child" policy, combined with increasing life expectancy in the country, has been the creation of a population bubble that is currently middle-aged but by 2040 will decrease the working-age population by over 110 million, or 11 percent of its overall population.[38] This shift has produced, among other things, a ballooning eldercare industry that appears likely to consume increasing shares of Chinese economic output in the coming decades.[39]

Those issues could pose significant constraints on Chinese domestic economic and foreign policies in the decades ahead.

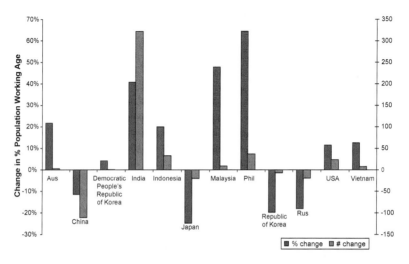

Figure 6.1. Working-age population change, 2010–40. (*Reprinted from* UN Population Division, World Population Prospects, 2010 revision [medium variant], http://esa.un.org/wpp/unpp/panel_population.htm.)

India, by contrast, has its highest concentration of population in a significantly younger cohort, which should allow it significantly more room for maneuver in its policy choices, particularly when compared to China. For example, the gap between India and China in terms of working-age populations will be roughly 400 million in India's favor by 2040. By 2030 India will possess roughly 100 million young men with at least a high school education, compared to only 75 million in China.[40] These demographic realities should lead Washington to expect India to play a greater security role in the Asia-Pacific.

The demographic developments in many of America's Asian allies, contrasted with the United States' relatively benign demographic condition, hold important consequences for America's military posture in Asia as well. As a recent report from the RAND Corporation notes, demographic trends in Asia make clear that if America seeks to keep its alliance system intact in the coming decades, it will need to "become an even more dominant partner" in the alliances than it is today—a prospect that when coupled with China's growing power implies both an even larger overall cost and a greater share of that larger cost accruing to Washington.[41]

But despite Japan's terrible predicament, the demographic picture in the Asia-Pacific hardly precludes other states from playing larger roles in securing their region. Countries like India, Indonesia, the Philippines, and Vietnam all can and should be expected to play a larger role. While Japan faces significant problems posed by economic and demographic challenges over the coming decades, it possesses advanced military technology, favorable geography, and, in extremis, the option of pursuing a "porcupine" strategy with a nuclear deterrent at its core. Japan's lack of any meaningful land warfare capability and severe fiscal and demographic constraints should lessen fears that Japan would use such a posture as a shield for an offensive strategy.[42] In addition, Japan may wish to work in concert with more demographically vital states to marry Japanese technology with manpower from these other states.

Military modernization in Asia. Economics and demographics are merely the foundations for America's security concerns in Asia. Washington focuses almost entirely on China's growing power. China has undergone an important qualitative and quantitative military transformation in the past decades. And in discussions about Asia in Washington, it is mostly China's military that looms large. China is presently increasing its capability to coerce Taiwan and to secure its SLOCs and, in general, is sowing fears that it may develop the ability to execute anti-access/area-denial campaigns to prevent the US military from being able to dominate East Asia.[43]

Importantly, geography and technology mean that other countries in Asia would not necessarily need to spend a dollar for a dollar to ensure their security in the face of Chinese economic and military growth. To the contrary, the fact that China's potential challenges are divided between maritime powers like Japan and land powers like India, Russia, South (and potentially North) Korea, and Vietnam means that China would need to field powerful ground forces in numerous areas as well as a powerful navy to establish anything like a Monroe Doctrine in Asia.[44] Moreover, Asian states would not necessarily need to field militaries that could defeat China outright. Instead, they could focus merely on raising the potential costs to China such that Beijing would be deterred from aggression against its neighbors.

In short, neither economics, nor demographics, nor military developments prove that Asian states could not provide a sufficient first line of defense against Chinese ambition. Should the United States do less to provide their security, there is reason to believe they would do more. Below I examine the idea that while Asian states could act as the frontline balancers, they would choose not to.

Objection Two: Other Countries Will Not Effectively Balance against China

The second potential objection to a more standoffish US policy on Asian security is theoretical: namely, that regardless of their capabilities, current US allies—as suggested above—would not increase their own efforts to hedge against Chinese power but instead would appease China, leaving their security at the mercy of the Chinese leadership. This is one side of a long-standing debate in security studies over whether states tend to balance against or bandwagon with power.[45] Without delving too deeply into theory, the objection is based on a particular theory and can only be answered on theoretical grounds and supplemented with evidence from history.

States that value survival will tend to balance against the power of potential rivals, although not always efficiently enough to prevent wars. If one views the international system as a competitive one in which security is frequently a zero-sum good between neighbors or rivals, states tend to balance against power to ensure control over their own destinies or, in extreme cases, their survival as political units. While these views are sometimes hard for Americans to understand—America's survival as an autonomous political unit has not been threatened in at least 200 years—they are far less difficult to appreciate for countries in other regions of the world.

Criteria for a nation's tendency to balance—such as consensus among elites about the nature of the threat, government vulnerability, and social cohesion—lead one to expect Japan to cohere and work to defend itself.[46] In fact, there is considerable evidence that all affected countries in Asia would be willing to do more to ensure their own security were America to do less on their behalf. Such evidence includes the recent joint statement issued by the Philippines and Japan marking a new "strategic partnership" and expressing "common strategic interests" such as "ensuring the safety of sea lines of communication."[47] More recently, as the Japanese prime minister, Yoshihiko Noda declared that Japan's security environment had grown "increasingly murky due to China's stepped-up activities in local waters and its rapid military expansion."[48] Likewise, the head of the Indian navy remarked that in the face of Chinese provocations there, "the South China Sea is an area of significant concern" for India.[49] A recent review of Australia's defense posture sounded similarly wary notes.[50]

These are only the most recent indications that other countries in the region would hardly shrug at Chinese power in the absence of US security guarantees. They see China as potentially threatening and would do more on their own without a security subsidy from Washington. Instead, Washington's constant repetition of its commitment to its allies' security allows these countries to avoid the necessary domestic debates about their security environments and what to do about them.[51]

Objection Three: Other Countries Can and Would Balance against China, but That Would Be More Problematic than the Current Approach

A final objection to restraint in the Asia-Pacific allows that America's Asian allies could and likely would choose to balance against China but argues that their doing so would cause dangerous arms racing in the region that would not result if America continued to shelter its allies. Accordingly, goes the logic—even at the cost of carrying a disproportionate share of the burden—it is better for Washington to take the lead on constraining China rather than cultivating dangerously destabilizing arms races that would encourage direct security competition among Asian states and with it a greater chance of war.

The most plausible version of this argument points out that the allure of a nuclear deterrent would be extremely powerful for a country like Japan. This argument raises questions about the implications of potential Japanese acquisition of its own nuclear deterrent on other countries in the region and the nuclear nonproliferation treaty itself.[52] It would also be helpful to point out that any prospective Japanese nuclear arsenal could serve only as a deterrent, since Japan lacks any meaningful ground warfare capability and faces severe demographic pressures that would make even a nuclear-armed Japan terrifically unlikely to attempt to replay the 1930s. Furthermore, China has its own nuclear deterrent and a massive conventional deterrent, both of which would give pause to any potential adversary.

More broadly, this objection fails to spell out why, exactly, regional balancing is clearly more risky to the United States than is America continuing to act as the balancer of first resort. As highlighted above, states in the region like Japan, whose rearmament is frequently rolled out as dangerously destabilizing, possess important demographic and economic constraints on their potential to generate power-projection capabilities. In other words, while countries in the region could do significantly more to enhance their ability to defend against potential Chinese aggression, no country has a realistic prospect at threatening Chinese territory. Put simply, Asian geography and the military requirements for producing security to current US client states favor defense.

Conclusion

This chapter argues that the Beltway foreign-policy establishment has flawed views on the rise of China and US China policy. That perception produces an inherently counterproductive policy: congagement. The flaws of congagement are coupled with the problem created by reassurance: free riding. In addition to shining a light on those misguided policies, this discussion suggests that questions remain about the future implications of demographic and economic change in the region, the impact of those changes on the ability and willingness of nations there to balance Chinese power, and the likely results of their doing so.

The Pentagon's plan to rebalance toward the Asia-Pacific will likely exacerbate those policy woes. The contradictions of congagement present the military with an unenviable task: consider China the primary adversary of the United States while the rest of the government encourages and enriches that adversary through trade and the financing of debt. Furthermore, due to continual American reassurance, our allies may struggle to perform as reliable partners in a future conflict, much as NATO countries did in Operation Odyssey Dawn in Libya.

In the coming years, Navy and especially Air Force assets are likely to bear the burden of those flawed policies. Air-Sea Battle, though not overtly aimed at China, is clearly meant as a response to Chinese anti-access/area-denial threats. Air Force efforts in long-range strike; cyber warfare; and over-the-horizon intelligence, surveillance, and reconnaissance will be key to fulfilling the execution of that concept—a concept designed to maintain a US military posture that is unfortunately built on unsound ideas about how the world works.

Moreover, as China continues to narrow the relative power gap between itself and the United States, China's ambitions are likely to grow, and America's ability to limit them is likely to shrink. The Air Force will be on the front lines of the Sino-US competition in the coming years. Therefore, while getting US China policy right is important for the country in general, it should be a particular concern for the men and women of the US Air Force.

Notes

1. Department of Defense (DOD), *Sustaining U.S. Global Leadership: Priorities for 21st Century Defense* (Washington, DC: DOD, January 2012), 2, http://www.defense .gov/news/Defense_Strategic_Guidance.pdf.

2. Gen Norton A. Schwartz, USAF, and Adm Jonathan W. Greenert, USN, "Air-Sea Battle: Promoting Stability in an Era of Uncertainty," *American Interest*, 20 February 2012, http://www.the-american-interest.com/article.cfm?piece=1212.

3. Some will no doubt object that the assassination of Archduke Franz Ferdinand and the September 11 attacks were hugely consequential events produced by non-state actors. While true on its face, this line of argument fails to juxtapose the impact of the events themselves against the enormity of the responses to them, which were produced by states. The supposed exceptions in fact prove the rule.

4. "How to Get a Date," *Economist*, 31 December 2011, 61, http://www.economist .com/node/21542155.

5. For an early formulation of this view, see Seymour Martin Lipset, "Some Social Requisites of Democracy," *American Political Science Review* 53, no. 1 (March 1959): 69–105.

6. In fairness to theorists of the democratic peace, it should be reiterated that this is a significantly dumbed-down application of their theory. On the democratic peace itself, see Bruce Russett and John Oneal, *Triangulating Peace: Democracy, Interdependence, and International Organizations* (New York: W. W. Norton, 2001).

7. On liberal institutionalist logic, see G. John Ikenberry, *After Victory: Institutions, Strategic Restraint, and the Rebuilding of Order after Major Wars* (Princeton, NJ: Princeton University Press, 2001).

8. G. John Ikenberry, "The Rise of China and the Future of the West," *Foreign Affairs* 81, no. 1 (January/February 2008): 37.

9. Richard Halloran, "Pacific Push," *Air Force Magazine* 94, no. 1 (January 2011): 46–50.

10. Maj Lawrence Spinetta, USAF, " 'The Malacca Dilemma': Countering China's 'String of Pearls' with Land-Based Airpower" (master's thesis, School of Advanced Air and Space Studies, Air University, Maxwell AFB, AL, June 2006), http://www .dtic.mil/cgi-bin/GetTRDoc?AD=ADA476931.

11. Dennis Blair and Kenneth Lieberthal, "Smooth Sailing: The World's Shipping Lanes Are Safe," *Foreign Affairs* 86, no. 3 (May/June 2007): 12.

12. See Zalmay M. Khalilzad et al., *The United States and a Rising China: Strategic and Military Implications*, RAND Corporation Monograph MR-1082-AF (Santa Monica, CA: RAND, 1999), http://www.rand.org/pubs/monograph_reports/2007/MR1082.pdf.

13. "Remarks by President Obama to the Australian Parliament" (address, Canberra, Australia, 17 November 2011), http://www.whitehouse.gov/the-press-office/2011/11/17/remarks-president-obama-australian-parliament.

14. Aaron Friedberg, *A Contest for Supremacy: China, America, and the Struggle for Mastery in Asia* (Princeton, NJ: Princeton University Press, 2011), 184.

15. John J. Mearsheimer, *The Tragedy of Great Power Politics* (New York: W. W. Norton, 2001), 271–72.

16. Jennifer M. Lind, "Pacifism or Passing the Buck? Testing Theories of Japanese Security Policy," *International Security* 29, no. 1 (Summer 2004): 92–121.

17. Victor D. Cha, "Powerplay: Origins of the U.S. Alliance System in Asia," *International Security* 34, no. 3 (Winter 2009/2010): 158–96.

18. Christopher Layne, "America as European Hegemon," *The National Interest*, no. 72 (Summer 2003): 17–29; Peter Liberman, "Ties That Blind: Will Germany and Japan Rely Too Much on the United States?," *Security Studies* 10, no. 2 (Winter 2000/2001): 98–138.

19. On active discussions about fighting China within the Pentagon, see Andrew Burt and Christopher J. Castelli, "Despite Improved Ties, China Weighs Heavily in Pentagon War Planning: Team Links AirSea Battle to China," *Inside the Navy*, 13 June 2011.

20. One recent study from the RAND Corporation suggests that in the event of a war, China could potentially ground the entire Taiwan air force before it could get into the air by cutting all of the runways at Taiwan's fighter bases. See David A. Shlapak et al., *A Question of Balance: Political Context and Military Aspects of the China-Taiwan Dispute* (Santa Monica, CA: RAND Corporation, 2009). On Taiwan's military efforts, see Justin Logan and Ted Galen Carpenter, "Taiwan's Defense Budget: How Taipei's Free Riding Risks War," *Cato Institute Policy Analysis* no. 600, 13 September 2007.

21. Shyu-tu Lee and Douglas Paal, "Responses: Disengaging from Taiwan: Should Washington Continue Its Alliance with Taipei?," *Foreign Affairs* 90, no. 4 (July/August 2011): 179–80.

22. Logan and Carpenter, "Taiwan's Defense Budget."

23. Peter Enav, "Taiwanese Youth Losing Taste for China Fight," Associated Press, 1 December 2011.

24. For a discussion, see Justin Logan, "What Does Hillary Think about Taiwan?," Cato@Liberty, 3 August 2007, http://www.cato-at-liberty.org/what-does-hillary-think-about-taiwan.

25. Michael Schiffer, "China's Military Modernization" (speech, Center for the National Interest, Washington, DC, 27 July 2011).

26. Donald Rumsfeld, "The US and Asia-Pacific Security beyond the War on Terrorism" (address, Shangri-La Dialogue, Shangri-La Hotel, Singapore, 4 June 2005), http://www.iiss.org/conferences/the-shangri-la-dialogue/shangri-la-dialogue-archive/shangri-la-dialogue-2005/2005-speeches/first-plenary-session-the-hon-donald-rumsfeld.

27. Dean Cheng, "The Influence of Seapower on China, or the Influence of Mahan on Yoshihara and Holmes?," *Asia Policy* no. 12 (July 2011): 145–46.

28. I borrow this formulation from Benjamin Friedman.

29. Dan Blumenthal et al., *Asian Alliances in the 21st Century* (Arlington, VA: Project 2049 Institute, August 2011), 5, 7–8, http://project2049.net/documents/Asian _Alliances_21st_Century.pdf.

30. Lind, "Pacifism or Passing the Buck?," 108–15.

31. A variant of this argument would be that countries would like to ally with one another against China, but the collective action problems with alliances would split the coalition.

32. Timothy Moe, Caesar Maasry, and Richard Tang, *EM [Emerging Market] Equity in Two Decades: A Changing Landscape*, Goldman Sachs Global Economics Paper no. 204 (New York: Goldman Sachs & Co., 8 September 2010), 13.

33. Mark L. Haas, "A Geriatric Peace? The Future of U.S. Power in a World of Aging Populations," *International Security* 32, no. 1 (Summer 2007): 112–47.

34. Nicholas Eberstadt, "Asia-Pacific Demographics in 2010–2040: Implications for Strategic Balance," in *Strategic Asia 2010–11: Asia's Rising Power and America's Continued Purpose*, eds. Ashley J. Tellis, Andrew Marble, and Travis Tanner (Seattle, WA: National Bureau of Asian Research, 2010), 250–52.

35. Demographers define *working age* as the group of a nation's citizens between 15 and 64.

36. Eberstadt, "Asia-Pacific Demographics in 2010–2040," 255–58.

37. Jack A. Goldstone, "The New Population Bomb: The Four Megatrends That Will Change the World," *Foreign Affairs* 89, no. 1 (January/February 2010): 34.

38. United Nations, Population Database, "World Population Prospects: The 2010 Revision," http://esa.un.org/unpd/wpp/unpp/Panel_profiles.htm.

39. Zhanlian Feng et al., "An Industry in the Making: The Emergence of Institutional Elder Care in Urban China," *Journal of the American Geriatric Society* 59, no. 4 (April 2011): 738–44.

40. Sonia Luthra, "India's Demographic Outlook: Implications and Trends: An Interview with Nicholas Eberstadt," National Bureau of Asian Research, 29 December 2011.

41. Martin C. Libicki, Howard J. Shatz, and Julie E. Taylor, *Global Demographic Change and Its Implications for Military Power* (Santa Monica, CA: RAND Corporation, 2011), 114.

42. On Japan's inability to project power on land (or indeed even to fight on land at home), see Lind, "Pacifism or Passing the Buck?," 96–97.

43. For a detailed study of Taiwan scenarios, see Shlapak et al., *Question of Balance*. On China's growing capacity to mount anti-access/ area-denial campaigns, see Vitaliy O. Pradun, "From Bottle Rockets to Lightning Bolts: China's Missile Revolution and PLA Strategy against U.S. Military Intervention," *Naval War College Review* 64, no. 2 (Spring 2011): 8–38.

44. The force requirements for dealing with a North Korean collapse, for example, are staggering and would likely attract profound Chinese interest, if not direct intervention. See Bruce W. Bennett and Jennifer Lind, "The Collapse of North Korea: Military Missions and Requirements," *International Security* 36, no. 2 (Fall 2011):

84–119. See also Robert S. Ross, "China's Naval Nationalism: Sources, Prospects, and the U.S. Response," *International Security* 34, no. 2 (Fall 2009): 46–81.

45. For discussion of balancing and bandwagoning, see Kenneth N. Waltz, *Theory of International Politics* (Reading, MA: Addison-Wesley, 1979), 125–28.

46. Randall L. Schweller, "Unanswered Threats: A Neoclassical Realist Theory of Underbalancing," *International Security* 29, no. 2 (Fall 2004): 159–201.

47. "Japan-Philippines Joint Statement on the Comprehensive Promotion of the 'Strategic Partnership' between Neighboring Countries Connected by Special Bonds of Friendship," issued in Tokyo, 27 September 2011, by Yoshihiko Noda, prime minister of Japan, and Benigno S. Aquino III, president of the Republic of the Philippines, http://www.kantei.go.jp/foreign/noda/statement/201109/27philippines_e.html.

48. Chester Dawson, "Japan PM [Prime Minister] Warns on Defense," *Wall Street Journal*, 17 October 2011.

49. Adm Nirmal Verma, quoted in "South China Sea an Area of 'Significant Concern': Navy Chief," *Times of India*, 17 November 2011.

50. Enda Curran, "Australia Defense Report Urges Northward Shift," *Wall Street Journal*, 30 January 2012.

51. Barry Posen, "The Case for Restraint," *The American Interest* online, November/December 2007, http://www.the-american-interest.com/article.cfm?piece=331.

52. Robert J. Art, for example, suggests that a nuclear Japan could "mortally wound" the Nuclear Non-Proliferation Treaty (NPT) or the nuclear nonproliferation regime generally. See Art, "The United States and the Rise of China: Implications for the Long Haul," in *China's Ascent: Power, Security, and the Future of International Politics*, eds. Robert S. Ross and Zhu Feng (Ithaca, NY: Cornell University Press, 2008), 293.

Chapter 7

Shadow Dancing in the Indian and Pacific Oceans

China, India, and America

Dr. Dhirendra K. Vajpeyi
Professor, Political Science, University of Northern Iowa

Introduction

All countries, irrespective of their geographical size or economic and political conditions, compete for power and influence to further their national interests. Countries with hegemonic histories—including colonial powers—do not like to share power or reluctantly share only that much power that does not erode their dominance. Alliances are sought to further consolidate their hegemony. They spend a tremendous amount of economic, political, and military resources to jealously guard these interests. Ideological virginity is sacrificed, and promiscuous political alliances are made and easily discarded. Such countries are quite suspicious of emerging "upstarts" as potential challengers/rivals, view their ascendency with caution, and try to contain or co-opt them as supplicant allies and strategic partners under their dominance. Post–World War II American foreign policy—foreign aid, formation of military pacts in Europe and Asia, and, now, Chinese expansion and policies in Asia and Africa—is directed toward maintaining or challenging the status quo in the global power equation. According to Robert Kagan, "Power changes nations. It expands their wants and desires, increases their sense of entitlement . . . , makes them more ambitious, . . . lessens their tolerance to obstacles, [and decreases] their willingness to take no for an answer."[1]

Globalization and sophisticated technologies have greatly impacted all aspects of our lives: strategic alliances are used to resolve potential conflicts in the twenty-first century. How will future conflicts/wars be fought, and what strategies will be employed? These conflicts are not likely to occur to acquire land but to satisfy increasing demands for natural resources by securing them in far-flung parts of the world—mainly in the Middle East, Asia, and Africa.[2] The ability to reach these areas will be crucial to who gets what and how much. Between the fourteenth and nineteenth centuries European expansion and colonization of Asia, Africa, and Latin/South America were due not to the Europeans' superior valor, bravery, or courage but to factors such as superior technology in such areas as arms and artillery.[3] In the absence of moral concerns, force, craft, and, above all, their superior naval technology enabled them to arrive at and control the shores of these Asian, African, and Latin/South American countries. As long as Brittania ruled the waves, it was the prime imperial power on the earth. Of course, the weakness and backwardness of most non-Western countries as naval powers and their internal problems also hampered their abilities to resist—and even caused them to lose to—smaller island nations such as Britain. In this context, control of sea-lanes of the Indian and Pacific Oceans played a pivotal role.

The following discussion addresses (1) the two emerging economic and political powers in Asia—China and India; their aspirations and strategies to be global power players, hence the competition; and political conflict in the region, mainly in the Indian-Pacific Oceans (the theatre stage); (2) their perception of each other and outsiders, mainly of the United States; and (3) the role of the United States in the region.

The Theatre Stage: The Indian Ocean

> This is the land you have been seeking,
> This is India rising before you.
>
> —Portuguese poet Luís Vaz de Camões
> *The Lusiads* (16th century)

The vast Indian Ocean is pivotal for commercial and military security because of its proximity to strategic locations. In the north it lies between the Indian subcontinent and Arabian Peninsula (southern and western Asia); to its west lies East Africa, and to its east lie Indochina and Australia (fig. 7.1). Robert Kaplan sees the Indian Ocean as "form[ing] center stage for the . . . twenty-first century." Its western reaches include the "tinderboxes of Somalia, Yemen, Iran, and Pakistan," and bordering it to the east are Indonesia, Malaysia, India, and Bangladesh. The region is plagued with pirates, drug smugglers, terrorist activities, and unstable and volatile regimes. He adds, "The Indian Ocean is also an idea. It combines the centrality of Islam with global energy politics and the rise of India and China to reveal a multilayered, multipolar world."[4] Surrounding the Indian Ocean are more than 30 countries, mostly poor—home to a third of the world's population.

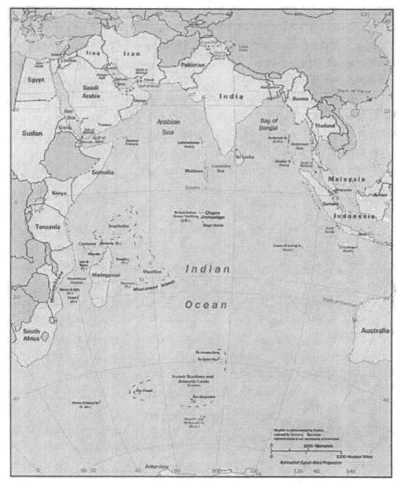

Figure 7.1. Indian Ocean area. (*Courtesy of* the University of Texas Libraries, the University of Texas at Austin, Perry-Castañeda Library Map Collection.)

Strategically it is also one of the most "nuclearized regions," with India, Pakistan, China, and a potentially soon-to-be nuclear power Iran. It is observed that access to and security of the Indian Ocean will influence not only the relationship among India, China, and the United States but also that of the Middle East and Central Asia.

From a global commercial point, the Indian Ocean is a "hydrocarbon transport route."[5] An estimated $200 billion of oil transits the Strait of Harmuz annually, while some $60 billion worth of oil transits the Strait of Malacca in route to China, Japan, and other East Asian countries.[6] Fifty percent of the world's merchant fleet, 90 percent of global commerce, and two-thirds of all petroleum pass through the Indian Ocean. With India's and China's increasing demand for petroleum, these sea routes will acquire greater importance and hence competition to control them. According to K. M. Pannikar, "India's economy is at the mercy of the power that controls the Indian Ocean."[7] Indian dependence on Middle East oil is almost total and, with its expanding economy, bound to increase. Also, approximately 3.5 million Indians work in the Middle East, sending about $4 billion per year to India. Similarly, China and the United States are heavily dependent on Middle East oil and their commercial ties. "This ocean" is therefore "the key to the Seven Seas."[8] It is here that "the rivalry between the United States and China in the Pacific interlocks with the regional rivalry between China and India" and that "in the 21st century, the destiny of the world will be decided."[9] And it is the Indian Ocean area that "will be the true nexus of world power and conflict in the coming years. It is here that the fight for democracy, energy independence, and religious freedom will be lost or won, and it is here that American foreign policy must concentrate if America is to remain dominant in an ever-changing world."[10]

The South China Sea (Nanyang) and China's Southeast Asia Neighbours

The South China Sea is a marginal sea that is part of the Pacific Ocean (fig. 7.2). It lies between Singapore and the Straits of Malacca and Taiwan. The South China Sea touches several countries—Taiwan, the Philippines, Vietnam, Malaysia, Singapore, Brunei, and the People's Republic of China (PRC)—and has often been called "China's Malacca challenge" and "a second Persian Sea" due to its strategic location and potentially rich oil and gas and vast fisheries resources.

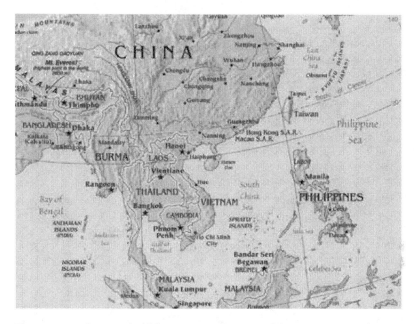

Figure 7.2. The South China Sea. (*Courtesy of* the University of Texas Libraries, the University of Texas at Austin, Perry-Castañeda Library Map Collection.)

According to the US Department of Energy, "the South China Sea could contain anywhere from 28 billion barrels of oil—a little less than double China's current proved reserves—to as high as 213 billion barrels, though analysts generally discount the higher figure as unrealistic."[11] Besides potential natural resources, the South China Sea's strategic location makes it a "pathway of the world's prime artery of trade. Over half of the world's merchant fleet, by tonnage, sails through the South China Sea each year, and it is considered to be one of the world's most important maritime choke points."[12] Even before 1949 China had considered the South China Sea a region of geostrategic interest and part of China's historical waters. It claims almost the entire ocean, including several islands in the zone, and has become assertive in recent years. However, six other sovereign states situated on the sea vehemently oppose China's unilateral assertion. Competing claimants include (see fig. 7.3 and table 7.1):

- Indonesia, China, and Taiwan over waters northeast of the Natuna Islands;

- the Philippines, China, and Taiwan over the Malampaya and Camago gas fields;
- the Philippines, China, and Taiwan;
- Vietnam, China, and Taiwan over waters west of the Spratly Islands, and Vietnam, China, Taiwan, Brunei, Malaysia, and the Philippines over some or all of the Spratlys;
- China, Taiwan, and Vietnam over the Parcel Islands;
- Malaysia, Cambodia, Thailand, and Vietnam over areas in the Gulf of Thailand; and
- Singapore and Malaysia along the Straits of Johor and Singapore.

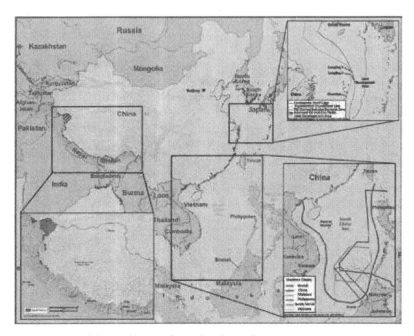

Figure 7.3. China's disputed territories. This map is an approximate presentation of PRC and other regional claims. China has remained ambiguous on the extent and legal justification for these regional claims. Three of China's major ongoing territorial disputes are based on claims along its shared border with India and Bhutan, the South China Sea, and with Japan in the East China Sea. (*Reprinted from* US Department of Defense [DOD], *Military and Security Developments Involving the People's Republic of China 2011*, Annual Report to Congress [Washington, D.C.: DOD, 2011], 16.)

Table 7.1. South China Sea, claims by country

Country	South China Sea	Spratly Islands	Paracel Islands	Gulf of Thailand
Brunei	UNCLOS	no formal claim	no	n/a
Cambodia	not applicable (n/a)	n/a	n/a	UNCLOS
China	all*	all	all	n/a
Indonesia	UNCLOS	no	no	n/a
Malaysia	UNCLOS	3 islands	no	UNCLOS
Philippines	significant portions	8 islands	no	n/a
Taiwan	all*	all	all	n/a
Thailand	n/a	n/a	n/a	UNCLOS
Vietnam	all*	all	all	UNCLOS

Source: US Energy Information Administration, Analysis Briefs, "South China Sea," March 2008, http://www.eia.gov/countries/regions-topics.cfm?fips=SCS.
*Excluding buffer zone along littoral states (calculations for buffer unknown)

These disputes involving multiple sovereign nations in the South China Sea have made it Asia's most dangerous point of conflict (see table 7.2). Prior to 1974, the PRC and South Vietnam each controlled part of the Paracel Islands. After a violent skirmish, China has controlled the whole of Paracel Islands. In a naval clash on the Spratly Islands, over 70 Vietnamese sailors were killed just south of Chigua Reef in March 1988.

Table 7.2. Military clashes in the South China Sea

Date	Countries	Military Clashes
1974	China, Vietnam	China seized the Paracels from Vietnam, with 18 of its troops killed in clashes on one of the islands.
1988	China, Vietnam	Chinese and Vietnamese navies clashed at Johnson Reef in the Spratlys. Several Vietnamese boats were sunk and over 70 sailors killed.
1992	China, Vietnam	Vietnam accused China of landing troops on Da Luc Reef. China seized almost 20 Vietnamese cargo ships transporting goods from Hong Kong from June to September.

Table 7.2 (*continued*)

Date	Countries	Military Clashes
1994	China, Vietnam	China and Vietnam had naval confrontations within Vietnam's internationally recognized territorial waters over Vietnam's Tu Chinh oil exploration blocks 133, 134, and 135. The Chinese claim the area as part of their Wan' Bei-21 (WAB-21) block.
1995	China, Philippines	China occupied Philippine-claimed Mischief Reef. Philippine military evicted the Chinese in March and destroyed Chinese markers.
1995	Taiwan, Vietnam	Taiwanese artillery fired on a Vietnamese supply ship.
1996	China, Philippines	In January, Chinese vessels engaged in a 90-minute gun battle with a Philippine navy gunboat near the island of Capone, off the west coast of Luzon, north of Manila.
1997	China, Philippines	The Philippine navy ordered a Chinese speedboat and two fishing boats to leave Scarborough Shoal in April; the Philippine navy later removed Chinese markers and raised its flag. China sent three warships to survey the Philippine-occupied islands of Panata and Kota.
1998	Philippines, Vietnam	In January, Vietnamese soldiers fired on a Philippine fishing boat near Tennent (Pigeon) Reef.
1999	China, Philippines	In May, a Chinese fishing boat was sunk in a collision with a Philippine warship. In July, another Chinese fishing boat was sunk in a collision with a Philippine warship.
1999	China, Philippines	In May, Chinese warships were accused of harassing a Philippine navy vessel after it ran aground near the Spratlys.
1999	Philippines, Vietnam	In October, Vietnamese troops fired upon a Philippine air force plane on reconnaissance in the Spratlys.
1999	Malaysia, Philippines	In October, Philippine defense sources reported that two Malaysian fighter planes and two Philippine air force surveillance planes nearly engaged over a Malaysian-occupied reef in the Spratlys. The Malaysian Defense Ministry stated that it was not a standoff.
2000	China, Philippines	In May, Philippine troops opened fire on Chinese fishermen, killing one and arresting seven.
2001	China, Philippines	During the first three months, the Philippine navy boarded 14 Chinese-flagged boats, confiscated their catches, and ejected vessels out of contested portions of the Spratlys.
2001	China, Philippines	In March, the Philippines sent a gunboat to Scarborough Shoal to "ward off any attempt by China to erect structures on the rock."
2002	Philippines, Vietnam	In August, Vietnamese troops fired warning shots at Philippine military reconnaissance planes circling over the Spratlys.

Source: US Energy Information Administration, Analysis Briefs, "South China Sea," March 2008, http://www.eia.gov/countries/regions-topics.cfm?fips=SCS.

The Association of Southeast Asian Nations (ASEAN) has been keen to ensure that the territorial disputes within the South China Sea do not escalate into armed conflict. As such, joint development authorities have been set up in areas of overlapping claims to mutually develop the area and to divide the profits equally without settling the issue of sovereignty over the region. This is more so in the Gulf of Thailand. Generally, China has preferred to resolve competing claims in bilateral negotiations. However, ASEAN countries favour multilateral talks, believing that they are disadvantaged in bilateral negotiations with the much larger China.

In July 2010, US secretary of state Hillary Clinton called for the PRC to resolve the territorial dispute peacefully. China demanded that the United States keep out of the issue. The US military released a statement on 18 August in which it opposed the use of force to resolve the dispute and accused China of assertive behaviour.

The Spratly and Paracel archipelagos are two groups of uninhabited islands located within the South China Sea and are subject to a complex territorial dispute involving neighbouring countries on fishing rights, the exploitation of crude oil and natural gas beneath the Spratly Islands, and the strategic control of a core position. Along with the territorial land claims on the islets, the disputes also involve the territorial waters of the various countries within the region. The nine dotted lines drawn by China to mark its claim cover around three-fourths of the total area of the South China Sea (fig. 7.4).

On 11 March 1976, the Philippine oil company discovered an oil field off Palawan Island, an island in the South China Sea claimed by the Philippines. These oil fields supply 15 percent of annual oil consumption in the Philippines. However, none of the countries claiming the Spratly Islands have granted concession offshore to avoid provoking a crisis. In addition, since the territorial dispute is not yet resolved, international oil companies have not showed much interest in exploring the area. On 17 September 2011, an influential Communist Party newspaper called on the Chinese government to use every means to stop the Oil and Natural Gas Corporation (ONGC) Videsh (India) from its exploration projects in the South China Sea in collaboration with Vietnam. The potential for a conflict—if not a war—is quite possible if ASEAN-brokered accords and international maritime law are ignored.

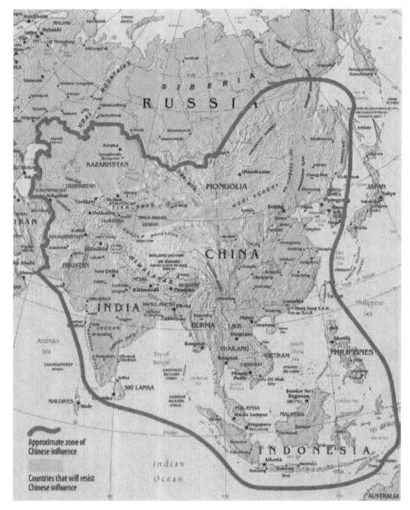

Figure 7.4. Approximate zone of Chinese influence. (*Adapted from* the University of Texas Libraries, the University of Texas at Austin, Perry-Castañeda Library Map Collection.)

On 20 July 2011, the PRC, Brunei, Malaysia, the Philippines, and Vietnam agreed to a set of preliminary guidelines to resolve the dispute. The PRC's assistant foreign minister, Liu Zhenmin, hailed the agreement as "an important milestone document for cooperation among China and ASEAN countries." Some of the early drafts acknowledged the need for "marine environmental protection, scientific research, safety of navigation and communication, search and rescue, and combating transnational crime."[13]

China's behaviour on these disputes has involved more "growling" than smiling. It has failed to convince its southeast neighbours about its intentions. The following are a few major examples:

- During the 1990s China unilaterally claimed the entire South China Sea to be its territorial waters and showed its willingness to enforce those claims.

- In the early 2000s China shifted slightly from "growling" to "smile diplomacy" to placate ASEAN.

- In March 2010 China declared the South China Sea as a "core national interest," similar to Tibet and Taiwan.

- In July 2010 Senior Colonel Geng Yansheng stated that "China has indisputable sovereignty of the South Sea, and China has sufficient historical and legal backing."

- On 10 September 2011, the Chinese navy harassed foreign vessels from Japan near the disputed island of Senkaku in the East China Sea.

- In October 2011 China's navy shadowed Indian navy ships on a friendly visit to Vietnam.

- In October 2011 China and Vietnam made a deal on sea disputes, agreeing to hold discussions twice a year. In response to China's aggressive behaviour, neighbouring countries are improving their defenses, naval forces, and bilateral cooperation (quadripartite "Arc of Democracy").[14]

The Pacific Ocean

The Pacific Ocean extends from the Arctic in the north to the Southern Ocean in the south, bounded by Asia and Australia in the west and the Americas in the east. The largest body of water on Earth, it borders 42 countries, including China, Australia, Brunei, Indonesia, North and South Korea, Malaysia, Singapore, the Philippines, Russia, Thailand, Vietnam, and the United States. The Japanese navy dominated it from 1914 until 1945. After the Second World War, the victorious American Navy thwarted Japanese dominance. America keeps a strong military presence in the region and considers itself to be a Pacific power.

The Players (the Actors)

China

The historic roots of Chinese civilization go back to 1600 BC, yet China is in many ways a new state. Its present political structure came into being in 1949 when, after decades of internal turmoil and struggle, the Chinese Communist Party (CCP) under the leadership of Mao Ze-dong and the long marchers successfully routed the Guomindang led by Chiang Kai-shek. The stated main objective of the new revolutionary regime was to establish a people's democratic political system and to initiate economic reforms by self-reliance and self-strengthening.

Mao romanticized and idealized "revolution and conflict."[15] Under his "helmsmanship" China was in a perpetual motion and revolution, going from one movement to another—the Hundred Flowers Campaign (1956), Great Leap Forward (1956–60), and Cultural Revolution (1966–69). These ideological spasms not only exhausted the Chinese people but also brought them immense suffering and adversely affected Chinese economic development. Between 1959 and 1961, 25 to 50 million Chinese starved to death in "one of the greatest human tragedies of the present time."[16]

During the Cultural Revolution the Chinese paid a heavy price. Total breakdown of legitimate authority throughout the country brought fanatic young Red Guards carrying Mao's "Little Red Book" to urban and rural areas of China. Thousands of innocent people were humiliated, unjustifiably arrested, tortured, and imprisoned. Millions of them were uprooted from their homes and sent to camps for hard labour and political reeducation. The Chinese national psyche was badly bruised for a long time to come.[17] It was only after Mao's death in 1976 that a more pragmatic leadership started to assert itself in undoing the damages of the past. In December 1978 at the Third Plenum of the Eleventh Central Committee of the CCP, Deng Xiaoping presented the "Four Modernizations" as a basis for China's economic transformation. However, the most far-reaching change occurred at the CCP's 14th Party Congress in October 1992, which called for an economic revolution linking China's future to the development of a capitalist-type market economy.[18] Major foreign policy decisions affecting China's role in the international sphere were also made. Intellectual freedom was encouraged as the fifth modernization. Hope for democracy was revived. The movement for democracy was, however, short-lived and like other "non-socialist movements" was snuffed out when the government cracked down in 1979. The Tiananmen massacre was brutal by any civilized standards. Unknown numbers of people, mostly young students, were killed. Leaders of the movement were arrested, and the supremacy of the CCP was restored. The CCP's commitment to the Four Modernizations—primarily geared to lift the faltering Chinese economy—continued. Despite weak international sanctions against China, it was anxious and determined to move out of long international isolation by opening its doors to foreign investment and experts. Close and cordial relations between China and Western democracies in general and America in particular brought immense prosperity to China, elevating its international status and influence.

The last 25 years have witnessed China moving from rags to riches. Its economic success has been unparalled in recent world history. As a result, Chinese perception of their role on the global stage has shifted tremendously. Also, economic prosperity has brought changes in the Chinese population's consumption patterns for commodities such as housing, clothing, food, and luxury items.[19] Supporting and sustaining its fast-paced industrialization requires natural resources, particularly for its energy needs. Hence, it must compete with other countries with similar needs. It is estimated that between 2006 and 2030, global energy needs will rise by 40 percent, and half of the demand will come from China and India. China's energy needs are consistently growing. It has invested in energy projects in more than 50 countries in the Middle East, Asia, and Africa. China seeks secure supply sea-lanes, particularly in the South China Sea and Strait of Malacca: in 2010 over 80 percent of China's oil imports passed through these sea-lanes (fig. 7.5).

Given China's growing energy demand, new pipelines will only slightly alleviate China's maritime dependency in either the Strait of Malacca or the Strait of Hormuz. The sheer volume of oil and liquefied natural gas imports to China from the Middle East will make strategic SLOCs increasingly important to Beijing. In 2009 a pipeline that will deliver up to 40 billion cubic meters (bcm) of natural gas per year from Turkmenistan to China via Kazakhstan and Uzbekistan commenced operation. Another natural gas pipeline designed to deliver 14 bcm per year from Burma is in the initial stages of construction and estimated for completion in 2013. Additionally, Beijing is negotiating with Moscow for two pipelines that could supply China with up to 69 bcm of gas.

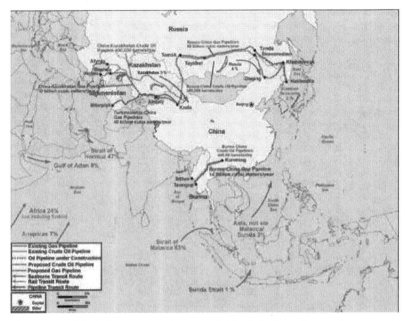

Figure 7.5. China's import transit routes/critical choke points and proposed/ under construction SLOC bypass routes. Boundary representation is not necessarily authoritative. (*Reprinted from* US DOD, *Military and Security Developments Involving the People's Republic of China 2011,* Annual Report to Congress [Washington, D.C.: DOD, 2011], 21.)

Chinese worldview. It has been observed that a "civilization's sense of its own place in the cycle of life matters."[20] As a country becomes more prosperous and strong, its aspirations, dreams, and goals are transformed along with its worldview. The "Power Shift" essays popular with younger Chinese diplomats state that "the tectonic plates that have defined Asia for the past half century are moving, and [China] is the chief agent of change as it resumes its historic role as Asia's central actor." A senior Chinese diplomat contends that it is now "far too powerful to be contained."[21] Chinese economic success is being felt around the world, and the global balance of power is shifting in China's favour. China has not been shy to flex its economic, political, and military muscles. China's recent prime minister, Wen Jiabao, no longer sticks to the script that China is a humble player in world affairs that wants to focus on its own economic development. He talks of China as a "great power."[22] It has a sense of manifest destiny that influences its worldview (its regional and global role) and formation of economic, diplomatic, and security strategies. China has a "steely ambition to become the Asian hegemon" by "disguising its ambition and hiding its claws" and by "smile diplomacy."[23] China is quite aware of its domestic social problems and its dependency on a mainly export-based economy to the United States, Europe, and other parts of the world. It is not ready as yet to bring out all its claws. China's 2010 Defense White Paper states that "China's future and destiny has never been more closely connected with those of the international community."[24] But China is greatly mistrusted in the region and has no real allies. Its aggressive policies in the region worry its neighbours about its intentions. China's dilemma is how to promote its "core" national interests (that often clash with others) without making regional and global actors too anxious about its ambitions and hegemonic agenda.

Chinese strategy. To achieve its goals both in domestic and international arenas, China aims toward "making the country prosperous[,] making the armed forces strong[,] and securing [its] status as a great power" by (1) accelerating its modernization of national defense and armed forces, (2) safeguarding national sovereignty, security, and national development goals, (3) maintaining domestic social harmony and stability, and (4) sustaining world stability and peace.[25] China's 2010 Defense White Paper sought to adopt a military strategy of "active defense" by enhancing national strategic capabilities conducive to Chinese development. The 2011 Defense White Paper discussed China engendering greater confidence in its own capabilities in relation to other major powers and also expressed concerns about US presence in the region.[26]

To achieve these goals, the Chinese have launched several diplomatic and military strategies in the region. The following briefly discusses these strategies and Chinese military preparedness.

String of pearls. According to a recent Pentagon report, China's armed forces are innovating capabilities that could extend their range into the Indian Ocean. Furthermore, China "has also made big investments in all of India's neighbours."[27] Robert Kaplan adds that the Chinese government "is building a large naval base . . . in Gwadar, Pakistan . . . ; a port in Pasni, Pakistan . . . ; a fuelling station on the southern coast of Sri Lanka; and a container facility with extensive naval and commercial access in Chittagong, Bangladesh," as well as roads linking Myanmar to China (fig. 7.6).[28] It is also planning an ambitious version of the Panama Canal across the Isthmus of Kra in

Thailand to connect the Indian Ocean to China's Pacific Coast and thus gain free access from East Africa to Japan and the Korean Peninsula.[29] From India's point of view, this "string of pearls" strategy is aimed to box in India in South Asia. The Chinese, however, do not see it as a threat to India and make semantic differences between "bases" and "places."[30]

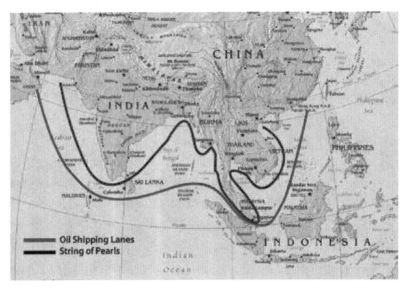

Figure 7.6. String of pearls. (*Courtesy of* the University of Texas Libraries, the University of Texas at Austin, Perry-Castañeda Library Map Collection.)

Chinese militarization. One of the most important components of the Four Modernizations has been military enhancement. China's spectacular economic growth and its huge foreign currency reserves have made it possible for Beijing to launch a massive militarization and technological modernization of all branches of the People's Liberation Army (PLA), creating unease among its neighbours and beyond. China faces no military threats to its borders. Its justification is to protect its national sovereignty and economic growth from external powers, non-state actors (pirates), and, often, mischief makers. Western military analysts are alarmed at what they see as a growing threat to American maritime supremacy in the Western Pacific. Chinese security specialists tend to scoff at the scaremongering (see fig. 7.7).[31]

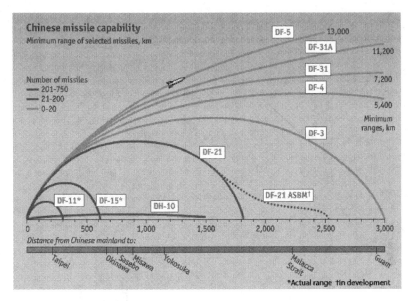

Figure 7.7. Chinese missile capability. (*Reprinted from* the Center for Strategic and Budgetary Assessments.)

Chinese militarization actions, in brief, have included:

- Improving their capacity to conduct high-intensity regional military operations, including anti-access and area-denial (A2AD) operations.

- Increasing ballistic and land-based cruise missiles with a range of 185 km.

- Developing anti-ship ballistic missiles.

- Growing capabilities to attack large ships including aircraft carriers—medium range (MRBM-DF 21 D)—in the western Pacific Ocean with a range exceeding 1,500 km.

- Modernizing their nuclear forces by adding a more survivable delivery system.

- Equipping naval forces with advance air-defense systems and modern anti-ship cruise missiles with a range exceeding 185 km.

- Building new naval bases at Yulin on the southernmost tip of Hainan Island.

- Purchasing a refitted and remodelled aircraft carrier (10 August 2011) for "research and training purposes."

- Improving sky-wave and surface-wave over-the-horizon radars, unmanned aerial vehicles, and other surveillance and reconnaissance systems over the eastern Pacific Ocean.

- Equipping China's air and air defense forces with 490 combat aircrafts within operational range of Taiwan.

- Trying to produce stealth aircraft—it was reported but not confirmed that Pakistan allowed the Chinese to see the American Navy SEAL Blackhawk helicopter downed during the Osama bin Laden operation.

- Upgrading their long-range surface-to-air missile (SAM) systems—China already has one of the largest such forces in the world.

- Improving intelligence collection and the maritime surveillance system.

- Developing their space and cyber warfare capabilities—in 2010 numerous computer systems around the world (including the United States, Japan, and India) were targets of intrusions that were believed to have originated in China. China denies it.

- Trying to acquire technology through illicit means, violating US custom laws—China is still dependent for key dual-use components of high technology on foreign sources, especially those not readily available through commercial or academic means.[32]

- Participating actively in foreign military engagements—the PRC conducts counterpiracy operations in the Gulf of Aden, counterterrorism, and search and rescue operations.

- Basing military attachés in 112 countries.

- Conducting combined military exercises to gain operational insights into others—in 2010 China conducted such exercises with Brazilian (Friendship), Peruvian (Peace Angel), Albanian, and Turkish forces.

Many other acquisitions would strengthen the ability of China's naval and air forces to operate in "distant seas."[33]

India

Indian worldview. India's cultural heritage is not only one of the most ancient but also one of the most extensive and varied. Its roots go as far back as the pre-Aryan Indus Valley civilization that flourished around the third millennium BC. Different systems of thoughts, beliefs, and practices have developed in India from the early dawn of human civilization. Throughout its history India has integrated heterogeneous elements that compose its national life. It has shown its "capacity to absorb other peoples and their cultural accomplishments, to synthesize them and develop a varied mixed culture" on the basis of universal values that constitute its present worldview about religion, politics, and relationships with other countries and peoples.[34] Three major cultural and political systems have most profoundly influenced the formation of India's worldview: the Aryan-Hindu-Buddhist, Muslim, and British/Western. Undoubtedly the most persuasive and dominant strain has been the Hindu heritage; however, the Indian worldview is not Hindu. India has been shaped over the centuries by its belief in tolerance and non-violence, as well as its Western heritage. These very attributes are also serving India today on its pathway to modernization and change.

Tolerance and secularism. The seeds of secularism and tolerance have been part of India's cultural and historical legacy. It was not only an ideological Westernized elite-driven impulse to proclaim India as a secular state but also a pragmatic decision. A country so vast in size and diverse could not survive a religiously dominated system. The Constitution of India (1950) has recognized and adopted symbols and philosophies from several religions (the tricolour national flag of India with Buddhist Chakra, the national slogan "the truth always prevails," principles of non-violence, and the Muslim practice of Sharia) and has secularized them. No parochial symbols such as the Hindu swastika or trident have been adopted in the public realm. Toleration of intellectual heterodoxy has influenced India's experiment with democracy.

Non-violence (ahimsa). The doctrine of non-violence and peaceful coexistence has been a cardinal virtue of Jain, Buddhist, and Hindu Indian cultural traditions. These have influenced Indian society and its political behaviour. Mahatma Gandhi relied on these doctrines to instil moral courage and self-discipline among Indians in their struggle for national independence.

Western/European heritage. The Europeanization of Indians, both Hindus and Muslims, began with the introduction of English education. Western education brought Indian intellectuals closer to Western ideas and views. The humanitarian writing of Edmund Burke, John Stuart Mill, John Locke, Jean-Jacques Rousseau, and Thomas Paine exposed Indian élites to ideas of equality, self-determination, and national freedom. British influence brought many social, economic, and political changes at various levels of Indian society. The British provided India a degree of unity it had not known for centuries, a liberal educational system, efficient and secular administration, and law and order. The constitution of the independent India incorporated many British practices and ideas including a parliamentary system of democracy. However, these changes and influences didn't totally transform basic structural forms and values of traditional Indian society and culture.

India and the United States. American presence and influence in pre-1947 India was almost non-existent except for some cultural and educational contacts. America's isolationist policy, its close relations with the British—despite President Roosevelt's sympathy for India's national movement—and mainly Euro-centric and Latin American–centric interests limited its presence in Asia and the Middle East. Japan posed no threat to American interests prior to Pearl Harbour, and China was an exotic land left mainly to Christian missionaries, adventurous tourists, and academics. The post-independent India under a non-aligned foreign policy of Prime Minister Jawaharlal Nehru, and later his daughter Indira Gandhi, disappointed and irritated American foreign policy makers. India's close relationship with Soviet Russia and China pushed America to support and sustain Pakistan as a useful and pliant ally in its Cold War national security strategies.

India as a rising power (post-1990) and its geostrategic role in the region. India struggled economically and politically between the 1950s and 1990s and was quite often called a "functioning anarchy" (John K. Galbraith) or "a wounded civilization" (V. S. Naipaul) with a "Hindu economic growth." It was quite irrelevant in the corridors of many world powers, better to be left alone to sort out its sordid situation.

The Indian struggle for independence had both economic and political objectives. Mahatma Gandhi often said that radical social and economic reforms were inevitable once political freedom was achieved. "The idea of economic equality was interlinked with political equality. . . . We wanted no change of masters from white to brown, but a real people's rule by the people and for the people and an ending of our poverty and misery."[35] The economic ideologies of various groups forming the Congress Party during the independence movement were dominated by urban intellectuals who favoured a socialist democratic India with emphasis on industrialization, land reforms, and planned economic growth under a socially aware public sector. The Gandhians, on the other hand, believed in local development centred around village self-sufficiency, small-scale industries, and handicrafts, with the state playing the role of a paternalistic and concerned—but not too interfering—authority. The Congress Party's approach was a combination of both Gandhians and Socialists. The philosophy of a planned economy was reflected in the Indian constitution promulgated on 26 January 1950. The public-sector-dominant Indian economy showed mixed results. On one hand, it contributed to tremendous government investment in industries crucial to economic development and national interests. On the other hand, it grew at a slower rate and was disdainfully characterized as a Hindu rate of growth due to an "unbelievably complicated system of restraints and rewards that, over the past four decades, has securely enclosed every aspect of Indian life. . . . India is a tiger caged."[36] Poor performance of the public sector in certain critical areas like power, coal, and steel led to loss of output and higher costs elsewhere in the economy.[37] As a result the Indian economy suffered, and by the 1990s India's house of socialism was in total shambles. "India had only two options: integrate with the world economy, or integrate with Burma," observed a cynical Anil Ambani of India's biggest family conglomerate. India decided to integrate with the world's economy and unchain the tiger.

The globalization and liberalization of the Indian economy has, since then, witnessed tremendous gains. According to Thomas Friedman, "India's economic revolution since 1990 has been a people-driven transformation: [the] biggest peaceful revolution in the last sixty years."[38] India's foreign currency reserves were less than $1 billion in 1991. India was almost broke and at the brink of defaulting. By 2006 the currency reserves rose to $140 billion! Its average annual economic growth has been 7 percent. According to the Indian government, Indians living in absolute poverty dropped from 34 percent to just 25 percent between 1991 and 2001. Edward Luce notes that "India in the early 21st century is an increasingly self-confident, materialistic and globalized place."[39] With increased economic growth and self-confidence, India's worldview concerning its role in the region and the world has changed. India's dangerous neighbourhood—an unstable rogue Pakistan, a troubled Afghanistan, Central Asia, and an ambitious and aggressive communist China—has forced Indian civil and military leaders not only to redefine and prioritize their country's national interests and strategies but to defend them as a regional power and global player.

India is now a nuclear power. Most Indians support and are quite proud of their nuclear status. India's nuclearization has put it in the same league as other nuclear states. However, India views its nuclear deterrent purely as defensive against two unfriendly nuclear powers—China and Pakistan—in the region and potentially Iran in the very near future. Here it must be noted that throughout its recorded history, India has never been a predatory—expansionist—power. It has used its soft power—religion, philosophy, and ideas of peace and coexistence—to spread its influence in pre-Islamic Central Asia, Indonesia, and Malaysia and precolonial Southeast Asia—Burma, Thailand, Vietnam, Cambodia, and even China.[40]

India and China. In their public pronouncements, both China and India proclaim to be "true friends and partners."[41] Despite their increasing trade relations, they have a serious mistrust toward each other, especially on the Indian side.[42] The 1962 Chinese invasion of northeast India; their differences on Tibet; claims on territories, including China's refusal to accept Arunachal Pradesh as Indian territory; and China's active assistance to provide missile, nuclear, and other advanced technologies to Pakistan pose strategic challenges for Indian policy makers. They also face statements such as "we can no longer accept the Indian Ocean as an ocean only for the Indians," differing views on the Chinese string-of-pearls strategy, as well as China's active involvement in Sri Lanka and Bangladesh.[43] India views these measures as a Chinese attempt to contain or box in India in the subregion. Hence, India has adopted a "look east" policy that includes "nurturing naval cooperation with Vietnam and Burma; . . . upgrading and modernizing its navy; . . . closer cooperation with other regional navies such as Australia, Indonesia, Japan, Singapore, and Mauritius; and [expanding] its naval presence as far west as the Mozambique Channel to as far east as the South China Sea."[44]

In addition to its diplomatic overtures, India is also making its presence felt in the vicinity. The Indian navy's maritime strategy is being coordinated with its foreign policy objectives. India has launched an ambitious program to acquire three more aircraft carriers by 2015 and 60 new surface warships. With 155 warships, India has one of the largest navies in the world. It is also planning to add six more submarines, including three nuclear-powered ones. As the competition between the two Asian powers escalates, India is investing more money to enlarge its navy (see fig. 7.8). In 2011 the Indian navy budget allocation was $15.4 billion, an increase of 14 percent over an earlier allocation.[45] India is introducing "long-range combat aircraft with mid-air refueling capability and landing platform dock ships for expeditionary warfare and humanitarian missions and is also developing an intercontinental ballistic missile with a strike range in excess of 5,000 km—all with the collective aim of influencing events far from home."[46] One interpretation of India's politico-military efforts is that they are "a repetition of the Monroe Doctrine, a forcible statement that external forces prejudicial to India's interest cannot be allowed to swim in the regional waters."[47] While both India and China aim to keep external forces out of their respective ocean zones, their perceptions of their own roles are quite different. Chinese diplomats assert that a "maritime order presided over by a capable, benevolent China" (remember Japan's pre–Second World War Asian prosperity doctrine), "excluding predatory Western sea powers such as America," would be beneficial to all Asian people.[48] India and most of China's neighbours are not convinced of a "benevolent" China's hegemonic assurances.

As in the past, China today covets its neighbours' land and tries to make them kowtow to the Middle Kingdom. China's reaction to India's assertiveness is mixed, posing a serious dilemma for its policy makers. China is suspicious of India's increasing presence not only in the Indian Ocean but also near the South China Sea. It is also concerned about India's strategic relationship with its neighbours and more so with the United States—the so-called axis of democracies.

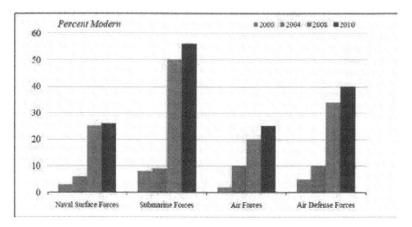

Figure 7.8. PLA modernization areas, 2000–10. This graphic compares the expansion of modern operational systems within the PLA in 2000, 2004, 2008, and 2010. (*Reprinted from* US DOD, *Military and Security Developments Involving the People's Republic of China 2011*, Annual Report to Congress [Washington, D.C.: DOD, 2011], 43.)[a]

[a]For surface combatants, *modern* is defined as multi-mission platforms with significant capabilities in at least two warfare areas. *Modern* for submarines is defined as those platforms capable of firing an anti-ship cruise missile. For air forces, *modern* is defined as fourth-generation platforms (Su-27, Su-30, F-10) and platforms with fourth-generation-like capabilities (FB-7). *Modern SAMs* are defined as advanced, long-range Russian systems (SA-10, SA-20) and their PRC indigenous equivalents (HQ-9).

China perceives India as its "most strategic adversary" in the region. Chinese commentators have repeatedly pointed out that "U.S.-India cooperation can lead to their 'unified strategy' on all major issues, which can change the strategic situation in South Asia."[49] Kaplan quotes the view of Zhang Ming, a Chinese naval analyst, that "the 244 islands that form India's Andaman and Nicobar archipelago could be used like a 'metal chain' to block the Western entrance to the Strait of Malacca on which China so desperately depends. . . . Once India commands the Indian Ocean, it will not be satisfied with its position and will continuously seek to extend its influence, and its east-ward strategy will have a particular impact on China."[50] Chinese reaction to Indian assertiveness has been to promote the string-of-pearls concept, support Pakistan, develop close relations with Burma, and implement massive investment in Sri Lanka and Nepal. China's strategy, therefore, is to "sideline India in its neighbourhood" via refusing to openly support India's membership in the United Nations Security

Council and using Pakistan "as a form of 'proxy deterrent' against India in its own backyard."[51] As one Chinese saying goes, "one mountain cannot accommodate two tigers"; but at the same time, it would be very difficult, almost impossible, for the dragon/python to swallow the elephant. There is no doubt that both China and India will potentially transform the geopolitical landscape.[52] "Geostrategically speaking, the Indian Ocean is a link of communication and oil transportation between the Pacific and Atlantic Oceans. . . . India is just like a giant and never-sinking aircraft carrier and the most important strategic point guarding the Indian Ocean."[53] The Chinese strategic goal is to keep India from being a rival and challenging its hegemonic dreams (see figs. 7.9 and 7.10).

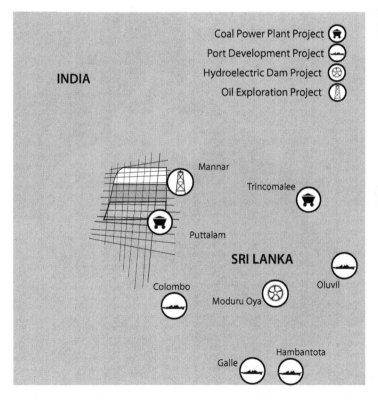

Figure 7.9. Locations of investment in key areas in Sri Lanka. (*Adapted from* R. S. Vasan, *Indo Sri Lanka Maritime Issues: Challenges and Responses*, South Asia Analysis Group, Paper no. 3787, 29 April 2010, www.southasiaanalysis.org/papers38/paper3787.html.)

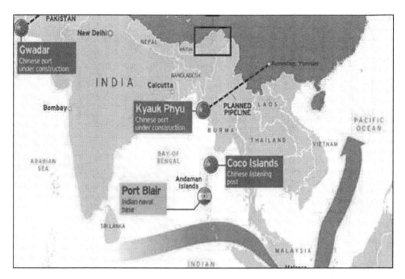

Figure 7.10. Chinese encirclement of India in Indian Ocean. (*Reprinted from R. S. Vasan, Indo Sri Lanka Maritime Issues: Challenges and Responses,* South Asia Analysis Group, Paper no. 3787, 29 April 2010, www.southasiaanalysis.org/papers38/paper3787.html.)

United States of America

The Spanish-American War provided the United States almost unhindered control in waters it considered important for its national interests. By 1914, with the construction of the Panama Canal, US dominance in the Atlantic and Pacific Oceans was secure. The canal allowed safe transit of American troops to theatres of war. During the Second World War, America was threatened mainly in the Atlantic and Pacific Oceans by Germany and Japan. During the Cold War, American presence was felt beyond its traditional two-ocean strategy. The British withdrawal from its Asian colonies left a strategic vacuum in an unstable area. The Indian Ocean became important for commercial and political reasons. The dependence of America and its allies, such as Japan and other West European countries, on Middle East petroleum created the need for a robust presence in the Indian Ocean. The former British island of San Diego Garcia, "leased" to America, provided an important strategic platform for the American Navy during the Vietnam, Iraq, and Afghanistan conflicts and a place to keep an eye on possible mischief makers, humanitarian aid, and, lately, pirates and terrorists. "For a century . . . American grand strategy has, through alliances backed by maritime power, aimed to prevent the rise of dangerous peer competition on distant continents."[54]

The recent rise of the PRC to become the Asian hegemon and challenge other powers in the region, especially the United States, has posed a serious strategic dilemma for American policy makers. China's lack of transparency, its aggressive behaviour in the region, and its military buildup is "potentially destabilizing," and by "most accounts, the [PLA] is on track to achieve its goals of building a modern, regionally focused military by 2020." The PLA, "motivated by expanding economic and security interests . . . is now venturing into the global maritime domain, a sphere long dominated by the U.S. Navy."[55] An *Economist* report assesses that "in sum, China's abilities to strike have soared far beyond seeking to deter American intervention in any future mainland dispute with Taiwan. Today China can project power out from its coastline well beyond the 12-mile (19 km) limit. . . . Ultimately, China seems to want to stop the American fleet from being able to secure its interests in the western Pacific."[56] Of late, the Chinese navy has not been cooperative with US Navy ships:

- In October 2006 a Chinese submarine stalked the USS *Kitty Hawk* in international waters.

- In November 2007 the Chinese denied the USS *Kitty Hawk* carrier strike group entry into Victoria Harbour when it asked for shelter from bad weather.

- In March 2009 Chinese navy ships harassed the USS *Impeccable* outside China's 12-mile territorial waters of the South China Sea.

China has also harassed other foreign vessels and issued veiled threats to them.

American policy makers are profoundly uncertain as to how to deal with China. Washington has given mixed signals. On one hand, Americans are worried about China's militarization (the new Prussia) and its goal to minimize American influence in the region. On the other hand, they observe that "China's navy has little operational experience beyond regional waters."[57] The heart of the problem is a profound uncertainty in both countries about where the relationship may lead. In many respects the two countries are in the same bed. They are "not just rivals for global influence; they are also mutually dependent economies."[58] This uncertainty between the two countries poses serious policy problems for potential allies of the United States in the region. Will America stand by them or leave them stranded by making deals with the Chinese?

Political scientist John Mearsheimer says that "America just cannot walk away from the region despite its 'to be or not to be' situation. America, as a hegemon of the Western hemisphere, will try to prevent China from becoming the hegemon of much of the Eastern hemisphere."[59] Secondly, its dependence on an unstable yet resource-rich strategic Middle East will not allow it to retreat from the Indian Ocean. Hence, America needs to rethink and constantly reevaluate its strategy in the Pacific and Indian Oceans in terms of its alliances and act as a necessary power balancer. America's dilemma is that it wants both solid commercial-economic ties with China and China as a responsible global power but, at the same time, feels threatened by China's increasing economic, industrial, and military might.[60] To accomplish its goal as a power balancer, as stated by Adm Robert Willard, head of the US Pacific Command, in his 2010 testimony to the US Congress, "Until . . . it is determined that China's intent is indeed benign, it is critical that we maintain the readiness of our postured forces; continually reinforce our commitment to our allies and partners in the region; and meet each challenge by the PRC . . . consistent with international law." Secretary of Defense Robert Gates observed in 2011 that "we are a Pacific nation. We will remain a Pacific nation. We will remain engaged."[61]

Overall, America looks uneasily on the rise of a political rival—an upstart China. Many policy makers in both countries feel that the balance of power has already shifted in favour of China. Today, "Barack Obama faces a China that is growing richer and stronger while remaining tenaciously authoritarian. Its rise will be far more nettlesome than that of his own country a century ago." Obama has said that "our future history will be more determined by our position on the Pacific facing China than by our position on the Atlantic facing Europe."[62] American commentators, policy makers, and politicians widely share the sentiment that "across the Pacific America faces a geopolitical rival that is also an effective economic competitor—a combination not seen since the Kaiser's Germany."[63] White House spokesperson Ben Rhodes said in November 2011 that the president will "be making it very clear over the course of the [Asian-Pacific summit] that the United States will continue to play the role it has throughout the last century in being the anchor of security and stability in the region and having the type of force posture in the

Asia-Pacific that can protect our interests as well as those of our allies in the region."[64] On 16 November 2011, President Obama announced that the United States will "deploy 2,500 Marines in Australia to shore up alliances in Asia. . . . The move prompted a sharp response from Beijing."[65]

Chinese perception of the United States. China's rise in Asia has been a "game changer," observes Seiji Maehara, a member of the House of Representatives of Japan. As chief policy advisor to the prime minister of Japan, Yoshihiko Noda called it the "dawn of a new dynasty."[66] Irrespective of these expressions, one thing is certain. The emergence of China has contributed to a power shift not only in Asia but globally. The Chinese worldview and position in the global power structure have changed immensely in the last decade or so. China has acquired a sense of manifest destiny and resists outsiders who deny it its long-due place in the international arena. China believes that it can afford to flex more of its muscles; however, Chinese diplomats take pains to convince their neighbours in the region and beyond that China's "peaceful rise" (*heping jueqi*) is benign. Most of China's neighbours and others mistrust those pronunciations: the Chinese talk about settling disputes but on their own terms.

China views America as a declining economic and political giant but a giant still capable of inflicting pain. The security specialists in China "tend to scoff at all the scaremongering" Americans indulge in.[67] The Chinese security specialists' counterargument to American paranoia is that America suffers from a post–Cold War "enemy deprivation" syndrome and aims to build a "Great Wall" around China. Its leaders, despite their steely ambition to be a superpower and hegemon, follow Deng Xiaoping's advice that the country "disguise its ambition, hide its claws, and bide for the time." The Chinese do not approve of American presence in the region, but they are also acutely aware of their limitations. At present, China does not have sufficient clout or the inclination to challenge America. China has serious domestic problems—environmental degradation, potential social unrest in Tibet, and an increasing gap between rich and poor—that make its leaders jittery. Despite manifold increases in its defense budget, the allocation in 2010 was about $160 billion, in contrast to the American defense budget of $500–$700 billion.[68] It is still dependent on foreign technologies and has an unfriendly neighbourhood on its land borders with India and Vietnam and at sea with most East Asian countries. And yet for all their internal challenges, the Chinese seem to want their nation to be a bigger player in the world. A 2006 opinion poll conducted jointly by the Chicago Council on Global Affairs and the Asia Society found that 87 percent of Chinese respondents felt that China "should take a greater role in world affairs." Most Chinese also believe that China's global influence "would match that of the U.S. within a decade."[69] China also wants to be left alone by outsiders, meaning the United States. It wants its own Monroe Doctrine but no pledges to treat others in the same fashion (see fig. 7.11).

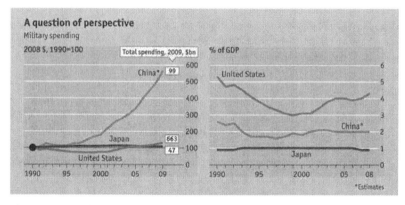

Figure 7.11. Military spending. (Chart developed by the Stockholm International Peace Research Institute [SIPRI].)

United States–India. Indian-US political and security relations could be analysed in two phases. The Nehru–Indira Gandhi era, mainly between 1950 and 1984, also coincided with the Cold War between the two superpowers, the Vietnam War, and the Soviet invasion of Afghanistan and other minor proxy entanglements between the two. India adopted a non-aligned foreign policy and drew closer to the Soviet Union due to American military aid to Pakistan and its outright hostility toward India during the Nixon presidency. The end of the Cold War and collapse of the Soviet Union created a security quandary for Indian policy makers. Several geostrategic factors, including the end of the Cold War, resulted in the limited thawing of the Indo-US relationship in the 1990s. However, as Admiral Willard points out, "Relations were by and large severed after the nuclear tests by both India [and] Pakistan."[70] He also notes that by 2002 many past misconceptions and new challenges—such as terrorism, Afghanistan, India's improved economic situation, and the somewhat more pragmatic political environment in both countries—renewed their engagement. Robert O. Blake, the Obama administration's point man for South Asia, observes that the US-India relationship "is rooted in the shared threat both countries face from international terrorism and the fact that India is situated in a dangerous neighborhood" and that Washington's "strategic relations with India will shape the world we live in, as the world settles into the still young—and at times turbulent—21st century."[71] Publicly, both India and the United States do not mention the increasingly assertive China in the region, but they do perceive China to be a potential destabilizing power in a relentless pursuit of its ambition to be a superpower and a hegemon in Asia. In public pronouncements, both India and the United States refrain from fuelling Chinese anxieties about emerging close relations between the two countries. Blake adds that "our engagement across the Asia-Pacific region, and our belief that India has a consequential role to play in the region, will not in any way deflect from our strong relations with China. In fact, we see great promise in bringing China, India and the United States even closer together, in formal capacities."[72]

However, India-US security relationships have been ramped up to levels that may have been unimaginable a couple of decades ago. Increased bilateral military exchanges, exercises, and capacity building have resulted in over 50 bilateral military exercises in the last six years. The United States hosted over 100 Indian military officers just in 2010. In terms of defense sales, it has made over $8 billion in defense deals with India for major programs such as the C-17 and C-130J. Maritime security is also another emerging area of cooperation. According to Assistant Secretary of State Blake, the United States was "elated" about India's decision to chair a plenary in 2012 of the Contact Group on Piracy off the Coast of Somalia.[73] The Indo-US civilian nuclear deal was one of the most positive and glaring examples of their improved and robust security and political relationship, but several areas of concern still need to be overcome in terms of their (1) developing an acquaintance with each other, (2) understanding how to work organization to organization, and (3) learning to trust each other's intentions (Cold War legacy). A few other tweaks in the relationship include India's own national and security concerns that may not always converge with America's—such as Indo-Iranian relations, India's abstention in the UN on Libya's no-fly zone, India's purchase of $10-billion European fighter jets instead of American jets despite President Obama's personal letter to Indian prime minister Manmohan Singh, and the stalled civil-nuclear deal.

According to Brookings Institution president Strobe Talbott, India and the United States are not now and may never be allies. Talbott states that "if India were an ally of the United States, there would be a treaty of alliance between us, like the one between the United States and Japan, the one between the United States and Korea, and the one between the U.S. and our NATO allies. . . . We are strategic partners."[74] However, India and the United States do have shared democratic values, and on several global and regional strategic and political issues their policies converge. Both countries realize that the "United States is the only world power capable of responding to aggressive and intimidating acts by China," and that could be a stabilizing factor in the region and beyond.[75] And it is not only the China factor that concerns India and US strategists but also the American concern that if America blinks, its global credibility as a power balancer and reliable partner—and not a mere paper tiger in the future—could be challenged by even lesser powers than China. So what is to be done?

Conclusion

The above discussion presented the following points:

- Despite massive military buildup by both China and India and the increased presence of the United States in the region, none of them want a conflict. They stand to lose more than gain.

- It is also clear that "the Asian seas today are witnessing an intriguing historical anomaly—the simultaneous rises of two homegrown maritime powers against the backdrop of U.S. dominion over the global commons . . . China and India. Their aspirations for great-power status and, above all, their quests for energy security have compelled both Beijing and New Delhi to redirect their gazes from land to the seas." While both China and India seem to have similar objectives, one would think that there is more room for cooperation at least on the second point. But given the India-China mistrust of each other, the trends are "worrisome."[76]

- China's one-party regime, lack of transparency, bullying of neighbours, arms sales to brutal regimes such as Sudan's and Libya's, transfer of nuclear technology to the region's most unstable country—Pakistan—and frequent temper tantrums about Tibet are of major concern. All the regional powers and others would like to see China as a constructive global partner. However, it needs to respect international codes of behaviour on commerce, currency, and security matters. It should likewise tone down its shrill, single-minded, self-righteous views about others.

- It is imperative that all regional powers and the United States do their best to convince China that their intention is not to contain China's peaceful rise.

- India and China are too big to be pushed around and contained either by each other or by outsiders. While both countries are still haunted by memories of humiliation and injustices heaped on them by Western colonialists, pragmatic considerations should prevail over past events by adopting either an expensive and futile use of hard power (the so-called realist approach) or of soft power (trade, democratization, respect for human rights, etc.). In an ideal world, the lions and the sheep drink together. However, in the real world, countries compete not only for power for power's sake but also to legitimize their regimes by providing more than basic necessities to their citizens. Hence, a bold approach is needed. It requires compromise, vision, tolerance, and respect for human dignity and the environment. An eye for an eye will leave the world blind (Mahatma Gandhi). Both India and China, the tiger and the dragon, will have to learn to live together. How both of them blend their ambitions and quest for peace will, to a great extent, determine global and regional security and prosperity in the twenty-first century.

- The role of the United States, both politically and militarily, is vital in the region. India and China should accept its presence. As discussed earlier, "for a century . . . American grand strategy has, through alliances backed by maritime power, aimed to prevent the rise of dangerous peer competitors on distant continents."[77] The United States was a Pacific sea power even prior to WWI. Post WWII brought US naval power beyond the Pacific to the Indian Ocean for strategic and commercial reasons. "In concert with [its] friends and Allies, the United States . . . will also continue adopting [its] forces, posture, and operational concepts to maintain a stable and secure East Asian environment."[78] It needs allies to build a concert of democracies (Japan, India, Philippines, Australia, Singapore, Indonesia, Malaysia, etc.)—"a string of pearls"—without threatening any regional power's ambitions, thus allaying fears of jittery countries. Such a NATO of democracies will assure security. Most of the Asian neighbours accept this premise. The main element of American foreign policy toward China must be long-term firmness, patience, and vigilance.

- India should also relax and try to improve its relations with Pakistan. Better relations are crucial to the stability and peace in the immediate South Asian region as well as in Central and East Asia.

- India and the United States are bound to cooperate. They share democratic values and several strategic global and regional concerns. Both of them could play a constructive role in the area and counterbalance any subversive presence, including piracy and terrorism. As noted above, India will not become a US ally in traditional terms but can be a partner. Much depends on how China and India manage their own relations and how they interact with others in their quest for peace and stability in the region and the world. A strategic cooperative triangle is the only hope for a noncombative-coexistence-driven framework for India, China, and the United States. A Sino-American understanding is crucial for the stabilization of the region.

- India will keep its options in view of its own national interests, which may not converge with either the United States or China. India needs to stand up and be tough not only in defining its national security goals but also in taking strong steps to protect them. It must convince its friends and partners of its dependability, get out of a failed shadow of a non-alignment policy that did not serve it well in 1962, and adopt a more pragmatic geopolitical strategy.

The region and the world need a balanced, cooperative relationship among an established democratic superpower and two emerging powers in Asia. To quote Robert Blake, "If we want to address, manage or solve some of the most pressing issues of the 21st century, India, China and the United States will have to coordinate [their] efforts."[79] While we hope for good relations among these three nations, as Richard Armitage says, "hope is not a policy."[80] The three powers have to accommodate one another's interests and translate diplomatic language into real, honest efforts.

Notes

1. Robert Kagan, quoted in "Less Biding and Hiding," *Economist* 397, no. 8711 (4 December 2010): 8–10.
2. Michael Klare, *Resource Wars: The New Landscape of Global Conflict* (New York: Henry Holt, 2001).
3. Jared Diamond, *Guns, Germs, and Steel: The Fates of Human Societies* (New York: W. W. Norton, 1998); and Jared Diamond, *Collapse: How Societies Choose to Fail or Succeed* (New York: Viking, 2005).
4. Robert Kaplan, "The Geography of Chinese Power: How Far Can Beijing Reach on Land and at Sea?," *Foreign Affairs* 89, no. 3 (May/June 2010): 17.
5. Ibid., 36.
6. James R. Holmes and Toshi Yoshihara, "China and the United States in the Indian Ocean: An Emerging Strategic Triangle?," *Naval War College Review* 61, no. 3 (Summer 2008): 44.
7. K. M. Panikkar, *India and the Indian Ocean: An Essay on the Influence of Sea Power on Indian History* (New York: Macmillan, 1945), 14.
8. Rear Adm R. Chopra (India), "A Seminar on Maritime History," *Sainik Samacher* 49, no. 4 (16–18 February 2002), 11.
9. Robert Kaplan, *Monsoon: The Indian Ocean and the Future of American Power* (New York: Random House, 2010), 9.
10. Kaplan, *Monsoon*, book jacket.
11. Patrick Barata and Chris Larano, "Drilling Plans, Disputed Seas," *Wall Street Journal*, 3 August 2011, 2.
12. *Maritime Disputes and Sovereignty Issues in East Asia: Hearing before the Subcommittee on East Asian and Pacific Affairs of the Committee on Foreign Relations, United States Senate*, 111th Cong., 1st sess., 15 July 2009, S. Hrg. 111-135, 32.
13. "South China Sea Agreement Reached," *Asean Affairs* online, 21 July 2011, http://www.aseanaffairs.com.
14. *New York Times*, 13 October 2011; Iskander Rehman, "Keeping the Dragon at Bay: India's Counter-Containment of China in Asia," *Asian Security* 5, no. 2 (2009): 141; and Richard Weitz, "Nervous Neighbors: China Finds a Sphere of Influence," *World Affairs* 173, no. 6 (March/April 2011): 6–14, tables 1 and 2.
15. Lucian W. Pye, *China: An Introduction* (New York: HarperCollins, 1991).
16. Fox Butterfield, *China: Alive in the Bitter Sea* (New York: Times Books, 1982), 348.
17. Ibid.
18. Cheng Chu-Yuan, "China's Economic Policies after the CCP 14th Party Congress," in Dhirendra Vajpeyi, ed., *Modernizing China* (Leiden: E. J. Brill, 1994), 7.

19. Lester Brown, *Who Will Feed China?: Wake-Up Call for a Small Planet* (New York: Norton, 1995).

20. Adam Gopnik, "Decline, Fall, Rinse, Repeat: Is America Going Down?," *New Yorker*, 12 September 2011, 40–47, paraphrasing German historian and philosopher Oswald Spengler.

21. "Survey: Reaching for a Renaissance," *Economist* 382, no. 8522 (31 March 2007): 4.

22. Ibid., 23.

23. Seth Cropsey, "Anchors Away: American Sea Power in Dry Dock," *World Affairs* 173, no. 5 (January/February 2011): 69.

24. PRC State Council, Information Office, *China's National Defense in 2010* (Beijing: PRC, 31 March 2010).

25. PRC defense minister Liang Guanglie, December 2010, quoted in US DOD, *Military and Security Developments Involving the People's Republic of China 2011*, Annual Report to Congress (Washington, D.C.: DOD, 2011), 9.

26. PRC State Council, Information Office, *China's National Defense in 2010* (Beijing: PRC, 31 March 2011), 30–33.

27. "A Himalayan Rivalry; India and China," *Economist* 396, no. 8696 (21 August 2010): 17–20.

28. Robert D. Kaplan, "Center Stage for the Twenty-First Century: Rivalry in the Indian Ocean," *Foreign Affairs* 88, no. 2 (March/April 2009): 22.

29. Ibid.

30. Daniel J. Kostecka, "Places and Bases: The Chinese Navy's Emerging Support Network in the Indian Ocean," *Naval War College Review* 64, no. 1 (Winter 2011): 61, 74.

31. "Less Biding and Hiding," 6.

32. David Wise, *Tiger Trap: America's Secret Spy War with China* (New York: Houghton Mifflin Harcourt, 2011), book jacket.

33. For details on China's acquisition, see US DOD, *Military and Security Development Involving the People's Republic of China, 2011*.

34. Jawaharlal Nehru, *The Discovery of India* (London: Meridian Press, 1946), 54.

35. Ibid.

36. Clive Crook, "A Survey of India: Caged," *Economist* 319, no. 7705 (4 May 1991): 1.

37. B. Morris, "Message from Bangkok," *Economic and Political Weekly*, 9 November 1990, 3912.

38. Thomas Friedman, foreword, in Nandan Nilekani, *Imagining India: The Idea of a Renewed Nation* (New York: Penguin, 2009), 5.

39. Edward Luce, *In Spite of the Gods: The Strange Rise of Modern India* (New York: Doubleday, 2007), 9.

40. A. L. Basham, *The Wonder That Was India: A Survey of the Culture of the Indian Sub-Continent before the Coming of the Muslims* (New York: Grave Press, 1959).

41. Sheela Bhatt, "China and India Are True Friends, Partners" (interview, Dehua Wang, director, Centre for South Asia Studies, Shanghai Academy of Social Sciences), *Rediff News*, 1 October 2009, http://www.rediff.com/news/report/chinese-expert-on-india-china-ties/20091001.htm.

42. Jonathan Holslag, *China and India: Prospects for Peace* (New York: Columbia University Press, 2010).

43. Zhao Nan, director, General Staff Logistics, Chinese navy, 1993, quoted in Maitra Ramtanu, "India-U.S. Security: All at Sea in the Indian Ocean," *Asia Times*, 6 December 2007, 11; R. S. Vasan, *Indo Sri Lanka Maritime Issues: Challenges and Responses*, South Asia Analysis Group, Paper no. 3787, 29 April 2010, www.south asiaanalysis.org/papers38/paper3787.html; and "Himalayan Rivalry," 17–20.

44. Ehsan Ahrari, "Strategic Moves in Southern Asia," *Far Eastern Economic Review*, 28 June 2001; and Kaplan, "Center Stage for the Twenty-First Century," 28.

45. Gabe Collins and Andrew Erickson, "India Plays Catch-Up with China: Asia's Titans Boost 2011 Defense Budgets," *China SignPost*, no. 29, 14 March 2011.

46. Rahul Bedi, "Getting in Step: India Country Briefing," *Jane's Defence Weekly*, 6 February 2008, 1. Bedi also cited in Walter C. Ladwig III, "India and Military Power Projection: Will the Land of Gandhi Become a Conventional Great Power?," *Asian Survey* 50, no. 6 (November/December 2010): 1163.

47. Bobb Dilip, "Cautious Optimism," *India Today*, 31 August 1987, 69.

48. Holmes and Yoshihara, "China and the United States in the Indian Ocean," 46.

49. D. S. Rajan, "China Worried by U.S.-India Military Cooperation," *India Abroad*, 9 October 2009, A31.

50. Kaplan, "Center Stage for the Twenty-First Century," 22–23.

51. Iskander Rehman, "Keeping the Dragon at Bay: India's Counter Containment of China in Asia," *Asian Security* 5, no. 2 (2009): 118; and J. Mohan Malik, "India and China Bound to Collude," in *Beyond Survival*, P. R. Kumarswamy, ed. (New Delhi: Sage, 2004), 4.

52. National Intelligence Council (NIC), *Mapping the Global Future: Report of the National Intelligence Council's 2020 Project, Based on Consultations with Nongovernmental Experts around the World* (Washington, D.C.: NIC, December 2004), http://www.foia.cia.gov/2020/2020.pdf.

53. Jian Hua, "The United States, Japan Want to Rope in India Which Cherishes the Dream of Becoming a Major Country," *Ta Kung Pao*, 4 June 2001.

54. Cropsey, "Anchors Away," 68.

55. US DOD, *Military and Security Development Involving the People's Republic of China, 2011*, 1.

56. "Fourth Modernisation," *Economist* 397, no. 8711 (4 December 2010): 7.

57. US DOD, *Military and Security Development Involving the People's Republic of China, 2011*, 2.

58. "Leaders: Facing Up to China," *Economist* 394, no. 8668 (6 February 2010): 11.

59. John Mearsheimer, quoted in Kaplan, *Monsoon*, 41.

60. "Friends, or Else," *Economist* 397, no. 8711 (4 December 2010): 13.

61. Robert Burns, Associated Press, "In Hawaii, Gates Stresses Commitment in Asia," *Navy Times*, 1 June 2011.

62. "A Wary Respect," *Economist* 393, no. 8654 (24 October 2009): 3–16.

63. David Frum, "Does America Have a Future?," review of *That Used to Be Us: How America Fell Behind in the World It Invented and How We Can Come Back*, by Thomas L. Friedman and Michael Mandelbaum, *New York Times*, 8 September 2011, BR1.

64. Jackie Calmes, "Obama Trip Stresses Ties to Economies across Pacific," *New York Times*, 12 November 2011.

65. Jackie Calmes, "A U.S. Marine Base for Australia Irritates China," *New York Times*, 17 November 2011, A3.

66. Michael Elliott, "The Chinese Century," *Time* 169, no. 4 (22 January 2007): 8.

67. "Fourth Modernisation," 6; and Robert Manning and Paula Stern, "The Myth of Pacific Community," *Foreign Affairs*, November/December 1994, 79–93.

68. "China's Military Rise," *Economist* 403, no. 8779 (7 April 2012): 28.

69. Elliott, "Chinese Century," 3.

70. Aziz Haniffa, "US-India Military Ties Robust but Lot to Overcome: PAC-COM Chief," *India Abroad*, 7 October 2011, A18.

71. Aziz Haniffa, "India, China, and the US Will Have to Coordinate Our Efforts," *India Abroad*, 7 October 2011, A18.

72. Ibid.

73. "Strategic Relations with India Will Shape World We Live In," *Rediff News*, 29 September 2011, www.rediff.com.

74. Stephen P. Cohen, "Strobe Has a Strong Personal Connection to India," *India Abroad*, 12 June 2011, M126.

75. *Maritime Disputes and Sovereignty Issues in East Asia: Hearing before the Subcommittee on East Asian and Pacific Affairs of the Committee on Foreign Relations, United States Senate*, 111th Cong., 1st sess., 15 July 2009, S. Hrg. 111-135 (opening statement, Hon. Jim Webb, US senator from Virginia), 3.

76. Holmes and Yoshihara, "China and the United States in the Indian Ocean," 41.

77. Cropsey, "Anchors Away," 68

78. Quote from DOD, *Military and Security Developments Involving the People's Republic of China 2011*, I. See also *Maritime Disputes and Sovereignty Issues in East Asia*, 111th Cong., 1st sess., 15 July 2009, S. Hrg. 111-135 (statement, Hon. Jim Webb), 15.

79. Haniffa, "India, China, and the US Will Have to Coordinate Our Efforts," A18.

80. "Friends, or Else," 13–15.

Other Sources

Friedman, Thomas L., and Michael Mandelbaum. *That Used to Be Us: How America Fell Behind in the World It Invented and How We Can Come Back.* New York: Farrar, Strauss and Giroux, 2011.

"Leaders: Facing Up to China." *Economist* 394, no. 8668 (6 February 2010): 11.

"Leaders: How China Sees the World." *Economist* 390, no. 8623 (21 March 2009): 13.

"Special Report: China and America." *Economist* 393, no. 8654 (24 October 2009): 3–16.

"Survey: Reaching for a Renaissance." *Economist* 382, no. 8522 (31 March 2007): 3–18.

Vajpeyi, Dhirendra. *Water Resource Conflicts and International Security: A Global Perspective.* Lanham, MD: Lexington Books, 2012.

Chapter 8

US Role in the Asia-Pacific Region

A Regional View

Dr. Rajeswari Pillai Rajagopalan
Senior Fellow, Observer Research Foundation, New Delhi

Introduction

In January 2012 the United States outlined its new defence strategy, *Sustaining U.S. Global Leadership: Priorities for 21st Century Defense.* The strategy states that while US interests are global, its security and economic interests are intertwined with developments from the Western Pacific and East Asia into the Indian Ocean region and South Asia. Therefore, the United States views its presence and influence in the Asia-Pacific as a necessary rebalancing toward this region.[1] This recent effort by the Obama administration is an attempt to rationalize its strategy after having overextended itself in the last decade in Iraq and Afghanistan. The fiscal compulsions and ever-changing dynamics of the Asia-Pacific also call for a far more agile and flexible US strategy. It must be able to respond to a variety of emerging challenges in the region while recognizing the changing nature of warfare. These realities have resulted in the United States initiating new proficiencies and strategies, including anti-access and area-denial (A2AD) operations. Succeeding in this environment warrants attention on a range of technologies—including developing new stealth bombers, enhancing missile defences, and improving the effectiveness of critical space-based capabilities and submarine technologies—while complementing new strategies and partnerships. The changing nature of warfare would emphasize information and communication networks in future operations while recognizing the vulnerability of these domains, thus making protection of these assets of new importance.

The United States' Pacific pivot has been much debated since the end of last year. This chapter addresses three specific questions: (1) how Asia-Pacific nations see the role of the United States in the region; (2) as China rises, how its neighbours in the region will react—whether they will bandwagon or balance—and (3) how states in the region are hedging their bets on the future. The discussion delves into the new alliances and partnerships that are likely responses in view of the new challenges.

Regional Perceptions of the US Role in the Asia-Pacific

The Asia-Pacific region does not present itself as homogenous either in terms of challenges and responses or history and cultural heritage. Each of the countries in the region has its own baggage of history that determines to a large extent its approach to the presence of external powers. Therefore, each country has responded to the US role and presence quite differently in the last nearly six decades.

However, for ease of understanding, the perceptions of Asia-Pacific countries toward the US role in Asia can be categorized into three mind-sets. First is the category of states with adversarial ties with the United States but that nevertheless perceive it as a necessary hegemon in the region. The second group is made up of American allies in the region that have looked to the United States as a protector and guarantor of security. These countries remain by and large clear about the role of the United States in the region, although variations and tensions have emerged in recent years. The third group of countries has maintained a certain neutrality, such as India, Vietnam, and Laos. Below, I elaborate on the response of each group to the US strategic presence in the Asia-Pacific.

Adversaries Yet Positive toward US Presence

Russia, China, and North Korea have maintained broadly adversarial ties with the United States. Their relations with the United States have been marked by ups and downs, including temporary Cold War–like situations in the last decade.

US-Russian relations have been difficult despite the intentions at the highest political level to improve bilateral relations. At the end of the Cold War, Russia was troubled by the US-led unipolar world—although it believed that US influence would decrease in coming years—and it continues to work toward a multipolar order. However, Moscow does not imagine this transition to multipolarity to be smooth, instead visualizing "growing chaos and a vacuum of governance and security" and a "multi-tier" order.[2] But a part of the problem has been the United States itself: the spread of the North Atlantic Treaty Organization to the east, the missile defence issue, as well as American criticisms of Russian domestic behaviour on issues such as Chechnya have made Moscow increasingly suspicious of Washington's objectives, driving it closer to China.

North Korea has had the most troublesome relationship with the United States. Though the United States has had troubled ties with North Korea, negotiations and dialogues on Pyongyang's nuclear programme have been important components of this relationship. US interests in North Korea are dictated by security concerns arising from its nuclear and missile programmes and their impact on regional security and Washington's alliance commitment to Tokyo and Seoul.

Pyongyang has been the most difficult not only in terms of its relations with Washington but also its regional security. North Korea's nuclear- and missile-related activities, along with its poor human rights record, have been of concern and have become the main plank for US engagement/disengagement with Pyongyang. The "military-first politics" of the regime at the cost of development in the region has been an area of concern. North Korea has continued to argue that its nuclear weapons and delivery vehicles, including missiles and conventional capabilities, are weapons of deterrence against possible South Korean, Japanese, or American military aggression. The leadership has also argued that this is one way to give North Korea international attention and that the world will engage with Pyongyang only under such conditions. This argument is difficult to sell beyond a point, given that the international community, and the United States in particular, has been engaged with Pyongyang in different formats—both bilateral and at a multilateral level through the six-party talks.

The regime under the leadership of Kim Jong-un, after the death of his father Kim Jong-il in December 2011, has displayed the same trend as far as its military policies and foreign relations are concerned. The recent failed attempt at a satellite launch is a reflection of continuity rather than a change in its policies and of an approach characterized by utter disregard for regional or international concern. Continuity in Pyongyang's future trajectory was a given considering that Kim Jong-il chose the youngest son and not the older one (who is considered a peacenik) to carry on with his legacy in Asian affairs.

Meanwhile, China has managed to emerge as the major fulcrum in Asian security and foreign relations. Of the three countries that have adversarial ties with the United States, China has been the most pragmatic one, exemplified in the kind of interrelations that it has worked out. The kind of economic dependency that Beijing has built around US-China interactions makes it difficult for either side to pursue a strategy of hostility beyond a point. China has accorded high priority to its economic engagement with Washington as it believes that is to its benefit. This trend will continue at least for the near term until it establishes a thriving domestic market as it concurrently explores fully some of the larger markets in Asia.

But Beijing has also built up closer ties, indeed quasi alliances, to counter the United States. Therefore, analyzing how Beijing has shaped its relations with some of these countries and the region is pertinent.

The China-Russia Tango. China and Russia hope that they will at least be able to replace the United States in the long term. Despite their old mutual wariness, especially traditional Russian suspicions of China, an anti-US plank has brought the two countries together as strategic partners. However, this is not to suggest that they have no differences. On the contrary, Russia remains highly suspicious of a rising China and what Chinese strategic objectives will be. Moscow is wary of the growing Chinese influence in the Central Asian republics[3] and the Far East.[4] China's growing military might in an asymmetric manner in favour of Beijing is another concern for Russia.[5]

While China believed that the unipolar power structure is only a transition toward a more multilateral one, it recognized the limits of openly countering the United States for a variety of reasons, from huge economic costs of a confrontation to potential domestic insecurity. Thus, China has made efforts to counter the "unilateral" power led by the United States by aligning with major powers such as Russia and strengthening bilateral and multilateral ties within the region, even at the cost of the United States. However, it is yet to make any serious dent in altering the geopolitical balance in its favour. Beijing has not succeeded even in forming a larger coalition of a nation that could potentially oppose Washington in the long run.

China's Integration Strategy. Meanwhile, China began to adopt subtler policies over the last decade as a way of countering and diminishing the US role in the region. For instance, while Chinese policies in Asia and in Africa have been both more passive and economic in nature, they are meant to alter the US-China balance in the longer term. Beijing was hoping that these policies could alter not only the US standing but also US relative power and influence in the region.

Also, the parallel diplomatic initiatives by both Washington and Beijing in Asia are creating their own dynamics. Beijing pursued its Asian diplomacy with a twin objective of reducing the regional states' reliance on the United States as a security guarantor and capturing economic space both in the trade and investment domains. However, its policy has been derailed to an extent because of China's own obdurate policy on territorial issues, especially in the South China Sea. This has raised new anxieties about China's long-term intentions and resulted in a situation where Asian states are seeking a greater role for the United States as well as developing new partnerships in Asia as a means to counter the growing Chinese might.

China and North Korea. China has a major role in Pyongyang's future trajectory. While on the surface Chinese interests seem congruent with those of the United States and other regional powers, they are in reality somewhat different. For example, Chinese and American perspectives on North Korean stability diverge. For the regional powers as well as the United States, stability would mean seeing a denuclearised North Korea at peace with its neighbours and also as a country that ensures a modicum of human rights for its people. Conversely, Chinese interests are primarily to ensure that there is no crisis that might prompt the influx of a large number of refugees into China. This makes them far more tolerant of North Korean misbehaviour. Additionally, Beijing is worried that any North Korean collapse would lead to a united Korea, in alliance with the United States, at China's borders. Therefore, Chinese interests are driven by narrower perceptions of North Korean stability.

This leads to almost unconditional Chinese support for the North Korean regime. Given that kind of support from China, North Korea has continued to adopt a defiant attitude in its dealings with its neighbourhood—Beijing being the only exception. Beijing has become almost the only friend of the North Korean regime, extending critical economic, political, and moral support. China remains North Korea's largest trading partner as well as an important source of food, fuel, and arms.[6] Given that Pyongyang's relations, particularly with Seoul, have declined drastically after the three nuclear tests, Beijing's bargaining power vis-à-vis North Korea should have gone up significantly, but paradoxically it does not appear to have done so.

Some analysts argue that the United States is dependent on China to put any serious pressure on North Korea. While this may be partly true, it is also possible that China has not put any such pressure on

North Korea because it sees it as a buffer state between itself and the US allies in its neighbourhood. Second, with the United States having been preoccupied with Iraq and Afghanistan, China has managed to create a vital strategic space in Asia by using problem cases like North Korea. China has emerged as the conduit for any dealing with North Korea, be it democracy, human rights, or weapon of mass destruction proliferation issues. Therefore, China does not want to lose that privileged position wherein the West has to route itself through Beijing to achieve some of its foreign policy objectives in North Korea.

On the other hand, some have argued that the West has over-estimated the Chinese hold on North Korea and that Beijing is unable to exercise any real influence on Pyongyang. Some experts note that China is beginning to reach a point of frustration with North Korea on some issues, including its increasingly belligerent behaviour and growing economic crisis, although the Cheonan incident or the recent failed satellite tests have established that Beijing has not really changed its policy toward Pyongyang.

Outlook toward the United States. However, even countries such as China, Russia, and North Korea have a tendency to see continued value in the US role in the region. They see the United States as a necessary stabilizing force. China, for one, has maintained that in the absence of US presence in the region, one would have seen more hegemonic tendencies there, including in Japan.

Meanwhile, the new US defence strategy has produced mixed reactions in Beijing. Specifically, different Chinese ministries and officials have responded to the US strategy paper differently in a move that is more deliberate than otherwise. Moving away from the open anti-American line of the yesteryears, Beijing has become more composed toward the US presence in Asia. For instance, Pres. Xi Jinping, making a cautious welcome to the US role in Asia, remarked, "We hope the United States will respect the interests and concerns of China and other countries in this region."[7] However, Ministry of Defense spokesman Geng Yansheng said in a statement on the ministry's website, "We have noted that the United States issued this guide to its defense strategy, and we will closely observe the impact that US military strategic adjustment has on the Asia-Pacific region and on global security developments." He added that "we hope that the United States will flow with the tide of the era, and deal with China and the Chinese military in an objective and rational way, will be careful in its words and actions, and do more that is beneficial to the development of relations between the two countries and their militaries."[8]

A commentary from Xinhua news was more blunt, stating that "the U.S. role, if fulfilled with a positive attitude and free from a Cold War–style zero-sum mentality, will not only be conducive to regional stability and prosperity, but be good for China, which needs a peaceful environment to continue its economic development. However, while boosting its military presence in the Asia-Pacific, the United States should abstain from flexing its muscles, as this won't help solve regional disputes."[9] China was also quick enough to warn that "if the United States indiscreetly applies militarism in the region, it will be like a bull in a China shop, and endanger peace instead of enhancing regional stability."[10] Furthermore, the Chinese assistant foreign minister, Liu Zhenmin, was reported to have told the *China Daily* that its neighbours should "discard their 'cold war mentality' when handling sensitive regional issues . . . in the wake of China's occasionally tense relations" in both the South China Sea and East China Sea disputes over the last year.[11] The *China Daily* reportedly talked about "forces outside the region," which could include both the United States and other powers, such as India, that have taken a more explicit stand in recent years.

While the American pivot and what it means for the region is being debated in all the Asian capitals, some American analysts, including Michael Green, believe that the Chinese have "brought this on to themselves to some extent because of their position on the Cheonan, on the South China Sea, [and] the Senkakus."[12] The incidents over the past few years vis-à-vis all of China's neighbours—India, Japan, and Southeast Asia—have made the neighbourhood nervous while bringing out the innate animosity and hostility that exists in the region, with most of the nations actively seeking a US comeback to "counterbalance" China. The incidents of the last two years have contributed to much of the region strengthening its relations with the United States while shaping few newer partnerships.

Having said that, China is also more confident of its interdependence in the region, saying that the economic interdependency between Beijing and the region will ensure that the pivot becomes a failure. An editorial in China's *Global Times* suggests that the United States has to be able to do more than simply give the region verbal assurances, essentially making the point that US support to the region has to be economic in nature if the region is to move away from relying on China. It further indicates that "China has gained more stakes when dealing with the US. It is hard to say whether the US holds more advantages in China's neighboring area. The potential for economic cooperation between China and its neighboring countries is great. China should learn to use this to protect its political interests. Any country which chooses to be a pawn in the US chess game will lose the opportunity to benefit from China's economy. This will surely make US protection less attractive."[13]

While Russia may not have openly commented on the US strategy and its new emphasis on the Asia-Pacific, it recognizes the importance of Asia in global politics. It also realizes that to be active in the Asian setting, Russia must emerge as a power that remains relevant (in addition to its science and technology capabilities and natural resources, including oil). Russia has accordingly aligned with China closer than ever before for two reasons: first, the geopolitical weight of Russia on its own may not be enough to impact global politics, but a Russia-China strategic combination cannot be overlooked; and, second, it is advantageous for Russia to manage the rise of China by keeping Beijing in the same tent rather than by being on opposing sides. Military ties have been an important aspect of this relationship, although China is moving away from a transactional defence trade relation to one of joint military exercises and display of the cumulative military might, which has been a new feature. The recent Russia-China joint naval exercise in the Yellow Sea is a case in point.

Nonetheless, recent Russian initiatives have been curious. Russia expressed strong reservations on China's approach to handling the South China Sea dispute, such as Beijing making claims on the entire region—most recently at the Association of Southeast Asian Nations (ASEAN) Summit in Indonesia. Moscow joined the Trans-Pacific Partnership (TPP), a trade and economic liberalization arrangement, indicating that it is in alignment with the United States and its allies on Asian security. Meanwhile, Moscow has also become active in Asia, giving a fresh focus to the region and playing a viable role in all of the regional security and economic groupings, such as the ASEAN Regional Forum and the East Asia Summit. Thus, Russia seemingly wants to go along with the United States, although not as a junior partner. Such tendencies reflect both the strengths and weaknesses of Russia. However, if Washington were to embrace Moscow as a major power in the new Asian game, Moscow might quite happily abandon Beijing. The United States has to adopt a long-term perspective and get over its Cold War inhibitions to embrace Russia for this major geopolitical change to occur.

US Allies

The second set of countries includes American allies such as Japan, Taiwan, Australia, and others that look to the United States as a security guarantor. These countries have been rather disappointed and worried about the United States' lack of focus in the Asia-Pacific in the last 10 years. So the United States' pivot role in the Asia-Pacific is seen as of great value. While US allies are more satisfied with this reorientation, they realize their greater responsibilities and role in ensuring stability in the region. This recognition has dawned on them in the last 10 years, when the United States was increasingly focused away from the Pacific and toward the Middle East and Afghanistan. US allies have been more forthcoming as well as unanimous in welcoming the United States back to the region, acknowledging its huge impact on regional security in balancing a rising China.

Regarding the US pivot and decision to send 2,500 Marines into Australia, Japan maintains that the Japan-US alliance will continue to be the linchpin of the US forward presence in Asia. However, the new strategic challenges and uncertainties call for certain adjustments in the US posture, which Tokyo welcomes as a positive step.[14] East Asian analysts were also quick to make the point that Beijing brought this on itself, stating that "[China] has only itself to blame. By throwing around its increasing weight over the last couple of years, China has unnerved much of East Asia [thereby] driving U.S. friends and allies even more firmly into Washington's arms."[15]

An editorial in *Yomiuri Shimbun* was even more forthcoming in acknowledging the importance of this new shift. It said, "It is significant that the United States, as a Pacific nation, has made the strategic decision to focus its foreign, security and economic policies on the Asia-Pacific region. . . . Obama assured his Asian allies that the cuts in U.S. defense spending to reduce fiscal deficits will not have a negative impact on this region. The new U.S. strategy is welcome as it will contribute to the region's stability and prosperity. The role of the Japan-U.S. alliance is certain to become more important."[16]

Australia, a staunch ally of the United States, has been concerned about the changing dynamics in Asia and is one of the most supportive countries in the region of US efforts to pivot back to Asia. Australia believes that it "has been a very secure country for many decades, in large measure because the wider Asia-Pacific region has enjoyed an unprecedented era of peace and stability underwritten by US strategic primacy."[17] As mentioned earlier, because the United States has been preoccupied with Afghanistan and Iraq, China has managed to carve out a crucial strategic space for itself that may not be easy to recapture. Canberra senses that the pre-eminent position of the United States in Asia itself may be in question with China's growing economic, political, and strategic might. Therefore, the United States' re-entry into Asia may not be easy and may face challenges. However, the decision by Canberra to station US troops on its soil brings out a certain amount of determination on its part to do all it can to prepare for the changing security equation as US power undergoes a gradual decline while other powers rise. For instance, the 2009 Australian Defence White Paper says, "The pace, scope and structure of China's military modernisation have the potential to give its neighbours cause for concern if not carefully explained, and if China does not reach out to others to build confidence regarding its military plans."[18] The growth of an economically powerful and militarily strong China has triggered much of the regional competition and insecurities. There is also the fear as to how a more mighty China will behave as it becomes even stronger in the years ahead. While many other factors may have also contributed to regional insecurities and arms competition, the double-digit growth of China's military and its lack of transparency have markedly upped the ante in recent years.[19]

This brings up the issue of how Australia would like to strengthen its security in the future. While the economic engagement between Australia and China has been flourishing, the increasing security concerns override the economic robustness and may dictate a much closer alliance with the United States in the future. Most recently, Australian defence minister Stephen Smith said that Australia could even be supporting the United States' spy operations out of some remote islands in the Indian Ocean, such as the Cocos Islands, in the future.

With Washington reportedly expressing some interest in the Cocos Islands as a potential base for surveillance aircraft and spy flights, Smith also acknowledges that "we view Cocos as being potentially a long term strategic location. But that is down the track."[20] Given the geographical location of the Cocos Islands, both US and Australian officials see them as the ideal site for manned US surveillance aircraft—Global Hawks and the newer version, the Broad Area Maritime Surveillance (BAMS) drone, due for operationalization by 2015.[21] However, given that China is Australia's largest trading partner, its military support of the United States is going to emerge as a complex puzzle. Canberra has to carefully juggle its security and economic interests.

South Korea, another US ally, has had mixed feelings about the US pivot. Over the years, Seoul has been doing a balancing act between Washington and Beijing, given the overbearing presence of China in its immediate neighbourhood. It sees the US pivot as complicated, although with certain benefits to Seoul. At least in conceptual terms, "it seems fairly straightforward that reducing military and economic tension in the Asia-Pacific by having the U.S. reaffirm its commitment to serving as an outside balancer in the region at a time when the rise of China has many worried would be beneficial for South Korea. Any subsequent increased U.S. leverage on China would also probably give Washington a better hand in negotiating with the North on its nuclear program—also a benefit for Seoul."[22] However, in overall terms, South Korea feels the situation is far more complex.

Meanwhile, Southeast Asian countries have responded differently to the United States' pivot given that different and competing interests have driven these reactions. Given the nature of the close economic relations that most of these countries have developed with China over the years, they cannot afford to completely ignore those compulsions and jump onto the US bandwagon. On the other hand, serious security concerns drive them away from Beijing and toward Washington. Chinese strategic trade linkages have become a problem not just for countries in Southeast Asia but in many other regions as well because they could jeopardize these profitable ties if they try to balance against China. This appears to be a deliberate attempt by China to create such strong economic interdependencies that it becomes difficult to steer away from Beijing. If we rewind back to 2001 during the first term of the Bush administration, we can see how the United States itself was constrained during the spy plane crisis in April 2001.

Some of the initial Southeast Asian reactions to the US pivot to Asia reflect these contradictory pulls. There was therefore a sense of caution in the reactions of these countries. Indonesian foreign minister Marty Natalegawa's initial statement was more of anxiety as to how the new US approach will play out in the region and whether it will fuel more tensions. While noting the danger, he said, "What I would hate to see is if such developments were to provoke a reaction and counter-reaction precisely to create that vicious circle of tensions and mistrust or distrust."[23] However, he did not shy away from pointing the finger at China to say that "one of the causes is the absence of China's transparency in their spectacular military buildup."[24] It was also reported that the Indonesian president, Susilo Bambang Yudhoyono, was in full support of US plans to re-focus on Asia.[25]

Other regional leaders, including Malaysian prime minister Najib Razak and Singaporean foreign minister K. Shanmugam, voiced similar concerns. Shanmugam made a categorical statement that ASEAN states did not want to be "caught between the competing interests" of major powers.[26]

Some of the initial cautionary remarks have become even more nuanced in recent months. For instance, Indonesia has been fairly receptive to the United States while also collaborating with China. This balancing effort was visible in the Indonesia-China joint exercises. On the other hand, Obama was warmly received during his November visit to Jakarta, and the United States and Indonesia have also increased bilateral military exercises. The United States is also selling more weapons to Indonesia.

Singapore, however, has been more forthcoming in its support to the United States. Speaking in April 2012, the Singapore defence minister welcomed the United States' continuing commitment to the region, arguing that he thought this would continue despite US budget problems. He went on to say that Singapore has given the US Air Force and Navy access to all facilities since 1990, including Paya Lebar Air Base and Changi Naval Base, and that this will continue into the future. Most significantly, he noted that despite the growing Chinese military might, Singapore would not replace the United States as its closest security partner.[27]

Neutral States

The third group of countries maintains a neutral stance toward the US role in Asia, which includes large powers such as India and some of the smaller countries in Southeast Asia such as Vietnam, Laos, and Cambodia. Vietnam of late has become much more open to the United States, whereas India continues to be the odd man out. Several reasons underlie India's ambiguities in this regard.

While India has been supportive of the US pivot in Asia, it is still presented with a complex game of managing multiple major power relations. On the one hand, India wants to partner with the United States, but on the other, it is worried as to how other countries in the immediate and extended neighbourhood would react. However, in the process of India keeping its feet in multiple camps, New Delhi appears to have every major country that matters annoyed with India's ambiguous policy approaches in recent years.

The Indian media may tell a completely different story. For instance, a *Times of India* editorial notes how Indian and American interests converge on this new vision for an inclusive Asia-Pacific framework:

> If East Asia is where the action is, then Indian diplomacy needs to focus here and make New Delhi a significant player in the region. India shares centuries-old cultural and civilisational links with East Asia which deserve to be leveraged. . . . While the Himalayas have limited (and blinkered) New Delhi's geopolitical vision, it now needs to see itself as part of a larger entity comprising not just South but East Asia as well. It must be more confident in pursuing its national interest through economic and security linkages in the region, refusing to be browbeaten by anybody else.[28]

Similarly, the centrist *Indian Express* editorialized that "Delhi ought to wake up to this new world order and utilise the opportunities thrown up to dynamically involve itself in shaping the new Asian security order."[29]

But another centrist paper, the *Hindustan Times*, states that the "idea of 'containing' a country like China never arises. The game is about trying to preserve sufficient autonomy of action for other Asian countries that they can resist when Beijing lapses into aggressive or bullying behaviour—of which there have been many recent examples. The South China Sea dispute is exactly this sort of an issue. India's role in this is minor—this is an arena at the fringes of Indian power."[30]

While the Manmohan Singh government had welcomed the United States' Asia pivot, its position in reality appears to be that it does not want to get in the middle of a US-China clash. New Delhi does not want to see the United States and China become hostile to each other and get into conflict situations where India will be forced to take sides. That could prove dangerous for India, being a neighbour. However, India does not want to see very close relations between the two countries as during the Clinton administration, where the United States and China try to jointly manage South Asia just as they did after the 1998 Indian and Pakistani nuclear tests. Neither is the November 2009 US-China Joint Statement, which created major uproar in India, forgotten by New Delhi. It can be concluded that China puts India in a fix—much as it does many other Asian countries—by restricting its options, given that it is the immediate neighbour.

Meanwhile, explaining some of the ambiguities in the Indian approach is not difficult. US policies toward China during the first year of the Obama administration were neither comforting nor reassuring to India. In fact, these policies have also contributed to the rising confidence levels in Beijing to take on its neighbours, or even the United States. The number of naval incidents involving Chinese with Japanese and American vessels in the last few years is a reflection of the new, confident China.

Meanwhile, smaller states such as Vietnam have become much more open to the idea of finding common platforms with the United States in recent years. From being once a foe, the United States has become a friend and partner across trade and strategic issues for Vietnam. The bilateral trade agreement between the two and Vietnam's participation in the TPP negotiations are indicators of the changed nature of the relationship between Washington and Hanoi. Most critically, the two sides identify each other as important strategic partners to ensure strategic balance in the region.[31]

Other smaller countries, such as Cambodia and Laos, have significantly improved relations with the United States in the wake of the unfolding uncertainties in the region. Obama's visit to Cambodia (the first by any US president) in November 2012 for the ASEAN Summit was an opportunity to narrow down the perceptional differences between the two sides, although the visit per se did not do very much on that front.[32] However, Cambodia is still juggling between Washington and Beijing as China is heavily involved in economic and developmental projects, creating a sort of dependency difficult to brush aside quickly.

As China Rises, Will Its Neighbours Bandwagon or Balance?

While there were suspicions earlier that countries in the Asia-Pacific region might bandwagon with China, such fears have been put to rest. These initial misgivings were driven by two reasons. First, the United States appeared to have forgotten the Asia-Pacific, having been drawn into the Middle East and elsewhere. Second, meanwhile, China was playing an excellent diplomatic game with its neighbours, creating the impression of being a benign power. Both of these have now proven wrong; the United States is back in Asia as a "resident power," and China is proving to be a threat that needs to be worried about.

What can change these assumptions? They may change under two circumstances: China starts behaving better and becomes more accommodative toward its neighbours, or the United States adopts a more isolationist strategy.

It may be only partially correct to say that the United States' Asia pivot is driven by China alone. However, China has been a major trigger for the changes witnessed in Asia. While China has continued to claim that it is "rising peacefully," its actions on the ground have sent a different message, particularly to its neighbours. China's growing military capabilities, including A2AD strategies, have prompted other countries to look for counter-measures, affecting the security-insecurity dilemma in Asia. Today, countries in the region have come to the firm conclusion that they need to look at actions and not words.

Ambiguity and lack of transparency regarding China's objectives or its military modernization have only added to the complexities. China's decision-making process—with a greater role or even an independent role for the People's Liberation Army (PLA)—may also be of concern. In some key instances, the PLA appears to have been in complete control rather than the Foreign Ministry or the political leadership. These include the 2007 Chinese anti-satellite missile test as well as the 2001 spy plane incident where the Ministry of Foreign Affairs was kept out of the entire decision-making process. It appears that the PLA disproportionately influences decisions during crises and on important foreign and security issues. Lastly, China's aggressive behaviour toward its neighbours, particularly those with whom there are unresolved territorial problems, is worrying. All of these have contributed to building new partnerships and to certain new aligning of forces in Asia and beyond.

Having said that, some of the broader trends—including the changing nature of warfare, the growing insecurities two decades after the end of the Cold War, and the gradual decline of the United States (or at least the perception of it)—may have also contributed to the changing dynamics in the Asia-Pacific.

Conclusion

The US pivot to Asia has provided new choices and options for countries in the region. It may be years before this strategy fructifies into something concrete. Hedging was the preferred strategy in Asia since the end of the Cold War. This has been replaced by greater willingness among Asian countries to consider the open balancing of China.

Meanwhile, it will do good if the United States and Russia can shed their Cold War inhibitions, take advantage of their mutual wariness of China, and strengthen bilateral relations while shaping a new regional architecture with the United States, India, Russia, Japan, and Australia as the principal actors. US-Russia relations are critical in this regard. It is also possible that as the US pivot gains traction, new bilateral and multilateral partnerships will emerge in the region and beyond.

Notes

1. Department of Defense (DOD), *Sustaining U.S. Global Leadership: Priorities for 21st Century Defense* (Washington, DC: DOD, 2012).

2. The Council on Foreign and Defense Policy, State University, Higher School of Economics and RIO-Center, *The World around Russia: 2017—An Outlook for the Mid-term Future,* Moscow, 2007, http://www.globalaffairs.ru/docs/2017_eng_reader.pdf.

3. Russia has also managed to keep the Shanghai Cooperation Organisation as a politico-security group rather than bringing out its huge economic potential.

4. The Far East remains an area abundantly rich in resources of all kinds, including water, and the territory is predominantly unoccupied. The Chinese might be tempted to extend their hold all the way up to the Far East in gaining a firmer grip of the region.

5. For instance, the Chinese development of intermediate-range missiles has been a major area of concern. In the absence of long-range missiles that could reach US cities, it is quite clear that Russia and India remain China's potential targets. Alexander Hrmchin, head of the Analytical Division of the Institute for Political and Military Analyses, suggests an interesting arrangement among all the nations that possess intermediate-range missiles with a range of 500 to 5,000 km. As of now, the majority of these missiles are in China. Hrmchin suggests that India, China, Iran, and other West Asian countries join and form an agreement on such missiles, though the agreement should be comprehensive. He adds that if China, for instance, does not join such an arrangement (China is certainly not going to join), it would become very clear who China is targeting. Alexander Hrmchin, "Without Panic and Hysteria," *Nezavisamaya Gazeta* (Independent Newspaper), 30 March 2007. I thank Nandan Unnikrishnan for bringing this source to my attention.

6. Jayshree Bajoria, "The China-North Korea Relationship," Council on Foreign Relations, updated 7 October 2010, http://www.cfr.org/publication/11097/chinanorth _korea_relationship.html.

7. Wu Jiao, "China Welcomes US Role in Asia-Pacific Region," *China Daily*, 16 February 2012, http://www.chinadaily.com.cn/china/2012-02/16/content_14618271 .htm.

8. "China Warns US to be 'Careful' in Military Refocus on Asia," msnbc.com news services, 9 January 2012, http://www.msnbc.msn.com/id/45926054/ns/world _news-asia_pacific/t/china-warns-us-be-careful-military-refocus-asia.

9. Yu Zhixiao, "Commentary: Constructive U.S. Role in Asia-Pacific Welcome, but Not Warmongering," Op-Ed, Xinhua news agency, 6 January 2012, http://news.xinhua net.com/english/indepth/2012-01/06/c_131346348.htm.

10. Ibid.

11. Hannah Beech, "The U.S. Military Eyes the Asia-Pacific: China's Response? So Far, a Shrug," *Global Spin* (blog), *Time*, 9 January 2012, http://globalspin.blogs .time.com/2012/01/09/the-u-s-military-eyes-the-asia-pacific-chinas-response-so -far-a-shrug.

12. Corey Wallace, "Dispatch Japan: The US 'Pivot' towards East Asia," *Asia Security Watch*, New Pacific Institute, 20 February 2012, http://newpacificinstitute.org /asw/?p=10415.

13. "US Asia-Pacific Strategy Brings Steep Price," *Global Times*, 18 November 2011, http://www.globaltimes.cn/NEWS/tabid/99/ID/684596/US-Asia-Pacific-strategy -brings-steep-price.aspx.

14. Andrew Shearer and Toshi Yoshihara, "Pacific President Leaves a Mark Down Under," Point of View, *Asahi Shimbun*, 17 November 2011, http://ajw.asahi.com/article /views/opinion/AJ201111170098.

15. Ibid.

16. "Japan-U.S. Alliance Growing More Important to Stability," *Daily Yomiuri*, 19 November 2011, http://www.yomiuri.co.jp/dy/editorial/T111119003100.htm.

17. Australian Government, Department of Defence, *Defending Australia in the Asia Pacific Century: Force 2030*, Defence White Paper 2009 (Canberra: DOD, 2009), para. 6.27, http://www.defence.gov.au/whitepaper/docs/defence_white_paper_2009 .pdf.

18. Ibid., para. 4.26.

19. For details on China's military growth and potential intentions of that force in the future, see an excellent essay by John J. Mearsheimer, "The Gathering Storm: China's Challenge to US Power in Asia," *Chinese Journal of International Politics* 3, no. 4 (Winter 2010): 381–96.

20. James Grubel, "Australia Open to U.S. Spy Flights from Indian Ocean Island," Reuters, *News Daily*, 27 March 2012, http://www.reuters.com/article/2012/03/28/us -australia-usa-idUSBRE82R03120120328. Cocos is seen as a potential alternative to the Indian Ocean Diego Garcia, whose current lease runs out in 2016, and the future course of action remains unclear.

21. Ibid.

22. Ben Hancock, "What the 'Asia Pivot' Means for South Korea," *Peninsula* (blog), Korea Economic Institute, 22 March 2012, http://blog.keia.org/2012/03/what-the-asia -pivot-means-for-south-korea.

23. "Indonesia Warns of 'Distrust' over US Troop Deal," *Asia One News*, 17 November 2011, http://www.asiaone.com/News/Latest+News/Asia/Story/A1Story20111117 -311120.html.

24. Mustaqim Adamrah, "'Vicious Circle of Mistrust' on the Rise," *Jakarta Post*, 12 May 2011, http://www.thejakartapost.com/news/2011/12/05/vicious-circle-mistrust -rise.html.

25. Erwida Maulia, "Signs Point to Marty's Isolation in the Palace," *Jakarta Post*, 26 December 2011, http://www.thejakarta post.com/news/2011/12/26/signs-point -marty-s-isolation-palace.html.

26. Michael Richardson, "US Must Sell Trans-Pacific Deal to Asia," Viewpoints, *Straits Times*, 21 November 2011, http://web1.iseas.edu.sg/?p=6025.

27. Chua Chin Hon, "US Expected to Keep Up Asian Military Presence: Ng Eng Hen," *Straits Times*, 7 April 2012, http://www.straitstimes.com/BreakingNews/Singa pore/Story/STIStory_786204.html.

28. "Eastward Ho," editorial, *Times of India*, 18 November 2011, http://articles .timesofindia.indiatimes.com/2011-11-18/edit-page/30410656_1_east-asia-summit -asia-pacific-trans-pacific-partnership.

29. "Return to Oz," editorial, *Indian Express*, 18 November 2011, http://www .indianexpress.com/news/return-to-oz/877314/0.

30. "The Message from Bali," *Hindustan Times*, 20 November 2011, http://www .hindustantimes.com/StoryPage/Print/771807.aspx.

31. For more details, see Raymond Burghardt, "US, Vietnam Begin Tough Trade Talks," *Asia Sentinel*, 1 March 2012, http://www.asiasentinel.com/index.php?option =com_content&task=view&id=4282&Itemid=238.

32. Julie Pace, "Obama in Cambodia Makes History as First President to Visit Country," *Huffington Post*, 19 November 2012, http://www.huffingtonpost.com/2012 /11/19/obama-cambodia-first-president_n_2157956.html; and Peter Baker, "Obama, in Cambodia, Sidesteps Ghosts of American Wartime Past," *New York Times*, 20 No-vember 2012, http://www.nytimes.com/2012/11/21/world/asia/obama-in-cambodia -sidesteps-the-ghosts-of-history.html.

Chapter 9

The Security Environment in the Asia-Pacific

An Australian Viewpoint

Dr. Sanu Kainikara
Air Power Development Centre, Royal Australian Air Force

Introduction

The collapse of the Soviet Union, even though the rapidity of its decline was unanticipated, brought about a general belief that the world would thereafter move on to becoming a more benign and peaceful place in comparison to the competitive years of the Cold War. It was also anticipated that the hegemony of the United States would ensure that the world became and remained a unipolar entity. In an overarching manner, there has been no direct challenge to US primacy in terms of power-projection capabilities; thus, it could be said that the world has indeed moved on to a unipolar state. However, the reality in terms of the security environment that has emerged after two decades is somewhat different. The world is today a much more volatile place as compared to the Cold War era, with even minor nations asserting their will through both overt and covert use of force. Further, the activities of nonstate actors are not exactly a new phenomenon since from the turn of the century these groups have taken centre stage in influencing the security environment.

Besides the volatility of the international security scenario, the globalisation of economies and trade has brought about a change in the concept of national security. It is no longer possible for a nation to isolate itself from the events taking place across the world and yet hope to maintain a prosperous and self-sufficient economy. This leads to security imperatives which dictate that a nation must be prepared to defend its interests wherever they may be, as opposed to the traditional concept of security that mainly involved safeguarding the sanctity of the physical borders of the country. The outward-looking

The views expressed in this paper are those of the author and do not necessarily reflect the official policy or position of the Royal Australian Air Force, the Department of Defence, or the Australian Government.

perception of security is now accepted as a necessity by all nations, with ramifications for international relationships and global as well as regional stability.

As early as the 1980s, there was tangible proof that global trade patterns were shifting, with the transpacific trade initially equalling and by the late 1900s overtaking the transatlantic trade both in quantity and value. The importance of the Asia-Pacific region stems not only from this shift but also from the dependence of Asian economic powers—China, Japan, India, and South Korea—on maritime trade conducted through the Pacific and Indian Oceans for their continued growth. They rely, to different degrees, on the import of energy resources through the sea lines of communication for their continued economic stability. This reliance stretches their strategic economic interests far beyond their power-projection capabilities, making it a security vulnerability. All the major Asian economic powers lack the military ability to protect their global interests, although these nations have made visible moves to redress this anomaly. However, global power-projection capabilities are not easy to develop and require long gestation periods to come to fruition. Even then, these economic powers are becoming increasingly influential in the international forums and are gradually altering the global order. The strategic power manipulations and manoeuvres for global dominance in the twenty-first century will be played out in Asia.

The United States has been, and continues to be, the predominant power in the Asia-Pacific region and has long-standing alliances with the major trading nations—Japan, South Korea, and Australia—and is carefully improving its relationships with India and a number of Southeast Asian countries. Even though the United States seems to have overstretched both its military and economic power over the past decade in conducting two simultaneous campaigns in Afghanistan and Iraq, it will retain its global lead for the foreseeable future. Indeed, all mature global economies look towards the United States as the catalyst for economic recovery.

Australia is firmly committed to its alliance with the United States and since World War II has based its security on the veracity of this alliance. Within this envelope Australia is compelled to develop its security policies in the context of the broader environment of Asia and the Pacific because of its geographic location. While the landmass of Australia is only marginally smaller than the continental United States, it has a fairly small population that is going through a fundamental change in its demographic make-up because of changed immigration trends and an ageing population. Its population is concentrated in the eastern seaboard because a major portion of the island continent is arid or semi-arid, making it unsuitable for profitable agricultural activities. Further, Australia sits uncomfortably at the extremity of the Asia-Pacific region as a "Western" nation and is not automatically considered as an Asian entity. This complex mix of virtual and physical positioning complicates its security perceptions to a great extent.

Australia's Strategic Interests

All nations face threats to their security in a broad manner—almost on a continuous basis. However, because they cannot all be ameliorated, it is always necessary to carry out a risk assessment of each threat based on the consequences of not neutralising a particular one. This process will also have to be continuous and ongoing since predicting the geopolitical risk cycle is impossible. Security risk assessment will have to be primarily based on the nation's enduring strategic interests so that passing or temporary threats, which may have the capacity to complicate and confuse the broader and overarching security requirements, can be identified and dealt with accordingly. Further, it will also be necessary to monitor events within the nation's region of interest to recognise the ones that could shift the balance of power between competing nations. Identifying the nation's enduring strategic interests is vital for long-term security planning and should then form the basis for developing clear national security policies. Enduring strategic interests are ones that must be protected even if they warrant the use of force.

Australia has four primary strategic interests. While they can be prioritised, they are also interconnected. In a geographic sense, these interests can be viewed as concentric circles emanating from the epicentre of Australia. The enduring strategic interests are a (1) secure Australia, (2) secure immediate neighbourhood, (3) strategic stability in the Asia-Pacific region, and (4) stable, rules-based global security order.

A Secure Australia

The primary strategic interest is the defence of Australia from direct armed attacks. Direct attacks could be carried out either by other states—a highly unlikely scenario under the current security environment—or by nonstate entities, a much greater possibility. Irrespective of their source, protecting the nation from such attacks is the first priority. In turn, this means that Australia must be able to control air and sea approaches, especially to the north from where the most likely threat would originate. This control could also involve neutralising hostile forces at their bases before they can be brought to bear directly on the nation or attacking them during transit. While this is comparatively easily achieved if the nation possesses adequate military capability, defeating nonstate entities could prove to be more difficult. Nonstate entities are best contained by a combination of military and civilian actions undertaken in a whole-of-government process. Australia has to be cognisant that it does not have the capability to negate the activities of a great power if one decides to operate consistently within its air and sea approaches. Therefore, Australia relies on strategic alliance with a global power—in this instance the United States—to ensure the protection of its air and sea approaches and to diminish the probability of another power with inimical interests dominating this vital area.

A Secure Immediate Neighbourhood

In order of priority, the next strategic interest for Australia is to have a secure and stable neighbourhood—Indonesia, East Timor, Papua New Guinea, and the South Pacific island nations. The primary goal is to ensure that they do not become a threat to Australia directly or indirectly. Even though the likelihood of any of these nations attacking Australia is remote, their development of military capabilities to influence activities of its air and sea approaches can also be counted as a direct threat. Australia, therefore, promotes diplomatic, economic, and cultural ties with its immediate neighbours while astutely maintaining a clear military superiority, making it difficult for these nations to challenge its primacy. More vital than ensuring such primacy is ensuring the stability of these nations, especially the smaller island nations. Instability can lead to these small nations becoming fragile and failing states, thereby threatening Australia's interests. Australia supports internal stability and good governance of these nations to avoid their becoming security risks. Within the neighbourhood, Indonesia is of particular importance. A fragmented and unstable Indonesia will have disastrous consequences for Australia's security because almost all threats to the nation's well-being will have to transit through the Indonesian archipelago. Furthermore, history demonstrates that any collapse of a regional nation, economically or in terms of law and order, results in an influx of refugees to Australia—bringing with them enormous security challenges.

Strategic Stability in the Asia-Pacific Region

The stability of the broader Asia-Pacific region—from North Asia to the Indian Ocean—is of enduring strategic interest to Australia. The nations of Southeast Asia are particularly important since any sustained projection of force against Australia would have to come through this area. Even if direct force is not applied, these nations could be used as bases to threaten trade and the supply of resources critical for Australia's economic well-being and development. It is felt that the rise of a regional power—which could use the threat of force to coerce smaller states—may be a destabilising force for the region. Therefore, Australia works to strengthen a regional security architecture that supports peaceful resolution of issues rather than resorting to bellicose use of force or coercion. From an Australian perspective, this regional architecture will have to include the United States, Japan, India, China, and Indonesia, as well as the smaller nations, in a cooperative manner. It also acknowledges that continued US engagement underpins the success of such endeavours.

A Stable, Rules-Based Global Security Order

There is firm belief within the nation that Australia can only be secure in a world that itself is relatively secure. Proponents of this view advocate a leading role for the United Nations (UN) as essential to ensuring that state-on-state aggression is avoided as well as in containing the inherent danger to global stability through acts of terrorism, civil war, state failure, and the security issues arising from climate change and competition for resources. Australia, as a responsible international citizen, assists the UN within its mandate to restore and maintain order when necessary and subscribes to the notion of "responsibility to protect." Towards this end, Australia contributes both economically and militarily to UN initiatives in different parts of the world, as far as possible and within its limited resources. Nuclear non-proliferation is another initiative that Australia supports in the international arena. In the broader global security environment, Australia believes that the United States is of primary importance in ensuring international stability and dealing with global security challenges.

The stated strategic interests recognise that Australia will have to be able to initiate and sustain decisive action in the defence of its sovereignty while being able to contribute effectively to maintaining both regional and global stability. However, Australia also recognises that its ability to influence events diminishes with distance from its shores, becoming perhaps only a token response to issues arising far away. Its security planning is therefore built on accepting that its capability to influence is limited and that such influence is highest closer to home.

Factors Affecting Australia's Strategic Outlook

National security planning must always take into consideration the global distribution of economic, political, and military power. Many nations around the world, even those without formal bilateral or multilateral alliances or agreements with the United States, base their security strategies on its strategic primacy. While this strategic primacy has not been effectively threatened, an increasing trend towards a multipolar world is noticeable in the changes visible in international strategic power realities. These evolvements are mainly driven by economic developments as well as by global demographic shifts and population movements, which in turn are driven by factors such as environmental changes, resource constraints, transnational crime, and fragile states that cannot provide effective governance to their population, resulting in civil wars and conflicts.

Developments in the Asia-Pacific region are critical to Australia's security. Most of the large economic powers—the United States, China, Japan, India, and Russia—have interests in this region that are likely to intersect and create tensions. The power equation can become volatile, with the chances of miscalculation increasing accordingly. Although the possibility of direct conflict between these nations is remote, indirect confrontation cannot be ruled out. This will increase uneasiness and create strategic instability, especially for the smaller nations of the region. Australia will not be immune to such changes and will have to carefully balance its diplomatic and economic initiatives with sufficient and effective power-projection capabilities.

Five fundamental factors directly affect Australia's strategic outlook. They are the (1) role of the United States in the Asia-Pacific region, (2) status of the South Pacific nations, (3) shift in global economic activity to the Asia-Pacific, (4) stability of Indonesia, and (5) strategic implications of the rise of China.

In addition, groups that perpetuate Islamic terrorism will be a destabilising factor and pose a direct threat to Australia and its interests. The activities of these nonstate entities will be concentrated in the Middle East and South Asia, especially in weak and fragile states. However, Australia plays a vital role in countering and diminishing this threat in the Southeast Asian region. While acts of terrorism create a high probability of threat to human lives and infrastructure, they do not as yet pose a long-standing strategic threat to the nation. Short-term effects, however, may result, and the nation relies on a constant vigil to neutralise the possibility of such attacks delivering more than a token threat.

The Role of the United States in the Asia-Pacific Region

The United States will remain the most powerful and influential nation in the global order for the foreseeable future and has recently shifted its security focus from Europe to the Asia-Pacific. This is so even while it is undergoing some of the worst financial crises that it has encountered in a long time. Australia believes that this strategic primacy will lead to a stable global strategic security environment, one that is conducive to economic growth and prosperity. However, it is also cognisant that emerging powers like China, India, Russia, and the European Union can exert global influence in varying degrees in a contextual manner. The United States has the ability to project power globally, although its capacity to position forces in a forward-deployed state has been diminished both through its long-drawn wars in Iraq and Afghanistan and the simultaneous financial crisis. However, forward-deployed forces are at times necessary to reassure partners and allies of its intent to influence a particular region.

This situation brings into focus the debate regarding the willingness and capacity of the United States to retain its strategic primacy in the Asia-Pacific region. From an Australian viewpoint, the willingness of the United States to stay engaged in the region is not in doubt, especially since the two nations have an enduring treaty alliance. However, the global distribution of power directly affects its ability to overcome any challenge to its primacy. The emergence of regional powers like China and India and the willingness of these nations to exercise their new-found power to further their interests could become a challenge to US activities in the Asia-Pacific region. In the past few years the US administration has clearly indicated its intention to remain fully engaged in the region, and Australia bases its security calculations on this being the case.

That the United States is somewhat stretched in its strategic capacity to enforce its will because of its preoccupation with Afghanistan and the "war on terror" is not lost on any nation or observer. This constrains the United States' ability to project power into any other region at will, making it dependent on its regional allies like Australia to maintain stability within their sphere of influence. Building regional security arrangements that can avoid the growth of one or multiple nations into regional hegemons therefore becomes a requirement. However, for the foreseeable future Australian security will be underpinned by the primacy of the United States in the Asia-Pacific region.

The Status of South Pacific Nations

Australia and the smaller nations of the South Pacific are indelibly connected through geography and a shared history. Ensuring the stability and prosperity of these nations is a strategic requirement since a vulnerable nation in its close neighbourhood automatically makes Australia also susceptible to the same threats. However, weak governance, corruption, crime, and social challenges create economic stagnation and political instability in many of the South Pacific nations. Unfortunately these same nations are also more prone to be at the mercy of frequent natural disasters. Their inability to deal effectively with natural as well as man-made calamities that become humanitarian crises tends to make these nations liable to become rapidly failing states with all the accompanying chaos. Australia will have to respond directly with appropriate humanitarian and security assistance to contain the spread of the destabilising influence to other nations.

Australia has to constantly build and sustain basic infrastructure, improve governance to a tolerable level, create law and order, and improve basic health and education standards to make certain that vulnerable nations do not deteriorate further from being fragile states to becoming failed states. It is in Australia's security interests to ensure that states with competing interests do not coerce weaker nations, either through economic inducements or the threat of force, into providing military basing facilities. Such a development is bound to constrain Australia's ability to operate freely in the region to pursue economic development. Therefore, Australia has a stake in encouraging that these nations continue to "look south" for stability and security rather than assume a posture of "looking north."

Irrespective of Australia's efforts, enduring cultural and political divisions in these states will break out into violence periodically and will have to be contained. Australia will need to monitor developments in these nations closely and be willing to intervene, unilaterally if required, to stabilise deteriorating situations. Such interventions will have to be a combination of military and civil agencies within a whole-of-government approach to national security. The difficulty in these actions is for the receiving nation to acquiesce to the intervention and for Australia to be seen as a helping hand rather than a regional hegemon or an occupying force. Maintaining this delicate balance in the prevailing international geopolitical environment will be a challenge.

The Shift in Global Economic Activity to the Asia-Pacific

The failure of the Soviet model made liberal market-based democracies that emerged after World War II the optimum model for governance and development of economies. An alternative model is unlikely to be realized anytime in the foreseeable future. Additionally, globalisation has fostered the interdependence of economies and linked states more closely to each other than ever before, creating a more interconnected and complex world. Globalisation has brought many benefits, but it has also increased the vulnerability—especially of smaller economies—to global shocks. The increased exposure of smaller economies to the vagaries of a global financial system makes them fragile and prone to becoming strategic security risks. Australia needs to closely monitor and carefully manage the numerous small and susceptible economies in its close proximity so that they remain viable.

A noticeable shift of economic weight and activity to the Asia-Pacific has occurred in the past decade, with the global financial engine gradually being established in the region. The current global economic crisis, affecting the Western economies more than the ones in Asia, is likely to accelerate this trend. Any change in economic power will have an almost immediate impact on strategic power and balance. Stability in these conditions can only occur with the major powers being ready and able to cooperate in a pragmatic manner. Competition for influence is unlikely to create a stable environment. Australia is fundamentally a trading nation and prone to be affected by the global economic volatility. In the contemporary geopolitical environment, the prosperity of a nation is equated to its stability and consequent economic vulnerability. Even slight changes in economic wellness can create threats to security far in excess of the actual volatility. This is an international situation. However, Australia—with its vulnerable neighbours—is more at risk than other nations. Added to this risk is that the larger economies of the region are becoming more assertive in their dealings with other nations.

Stability of Indonesia

In the past decade, Indonesia has managed a remarkable transition from autocracy to multiparty democracy. Far-reaching economic reforms have accompanied this evolution, creating a positive trend in the nation's development. Predictions are that Indonesia will continue to grow into a stable and strong nation with sufficient social cohesion to make it a prominent power in the region. The largest country in Southeast Asia, Indonesia is already an important and influential element in regional forums. It also harbours ambitions of playing a visible and constructive role in international affairs commensurate with its status as the world's largest Muslim majority democracy. The size of Indonesia's economy makes it critical to the success of any regional alliance mechanism that is developed and one of the foundations of regional security.

Stability of the Southeast Asian region is dependent on Indonesia continuing to pursue democratic reform and evolving into a mature democracy. If it lapses into authoritarian rule or becomes overly nationalistic in its approach to bilateral and multilateral relations, the region has an increased chance of being destabilised from a security and trade point of view. The shift in economic activity to the Asia-Pacific will bring with it a certain amount of great-power rivalry into the region. A cooperative relationship between Australia and Indonesia will be able to prevent such rivalries from becoming confrontational while continuing to improve the economic status of the smaller nations in the region. Security of the region hinges on the ability of Indonesia to develop positive relations with its neighbours through entrenched democracy that provides the foundation for the nation to move towards economic prosperity. A fragile Indonesia will be a destabilising influence across the region.

The Strategic Implications of the Rise of China

It is stating the obvious when predictions are made that—barring some unforeseen major setback—China will be a major driver of both the regional and global economy in about two decades. China is Australia's largest trading partner, and therefore Australia's own economic growth is intrinsically connected to China's growth. Setbacks in China's economy can have an immediate and palpable impact on Australia's economic well-being, creating a ripple effect on its stability and security.

Uninterrupted economic growth will automatically transform China into an ascendant strategic influence. In addition, China has clearly demonstrated an unambiguous ambition to become a global power. China's foreign policy is oriented towards achieving this goal and is heavily influenced by its peculiar sense of nationalism. China uses its nationalism as a tool both to control domestic challenges and to influence its relationships with other nations. Accordingly, its foreign policy spans the entire spectrum from benevolence to aggression in a contextual manner according to Chinese whims. The other side of the coin is the build-up of China's military capabilities to portray a credible power-projection capability. An arrogant foreign policy, backed by a well-developed and booming economy and growing military might, is an unsettling element in international relations. When this is accompanied by less-than-transparent developments in military capabilities and territorial disputes with almost all neighbours, other nations are bound to be concerned. This situation can rapidly deteriorate into confrontational politics that destabilise the region. At the moment, China is reluctant to incorporate sufficient confidence-building measures to dispel the concerns of its neighbours and demonstrate that its military build-up is essentially benign and in keeping with the status of a growing power.

By far the two most important factors in the strategic rise of China and its impact on the security environment are US-China and Indo-Chinese relations. Chinese initiatives to integrate Taiwan remain a pressure point in these relationships.

The China policy being pursued by successive US administrations has a fundamental contradiction—there is a policy of engagement for mutual benefit in economic dealings and one of engagement to ensure that China remains "responsible" and indirectly subordinate to the United States in terms of security issues and building regional stability. The first could easily shift the balance of economic power, and the second is an indication of how the United States views the rise of China: warily and with concern. The United States is also gradually realising that in its relationship with other Asian nations, common interest against a belligerent China does not always translate to firm alliances. This is evident in the United States developing bilateral relationships with Vietnam and Indonesia. The United States faces geographical, economic, and technological challenges from China, and the nations of the region are keenly observing how the global power deals with them. While the situation is not in any way as confrontational as the Cold War, an ever-present layer of tension underlies all US-China dealings. This climate is not conducive to stability in the Asia-Pacific.

From an Australian perspective, the best way forward would be if the US-China relationship can be progressed through accommodation rather than confrontation. This is not only economic pragmatism but also a basic requirement to continue the stable growth of the region. To achieve this, the United States will have to start building partnerships with the nations of the region rather than attempting to continue the earlier relationships that hinged on the regional states being subordinate to US hegemony. Again, this tactic is a logical way to approach the emerging situation wherein the influence of the United States—economic, military, and diplomatic—is seen to be waning in the Asia-Pacific and the ability of the United States to be the single stabilising force in the region is being actively debated. The region is monitoring and focusing on what the United States is not doing in the region—rather than what it is doing—whether due to its preoccupation with other areas or the financial crisis creating a lack of capacity to deliver on two disparate fronts. Australia has to do a delicate balancing act and exert its influence on both of these nations to try and maintain a status quo situation that does not deteriorate.

The relationship between India and China—at times confrontational and at times reconciliatory—is not only interesting to monitor but also of critical importance to the stability of the greater Asian continent. India is becoming more important economically and has increased its external engagement considerably in the past decade. It clearly seeks to continue its development and also covets recognition as a major power with global interests. India's primary focus is on the Indian Ocean and only peripherally on the Asia-Pacific region. However, it must be stated that when democracy in Fiji—supported by its majority Indian-origin population—failed, it was not unnoticed in India's strategic calculations. In this scenario, China's forays into the Indian Ocean, ongoing border disputes with India in the east, and occupation of territory in the north that India claims as its own have been treated with extreme scepticism in India. However, even under this extreme situation India does not consider the concept of "strategically containing" China as a viable option. The so-called quadrilateral alliance—the United States, Japan, Australia, and India—mooted a few years ago was considered only a basic security understanding rather than a mechanism to either monitor or contain China.

Indo-Chinese interaction will, of necessity, have to be bilateral. This is an imperative and not an option for both the nations. Third-country participation will only be an adjunct and is not a critical factor to be considered. The primary competition between the two nations will be for greater influence in the Indian Ocean, now one of the most important global sea routes carrying energy resources between the Middle East and Asia. Further, significant interstate conflicts ongoing on the periphery of the Indian Ocean could become potential flashpoints drawing external powers to the region. The Indian Ocean is gradually becoming host to great-power naval presence and the ensuing struggle for primacy between them. This crucial maritime region is likely to see increased militarisation by external powers competing for strategic influence, China amongst them. The Indian response to Chinese activities in the region could trigger confrontation that both nations do not want in the current environment. With a vested interest in the Indian Ocean remaining peaceful and stable, Australia will need to factor in its centrality to the nation's security calculus.

The Indo-Chinese relationship and diplomatic sparring is a classic case of economic realities overcoming even geopolitical concerns. It also shows that maturity in dealing with foreign affairs in a deliberate manner can and does tend to keep minor confrontations from becoming full-blown crises. However, the Indian Ocean will remain a contentious issue between India and China, adding to the tensions of the region as well as to speculations regarding China's intent in the region.

An Australian Perspective on Its Security

Australian security is built on an alliance-based strategy primarily due to its lack of demographic depth, technological base, and resource availability to implement a stand-alone policy on protecting its interests and defending its borders. Australia's strategic posture is defined through its alliances, bilateral and multilateral defence agreements and relationships, and membership in regional and global security forums. These networks reduce the potential for confrontation over contentious issues and provide the wherewithal for long-term security and stability. Building such relationships requires a dedicated investment of national resources and a long-term commitment, while nurturing them to function even under extreme pressure requires patience and skill. However, success in these endeavours will secure the nation better than having a potent but stand-alone security force.

Australia has a history of international engagement through contribution to the wars of its significant partner nation—Great Britain until the beginning of World War II and the United States thereafter. The rationale was that by combating instability and threats far away from Australia's shores, the security of the region and the nation could be ensured. While this concept has been interpreted in various ways, the primary premise remains true even today. This belief is further reinforced by Australia's ambition to be a responsible international citizen and by the peculiarity of its geographic situation—it does not share a geographic border with any other nation and is sufficiently remotely situated to avoid casual contact with belligerent forces. In effect, Australia has used the contribution of its military forces to distant wars as an insurance against a direct threat to its sovereignty, a repeated pattern since its participation in the Boer War.

Australia could face two primary types of challenges to its security—geopolitical and military technological. Geopolitical confrontations will threaten stability and security in the long term and must be carefully addressed. Although their impact may be felt only gradually, they have the potential to spiral out of control into greater confrontations with far greater detrimental consequences to the security environment. On the other hand, military technological challenges are potentially disruptive events with more immediate effects. Within Australia's area of interest, more regional militaries are building their capabilities through direct modernisation achieved through capital acquisitions and enhanced by the networking of their advances. The developments that will lead to these militaries becoming power-projection tools have the capacity to change the regional distribution of power. Further, the Australian Defence Force could become constrained in its ability to operate freely in certain areas if the alteration of the power equation is inimical to Australia's interests and could be the beginning of the emergence of a strategic risk. The global financial crisis could perhaps slow down this regional trend and stop it from becoming a full-fledged arms race with all the attendant issues that arise.

The fundamental policy that Australia follows is to avoid the use of force or even to threaten its use as far as possible. This is in keeping with its inherent belief that the use of force will bring about only temporary respite in a confrontation, and then only if one side emerges as a clear winner, and that the diffusion of a confrontation is best achieved through dialogue and accommodation. Towards this end Australia has always supported, to the extent that its limited resources permit, all UN initiatives aimed at peacekeeping and stabilisation of volatile regions. This effort is a major factor in Australia's security outlook and is expected to yield dividends towards securing the nation and its interests.

Developments in the Asia-Pacific region and in the broader Asian context will have a salutary impact on Australian security. However, even military build-up by regional nations will not pose an existential threat to Australia. This is the result of Australia's inherent stability, mature democratic process, and power-projection capabilities. Although the possibility of a military threat is extremely low, increased military activity in the region can gradually constrain or constrict Australia's freedom to operate in an unrestricted manner. This is in contrast to the assured freedom that continued US primacy in the region will provide. A challenge to US primacy will be particularly visible in the direct impact it will have on the ability of Australia to pursue its developmental and economic objectives.

Australia is essentially a Western democracy that is geographically situated in the Asia-Pacific. In the past four decades or so, it has made concerted attempts to become part of the Asian collective economic and security forums and has been marginally successful in getting accepted by the Asian nations on an equal footing. This could stem from the anti-colonial ethos of a majority of the nations that were erstwhile colonies of Western powers as well as the "White Australia" policy pursued by successive Australian governments till the 1960s. From a security perspective, this is a nebulous situation and needs careful handling. Australia has both initiated bilateral arrangements with its neighbours and proposed an Asia-Pacific multilateral forum to discuss collective security and resolve outstanding issues in an amicable manner. Since the Association of Southeast Asian Nations (ASEAN) exists as a long-standing entity, this initiative has not gained much traction amongst the Asia-Pacific nations. While animosity towards Australia has certainly diminished and it is looked upon as a benign and helpful nation, it still lacks open inclusivity within the region. Open acceptance as part of the region is still a far-away objective for Australia.

A major factor continuing to plague Australian security is its limited control over factors that affect its security and strategic outlook. This leads to a situation where, at times, Australia has been reactive to emerging security issues rather than being proactive on a long-term basis to mitigate challenges that can be predicted. Further, Australia is a middle power and does not have the abundance of power essential to enforce its security needs through the employment of its foreign policy, economic initiatives, or the actual application of force. This is an unenviable situation for any nation and could lead to difficult security challenges if not prudently alleviated at an early stage in their emergence.

Australia's security and regional stability depend on its ability to influence the major powers—the United States, China, India, Japan, and Russia—to share leverage within a collective leadership model that will provide an environment conducive to mutual development towards prosperity.

Conclusion

Nations have always faced threats to their security and have dealt with them in different ways according to their own definitions of national security and perceptions of the nation's requirements to prosper. This is a common thread across time and applicable to all nations. The changes that can be observed are brought about mainly through the evolving definition of security that now transcends the traditional concept of the protection of the physical entity of the state. In fact, definitions of security now encompass even non-quantifiable, vague, and ever-evolving concepts such as "respect" for universal, national, and human values.

Globalisation facilitates integration and interdependence among nations and has brought about unprecedented human development, as well as the spread of people, ideas, and education. It has immense potential for poverty alleviation and provides economic opportunities for individuals and nations as never before. However, globalisation has also contributed to increased inequality among, as well as within, nations and to greater vulnerability of nations to global shocks and crisis. In effect, the security and stability of nations have become even more fragile with new system risks brought about through the same interdependence that brings prosperity. Essentially, the security threat threshold is lower than even a decade ago.

Australia functions under a basic disadvantage of having to base its security on another nation's ability and willingness to retain its primacy in the Asia-Pacific. It does not have the power—economic or military—that would automatically translate to political and diplomatic influence to change the course of events or even to alter the status quo. The other factor is that there is bound to be a tug-of-war between the United States and China for supremacy in the Asia-Pacific, if one is not already under way. In these circumstances, Australia could assume the role of an honest broker to ensure that diplomatic or economic confrontations and competition do not evolve into all-consuming force-projection issues and military conflicts. This is the only way to ensure regional stability and thus strengthen its security. Regional security is an essential and critical contributory factor to achieve prosperity. It will not be amiss to state that over the past decade, Australia has established sufficient credentials with both the United States and China to achieve this status.

References

Australian Department of Defence. *Defending Australia in the Asia Pacific Century: Force 2030*. Defence White Paper 2009. Canberra: Commonwealth of Australia, 2009.

Australian Government. *Advancing the National Interest*. Australia's Foreign and Trade Policy White Paper. Canberra: Commonwealth of Australia, Department of Foreign Affairs and Trade, 2003.

Kainikara, Sanu. *Australian Security in the Asian Century*. Canberra: Air Power Development Centre, 2008.

Chapter 10

Conflict and Diplomacy in the South China Sea

Dr. Sheldon W. Simon
Professor, School for Political and Global Studies
Arizona State University

Abstract

Disputes over sovereignty and freedom of navigation in the South China Sea (SCS) involve not only the claimants (China, Taiwan, Malaysia, Philippines, Brunei, Vietnam) but also major maritime powers whose ships regularly move through these waters (the United States, Japan, India, Australia). Among the claimants, China is the most ambitious and ambiguous. The People's Republic of China (PRC) claims include all land features in the sea and arguably the entire SCS itself. Two starkly different approaches to the SCS conflict are discussed: (1) diplomacy among the claimants either bilaterally—advocated by China—or multilaterally endorsed by the Association of South East Asian Nations (ASEAN); or (2) in the event that diplomacy fails, a buildup by claimants of their naval and air capabilities—potentially to assert their rights through force. As the primary naval power in the region insuring freedom of navigation, the United States has an important stake in the peaceful resolution of the SCS disputes. Not only because of Washington's support of ASEAN multilateral diplomacy but also because of its security commitment to the Philippines (a claimant), the United States could become involved if the dispute becomes an armed conflict. As the United States shifts more military resources to the western Pacific, it is also ramping up its diplomatic support for the SCS littorals whose maritime policies are consonant with Washington's.

Introduction

The general consensus for some time has been that only two confrontations in eastern Asia could lead to conventional war: a blowup

---

The author wishes to thank his graduate assistant, Jacqueline Schneider, for research support.

on the Korean peninsula and/or war between China and Taiwan across the Taiwan Strait. While the probability of either contingency thankfully is low—at least in the short term to midterm—should either occur, it is highly probable that the great powers would be involved, specifically the United States and Japan. These potential hot spots are in Northeast Asia. However, another East Asian conflict venue looms on the horizon—this time in Southeast Asia (SEA). Over the past two decades, the SCS has been the source of politico-economic-military disputes among several of the region's littoral states (Malaysia, Vietnam, the Philippines, Brunei) as well as China and Taiwan, with the United States, Japan, Australia, and India as maritime powers professing a vested interest in freedom of navigation and potential exploration and exploitation of the seabed's petroleum and natural gas.

The SCS is semienclosed and bounded by China on the north, the Philippines in the east, Vietnam in the west, East Malaysia and Brunei in the southeast, and Indonesia and Malaysia in the southwest. One-third of world trade and half of its oil and gas pass through these waters—therefore, freedom of navigation is essential. The SCS is also rich in marine life, a staple for Asian diets and a major source of employment for millions of inhabitants in coastal communities. The SCS is ostensibly governed by international law, particularly the 1982 United Nations Convention on the Law of the Sea (UNCLOS) to which China, Japan, South Korea, and all 10 ASEAN countries have adhered. Geographic features within the SCS are subject to competing claims of sovereignty, the most contentious being the SCS's central Spratly Islands. All claimants occupy some of the features of the Spratlys. Vietnam claims sovereignty over all the Spratly Islands, while China claims sovereignty over all the territorial features in the SCS. There has been no judicial test of these claims, meaning that they are yet to be resolved through negotiation, arbitration, adjudication, or the use of force.

China's claim is the most extensive and the most ambiguous. Where other claimants base their descriptions on specific geographical features and their adjacent waters, Beijing insists on ownership of the entire SCS. In an official submission to the UN in May 2009 on the outer limits of its continental shelf, China attached a map with nine dashed lines forming a "U" that enclosed most of the waters of the SCS. If China is claiming the totality of the SCS based upon historical discovery and use, the claim is not consistent with the 1982

Law of the Sea Convention. Further complicating this situation are the characteristics of the features in the SCS. They encompass small islands, rocks, low-tide elevations, and artificial islands. Of these, only islands and rocks are entitled to 12-nautical-mile (nm) territorial seas. In addition, only islands are entitled to 200 nm exclusive economic zones (EEZ) and a continental shelf. The UNCLOS treaty states that the difference between a rock and an island is that the latter is capable of sustaining human habitation or economic activity. In its 2009 submission to the UN, Indonesia contends that all the features in the SCS are rocks, not islands, and therefore may not be the basis for 200 nm territorial sea claims.[1] Although not a Spratly claimant, Indonesia's submission is designed to foreclose any Chinese argument that their territorial waters include the rich fishery and seabed petroleum area north of Indonesia's Natuna Islands.

Although the issue of sovereignty in the SCS is fundamentally bilateral among state contenders, ASEAN—a multilateral organization—has become involved, primarily through its efforts to promote the peaceful development of SCS resources while sovereignty claims are sidelined. Within ASEAN, the features claimed by Malaysia, the Philippines, and Brunei are also claimed by Vietnam. So these claimants are arrayed not only against China but also against each other. Moreover, ASEAN states take varying positions on the SCS dispute: Laos, Cambodia, and Burma lean toward China; Malaysia and Indonesia are cautious about US involvement; Thailand and Singapore are neutral; while both Vietnam and the Philippines welcome an American role.[2] ASEAN has played a diplomatic role in efforts to resolve the standoff. The association was instrumental in negotiating the 1992 Declaration on the Conduct of Parties in the South China Sea (DOC) among the claimants and subsequently backed the creation of a China-Philippines-Vietnam Joint Marine Seismic Undertaking (JMSU). The JMSU was an agreement among the three to explore seabed resource potential in some of the overlapping areas they claimed. It lapsed in 2008, and no results have been made public. As for the DOC on how claimants could develop the features they occupied so that conflict among them would be minimized, no meaningful implementation was ever reached.

Conflict and Diplomacy:
Alternative Approaches to the South China Sea

Sam Bateman, an eminent Australian naval strategist, has labeled the South China Sea a "wicked problem" for maritime security. By that he meant that many states were involved and that they hold different interpretations of the Law of the Sea, have conflicting sovereignty claims, and have been engaged in managing the risks of greater naval activity in the region.[3] Essentially, states with SCS claims can manage these risks in two ways: building their own naval and air capacities to enforce their interests and/or negotiating with their rivals either bilaterally or through regional arrangements. First, we examine hard power capabilities among the SCS Southeast Asian claimants and then the diplomatic venues available to them before turning to China's position in the dispute and finally to the actions of external stakeholders—the United States, Japan, and India.

Southeast Asian armed forces over the past decade have acquired "fourth generation" fighter aircraft, submarines, air-to-air and air-to-ground weapons, frigates, amphibious assault ships, antiship cruise missiles, and new command, control, communications, computer, intelligence, surveillance, and reconnaissance (C4ISR) systems.[4] Arms imports to Indonesia and Malaysia have gone up 84 and 722 percent, respectively, between 2000 and 2010. Vietnam has spent $2 billion on six state-of-the-art *Kilo*-class Russian submarines and $1 billion on Russian jet fighters. Malaysia just opened a submarine base in Borneo. The Philippines committed $118 million in 2011 to purchase a naval patrol vessel and six helicopters to provide a security perimeter for a joint natural gas venture with Shell Philippines.[5] Though primarily a land power, Thailand has considerable maritime interests, including the protection of offshore oil and gas resources. Bangkok has not only acquired frigates from the United States and Britain and offshore patrol vessels from China but is also negotiating with Germany for the purchase of refurbished submarines.[6] Thailand participates in the Malaysia-Indonesia-Singapore "Eyes in the Sky" component of the antipiracy Malacca Strait Patrols. Additionally in September 2011, Indonesia and Vietnam agreed to establish joint patrols on their maritime borders to improve their SCS monitoring capabilities. Indonesia's EEZ overlaps China's claim within the nine-dash line.

The larger questions are whether the Southeast Asian acquisitions are sufficient to balance China's growing naval presence in the region and whether they can be interpreted as an arms race. In fact, the new ships and aircraft acquired by Southeast Asian armed forces are relatively few in number and hardly a match for the growing air and naval assets of the People's Liberation Army. Moreover, elements of an arms race seem to be absent. An arms race requires mutually acknowledged public hostility among the actors, leading to the acquisition of weapons based on anticipated military operations against one another. The purchases are made on an escalating tit-for-tat basis designed to neutralize any temporary advantage the adversary possesses. Although Southeast Asian arms buildups may in part be a function of China's behavior, a more plausible explanation is found in the modernization of obsolete systems and greater attention to maritime interests in light of the EEZs within the UN Law of the Sea. Nevertheless, these states are acquiring standoff precision strike, airborne, and undersea attack capabilities, as well as some expeditionary amphibious warfare, and improved C4ISR networks. None of these, however, is designed to achieve superiority but rather to maintain the status quo. There is, therefore, an arms dynamic but not an arms race.[7]

Southeast Asian Spratly claimants have also confronted each other: Malaysian air force fighters drove off Filipino military aircraft near Investigator Shoal in 1999; Malaysian and Indonesian ships clashed over the Sipadan and Ligatan Islands in the Celebes Sea in the 1990s and more recently over the Ambalat Islands in 2008–9. Both countries have increased their deployments in these waters off Sabah.[8]

Multilateral Diplomacy

With so many overlapping maritime zones, unsurprisingly several Southeast Asian regional forums have addressed these issues, including ASEAN itself as well as the ASEAN Regional Forum (ARF), the ASEAN Defense Ministers Meeting Plus (ADMM+), and the East Asia Summit (EAS). Discussions within these groups have revealed a lack of agreement on key Law of the Sea issues, including innocent passage based on EEZ rights and obligations.[9] The PRC views its EEZ as an extension of its national waters, meaning that no country's naval ships have the right to move through these waters without China's permission, nor may they engage in military surveillance. Beijing's idiosyncratic interpretation of the EEZ provision does not conform to the vast majority of UNCLOS signatories who agree that the 200 nm zone stretching from a country's baseline can be regulated by its littoral state only with respect to economic activity, not military movement or surveillance.

The Philippines, Vietnam, and Indonesia have been particularly keen to use ASEAN-derived regional diplomacy to embed China in a regional maritime consensus. While cooperation has increased on nontraditional security concerns such as humanitarian assistance, disaster relief, and counterpiracy, consensus on the SCS has been elusive.[10] In 2010 China became more assertive in its SCS sovereignty claims, clashing with both Philippine and Vietnamese fishing boats and an oil exploration vessel. Philippine president Benigno Aquino responded diplomatically, filing letters with the UN delineating Philippine sovereignty claims and, in June, launching a new initiative calling for the SCS to become a zone of peace, freedom, friendship, and cooperation where disputes could be cooperatively addressed. The Philippine president also pledged in July to bring its SCS dispute before the UN International Tribunal on the Law of the Sea. Vietnam joined the Philippine UN submission.[11] Hanoi and Manila also joined hands to call for a meeting of ASEAN maritime law experts in Manila, where, in September 2011, they agreed that UNCLOS should be the basis for resolving territorial disputes. The Philippine plan centers on marking out disputed areas of the SCS where claimants could agree on joint development while setting sovereignty claims aside. Areas not in dispute would be the exclusive preserve of the country owning them. Manila specifically cites the Reed Bank, where it has granted oil and gas exploration permits. Reed Bank is within the 200 nm EEZ of the Philippines. The ASEAN experts presented their report at the November 2011 Bali East Asian Summit. In an attempt to preempt expected PRC opposition, Philippine foreign secretary Esteban Conejos stated that the proposal is designed to separate sovereignty claims from exploration opportunities.[12]

The ASEAN states agree that the crux of the SCS dispute centers on China's nine-dash line claim, officially sent to the UN in 2009. Writing to UN secretary general Ban Ki-moon in April 2010, Beijing asserted that China was "fully entitled" to a territorial sea extending 22 kilometers from the baselines of the Spratly Islands and an EEZ out to 370 kilometers from these baselines as well as a continental shelf extending possibly further. These claims would give China extensive national security rights and control over natural resources throughout the SCS. In making these demands, Beijing invoked not only the 1982 UNCLOS but also two of its own laws: the 1992 Law on the Territorial Sea and Contiguous Zone and the 1998 Law on the Exclusive Economic Zone and Continental Shelf. Moreover, when Beijing ratified UNCLOS in 1996, its reservations rendered that ratification largely meaningless because, as one of the disclaimers stated, China reaffirmed "sovereignty over all archipelagos and islands" listed in its 1992 law. These assertions about the Paracel and Spratly Islands as well as other SCS features would mean that little of the South China Sea would remain outside some form of Chinese jurisdiction. PRC policy abjures any negotiation on sovereignty and confines its diplomacy to the joint development of SCS resources with the understanding that these arrangements would be temporary because China retains sovereignty.[13]

The PRC has pressured international oil companies as early as 2006 not to sign exploration contracts with Vietnam. These companies included Chevron, ExxonMobil, ConocoPhillips, Japan's Idemitsu, British Petroleum, and Malaysia's PETRONAS. All were told that such contracts would violate China's sovereignty. Only ExxonMobil decided to stay on. Chevron noted that in abandoning its Vietnam exploration plans, it obtained a large natural gas concession agreement from China in Sichuan Province—considered by Chevron to be a significant opening into China for the US oil company.[14]

The United States, the Code of Conduct, and South China Sea Diplomacy

Diplomacy in SCS disputes has dominated US actions in SEA over the past two years.[15] Beginning with the ARF meeting in July 2010, the Obama administration decided to play a major role in promoting resolution of the Spratly Islands imbroglio while laying down a marker that SCS stability for maritime commerce constituted a significant US interest. ASEAN's first-ever declaration on the SCS was issued long ago in 1992. Ten years passed before ASEAN and China agreed in 2002 on a DOC, a set of principles that was supposed to stabilize the status quo, though it was nonbinding and lacked any enforcement mechanism. ASEAN's 2011 leader, Indonesian president Bambang Yudhoyono, stated at the association's 44th Ministerial

Meeting in July 2011 that the ARF should "finalize the long overdue guidelines because we need to get moving to the next phase, which is identifying elements of the Code of Conduct."[16]

The United States backed ASEAN initiatives with respect to the Code of Conduct when at the July 2010 ARF, US secretary of state Hillary Clinton said, "The United States, like every other nation, has a national interest in freedom of navigation, open access to Asia's maritime commons, and respect for international law in the South China Sea. We share these interests not only with ASEAN members and ASEAN Regional Forum participants but with other maritime nations and the broader international community."[17] In effect, Clinton articulated what she believed was the consensus among most of the world's maritime powers. She also proposed that ASEAN serve as a multilateral venue for SCS negotiations—a prospect supported by the four ASEAN claimants (Malaysia, Philippines, Vietnam, and Brunei) but vigorously opposed by China.

The Obama administration has emphasized the importance of Asian politico-security organizations led by ASEAN, the ARF, the EAS, and the ADMM+. US secretaries of state and defense have attended the ministerial meetings, and the president attended the EAS in November 2011. Washington sees ASEAN as an institution essentially supportive of international law, the peaceful settlement of disputes, and implicitly the territorial status quo under which maritime commerce and resource exploitation can be peacefully conducted. While the United States insists that it does not take sides on territorial disputes and has no stake in them, it also holds that the disputes must be reconciled according to customary international law, meaning the 1982 UNCLOS under which there are rules for fixing maritime boundaries via EEZs. Application of these principles would invalidate China's claims to most of the South China Sea in favor of the littoral states.

Despite current US economic problems and the prospect of a significant decline in its defense budget over the next decade, military officials insist that Washington will maintain a "continuous presence" in Asia and will sustain its exercises with and assistance to ASEAN states' defense forces, according to US Pacific Command (USPACOM) commander Adm Robert Willard as reported in the 18 July 2011 issue of *Defense News*. The Obama administration's relatively relaxed "steady-as-she-goes" assessment of SCS tension probably reflects its belief that SEA is a pro-United States region and that American reassurance depends on Washington upgrading its diplomatic activity alongside an already robust security presence. Increasingly, PACOM features its unparalleled humanitarian relief capabilities as a form of military diplomacy. More generally, the Defense Department is also assisting ASEAN states in developing coastal monitoring and patrol capabilities. If one adds capacity building to internationalizing the SCS disputes, these constitute an easy and low-cost way for the United States to inject itself into Southeast Asian regional politics.

US diplomacy designed to implement the foregoing Southeast Asian strategy was displayed at the ASEAN Summit in May, the Shangri-La Dialogue in June, and the ARF in July 2011. The US ambassador to the Philippines, Harry Thomas, endorsed the SCS statement issued at the ASEAN Summit in May, which averred that ASEAN consultations are perfectly appropriate before any meeting with China on territorial disputes and that "all claimants should sit down at the negotiating table."[18] In effect this was a confirmation of an independent ASEAN role in the SCS negotiations separate from the bilateral negotiations with each claimant preferred by China. The ASEAN approach was also endorsed by the secretary of defense, Robert Gates, at the Shangri-La Dialogue on 4 June 2011. Subsequently, in late June, US assistant secretary of state Kurt Campbell at the inaugural United States–China Asia-Pacific Consultations in Hawaii repeated American support for "strengthening the role of regional institutions on the challenges facing the region."[19]

Although the July ARF meeting in Bali did not see a replay of the previous year's China–United States acrimony over an ASEAN role in resolving the South China Sea disputes, Secretary Clinton reiterated the need for ASEAN participation as well as a US "strategic stake in how issues there are managed."[20] When China and the 10 ASEAN members announced an agreement at the forum on a set of guidelines to advance the 2002 Declaration of Conduct of Parties in the South China Sea, Assistant Secretary Campbell called them "an important first step . . . [but] clearly it's just that: a first step."[21] The guidelines cover the easiest issues for cooperation: maritime environment, infectious diseases such as severe acute respiratory syndrome (SARS), transnational crime, and navigation safety—collectively known as nontraditional security. They fail to address the most critical issues—energy exploration and military tensions.

In the aftermath of the guidelines agreement, Secretary Clinton called on SCS rivals to back their claims with legal evidence—a challenge to China's declaration of sovereignty over vast stretches of the South China Sea. More specifically, she urged that they "clarify their claims . . . in terms consistent with customary international law . . . derived solely from legitimate claims to land features."[22] As stated above, this means that the claims should be delineated according to the 1982 UNCLOS by which EEZs could be extended only 200 nm from the land borders of littoral countries. (Ironically, Washington itself has not yet ratified the UNCLOS, though US authorities have stated that they will abide by its provisions.) Secretary Clinton went on to praise Indonesia's leadership role in ASEAN, looking forward to its help in settling the conflicts.

In fact, the guidelines do not create a proper code of conduct for navies or air forces involved in the SCS disputes. There are no provisions for how contending ships or aircraft should behave toward one another; nor are communications channels established in the event of such contact. In the past year, the United States has engaged in joint naval and air exercises with all the Southeast Asian claimants—Vietnam, Malaysia, the Philippines, and Brunei. Some of these exercises include protocols for appropriate military relationships.

Washington's emphasis on multilateral diplomacy for the SCS underlines the point that ASEAN as a whole as well as other states has significant interests in the region that go beyond the territorial disputes between the five states and China. Secretary Clinton has established the United States as a de facto party in the facilitation of a peaceful settlement. After all, Washington has a security treaty with one of the claimants, the Philippines, which could potentially draw the United States into the conflict. Hence, it is understandable that the United States prefers a negotiated future that takes into account the interests of maritime trading states, China, and the ASEAN countries. These concerns will continue to dominate Washington's Southeast Asian diplomatic agenda as well as ASEAN's politico-security relationships with both China and the United States.

The United States and the Philippines:
A Special South China Sea Relationship

Of the four ASEAN states with claims to some of the SCS islets, the Philippines has the weakest enforcement capability.[23] Its armed forces are underfunded, ill equipped, and, with the exception of its special forces, poorly trained. The air force flies virtually no combat aircraft worth that designation, and the navy's ships are Vietnam War vintage and barely seaworthy. While the current Aquino government and its predecessor devised plans to modernize the armed forces, emphasizing the navy and air force, so far little has changed. Manila's alternative is to strengthen defense ties with the United States, encourage Washington to reiterate its commitment to freedom of the seas, support former secretary Clinton's call for a multilateral negotiated settlement to the disputed maritime claims, and insist that the United States honor its mutual security treaty with the Philippines.

Washington has assisted the Philippines in establishing the Coast Watch South program, helping fund 17 coastal watch stations in southern Philippine waters. The United States is also discussing the construction of an additional 30 coastal watch stations to prevent smuggling, drug trafficking, and terrorist movements between Mindanao and Borneo. The US Coast Guard has refurbished a 40-year-old *Hamilton*-class cutter for the Philippines. It is the biggest ship ever acquired by the Philippine navy and is deployed off Palawan near the Spratly Islands. Additional retired *Hamilton*-class ships could also be sold to the Philippines.

In early June 2011, the Philippine Embassy in Washington announced that it was shopping for excess US defense equipment under the Foreign Military Sales program. Amb. Jose Cuisa Jr. asked his country's Department of National Defense and Armed Forces to provide him with a wish list of military equipment needed to shore up the country's defenses. In late June, Philippine foreign secretary Albert Del Rosario, speaking at the Center for Strategic and International Studies (CSIS) in Washington, tabled a new approach to acquiring US military items by leasing rather than buying them. At a subsequent joint news conference, Secretary Clinton stated that the United States is "determined and committed to supporting the defense of the Philippines" and is working with that nation "to determine what are the additional assets that the Philippines needs and how we can best provide those."[24] Philippine president Benigno Aquino III has allocated $254 million to upgrade the navy, and the visiting foreign secretary noted that "an operational lease [of] fairly new equipment" would permit his country to stretch the purchasing power of that sum. (However, the United States has not leased military equipment to other countries since the end of World War II.) Manila's wish list includes frigates, modern combat aircraft, and two submarines. While the United States regularly provides military assistance to the Philippines, local critics complain that the equipment is frequently "thirdhand" after being extensively used in Thailand and South Korea. Washington has also agreed to boost Philippine intelligence capabilities in the SCS by sharing US intelligence.

In addition to acquiring more military hardware to defend its SCS claims, Manila is also seeking an unequivocal US commitment to defend the Philippines in the event of a military confrontation with China. Philippine legislators and media commentators emphasize that US statements about Washington's obligations under the 1951 Mutual Defense Treaty between the Philippines and the United States are ambiguous. Manila's argument is based on a letter exchanged between foreign affairs secretaries Cyrus Vance and Carlos Romulo in 1979, in which the Philippines claims that an armed attack on Philippine forces anywhere in the Pacific, including the SCS, will trigger a US response. The American commitment, according to this interpretation, is not confined to the Philippine metropolitan territory. In recent months, the US position on the question of its obligation seems to stop short of an automatic involvement with US forces. In late May 2011, Ambassador Thomas stated on board the visiting US aircraft carrier USS *Carl Vinson* that "we are dedicated to being your partner whenever you are in harm's way." Nevertheless, on 12 June, embassy spokesperson Rebecca Thompson responded to a Malacanang statement that the United States would honor the Mutual Defense Treaty if Manila's spat with China escalated to war by saying that "the US does not take sides in regional territorial disputes."[25] After Philippine media pushback that Washington was reneging on its commitment, Thompson attempted to smooth the troubled diplomatic waters by saying, "When I said, 'The U.S. does not take sides in regional territorial disputes,' I was talking about the current dispute over boundaries—an issue separate from what the U.S. would do in the hypothetical event of conflict."[26] President Aquino put a positive spin on the discussion by claiming, "Perhaps the presence of our treaty partner, which is the United States of America, ensures that all of us will have freedom of navigation (and) will conform to international law."[27]

Washington's interpretation of the scope of the Mutual Defense Treaty seems to be that the Spratlys are located in a part of the Pacific Ocean. Therefore, Manila could invoke the treaty if its forces were attacked in the area it claims. This would lead each signatory to consult and determine what action, if any, it might take. The implication is not that the United States would be required to use force. Rather, because the United States is a treaty partner with the Philippines, China cannot assert that events in the SCS, including the contested islands, are not any of Washington's business.

Other Significant External Actors: Japan and India

For Japan, the East Asian seas serve two strategic goals: by monitoring its sea and air spaces, Japan engages in burden sharing with the United States and reinforces the American commitment to Japan's own security. By extending antipiracy assistance to SEA, Tokyo protects its own sea-lanes and demonstrates that it is also a regional security partner to other littoral states. Since 2000 Tokyo has concluded antipiracy training agreements with several Southeast Asian states. The Japan coast guard holds training exercises annually with Southeast Asian counterparts as well as with India. In the past few years, Tokyo has provided grants to Indonesia, the Philippines, and Malaysia to enhance maritime security.[28]

Japan has also established "strategic partnerships" with India and Australia which include cooperation in disaster relief operations and an acquisition and cross-servicing agreement with Canberra. Possessing two helicopter carriers, Japan could play a significant role in containing China's expanding submarine capabilities. And Tokyo's plans for a new fifth-generation F-X fighter are also designed to prevent China from gaining air superiority in Japan's vicinity.[29]

In September 2011, Japanese and Philippine officials discussed the creation of a "permanent working group" to coordinate their policies pertaining to Asian maritime disputes. Undoubtedly, Manila has the SCS claims in mind. A Philippine spokesman said, "Just like the U.S., Japan is also a stakeholder in the quest for peace and stability in the (South China Sea). So this is a matter of common interest to the two countries."[30] In a Tokyo meeting with ASEAN defense officials at the end of September 2011, Japanese vice-minister of defense Kimito Nakae stated that the Japan-ASEAN security relationship has matured to the point where Japan can play "a more specific cooperative role" on regional security issues. Mr. Nakae also said that resolving maritime problems requires stronger cooperation from Japan, the United States, and others.[31]

These combined security concerns in the SCS led to a September 2011 military cooperation agreement between Japan and the Philippines to expand joint naval exercises. China's recent assertive behavior in the SCS constitutes not only a direct challenge to Philippine claims but also an implicit threat to Japan's oil and raw material lifeline. (Japan's dependence on foreign oil sources is nearly 100 percent, of which close to 90 percent passes through the SCS.) Tokyo now regularly voices concerns about China's dominance in these waters at ASEAN-sponsored gatherings. Both Japan and the Philippines have endorsed a multilateral approach to the SCS, compliance with freedom of navigation, and a binding code of conduct under established international law. All of this is a none-too-veiled riposte to Beijing's insistence on exclusively bilateral negotiations to resolve disputes in the region.[32]

India's naval extension from the Indian Ocean into the SCS may be understood along several dimensions: the desire to become an Asian power, not just an Indian Ocean actor; after considerable investment in its navy, the fact that India now has the capability to deploy to eastern Asia and balance China not only along the Sino-Indian land border but on the sea as well; and investment in SCS energy exploration for India's rapidly developing economy. Within the decade, India will have three aircraft carriers equipped with fourth-generation MiG 29-K supersonic strike aircraft. On the other hand, even with three carriers, its total air complement would only be 92 fighters—a very limited land bombardment capacity. Moreover, a three-carrier fleet means that only one will be deployed at all times, hardly sufficient for both the Indian Ocean and SCS. Additionally, aircraft carriers are normally protected by surface combatants, and most of India's surface ships are old and obsolete. Even more problematic is the Indian air force. To operate in the SCS region would require in-flight refueling, for which it has only six aircraft. An expeditionary strike force of 60 planes would need at least 15 tankers. Finally, there is no strategic plan for aircraft acquisition; they have been purchased piecemeal without coordinating weapons types or refueling aircraft. In short, while India clearly dominates the Indian Ocean, its capability to be a significant military actor in the SCS is insufficient.[33]

A method by which India can enhance its military clout involves deepening ties with the United States and its regional allies and partners. Relations with Japan, Indonesia, and most recently Vietnam are illustrative. A "strategic partnership" between Japan and India was announced in 2005. Expanded to the notion of an "arc of freedom and prosperity," values-oriented diplomacy linked India, Japan, Australia, and the United States. In 2007 Japanese prime minister Shinzō Abe proposed the "Quadrilateral Initiative" through which the United States, India, Japan, and Australia would create a formal security dialogue. In both 2007 and 2009 trilateral exercises were held in the Indian Ocean and western Pacific among Indian, Japanese, and American navies.

A joint security declaration in 2008 pledged Japan and India to coast guard cooperation and consultation within existing regional multilateral institutions as well as sharing experiences from nontraditional security activities such as peacekeeping and disaster management. The emphasis here is on political rather than military cooperation, reflecting Japan's prohibition under its "peace constitution" to become involved in collective defense (though military collaboration with the United States is a notable exception). From Delhi's perspective, Japan-Indian security ties help to legitimize an Indian role in eastern Asia. In turn, Tokyo obtains an implicit Indian pledge to provide security for Japanese shipping in the Indian Ocean, an understanding that also seems to be endorsed by the Obama administration.[34]

For India to sustain an active maritime security role in the SCS, it also needs approval from the Southeast Asian littoral. Indonesia has provided that as India assists the development of Jakarta's naval capabilities. Beginning in 2002, the two countries have undertaken "coordinated" patrols through the Andaman Sea at the northern entrance to the Malacca Strait, involving ships and aircraft. These patrols are directed from an Indian command in the Andaman Islands. By categorizing itself as a "funnel state" to the Malacca Strait, India justifies a greater security role for itself. The United States appears comfortable with this growing Indian security role.[35]

The most striking evidence that India intends to be an SCS security participant is found in its deepening ties with Vietnam. By seeking docking rights for its warships and posting long-term naval instructors at both Cam Ranh Bay and Nha Trong, Delhi is entering into China's strategic backyard. India has also agreed to help Vietnam ready a new fleet of submarines and is engaged in talks with Hanoi over hydrocarbon exploration off Vietnam's coast. India's largest oil company, ONGC Videsh, plans two oil exploration projects with Petro Vietnam in SCS waters also claimed by China. Beijing has labeled India's meddling in the region an attack on China's sovereignty.[36]

Implications for the United States

In October 2007, the United States issued a new maritime strategy, *A Cooperative Strategy for 21st Century Seapower* (CS21). It avers that "credible combat power will be continuously postured in the Western Pacific and Arabian Gulf/Indian Ocean" to defend "vital interests" and assure friends and allies of America's commitment to regional security and open sea lines of communication and commerce. In recent years, the United States has modified its Asia-Pacific defense posture to bring forces closer to Asian sea-lanes. It has also upgraded its Pacific Fleet surface combatants, deployed *Los Angeles*–class submarines to Guam, and is shifting vessels from the Atlantic Fleet to the Pacific Fleet. Some of the new littoral combat ships are also scheduled to be stationed permanently in Singapore. These developments are components of the Obama administration's plan to enhance its Pacific presence as American forces leave Iraq and Afghanistan.[37]

The strategic principle behind this plan is the Air-Sea Battle doctrine described in the 2010 *Quadrennial Defense Review* (QDR). Air-Sea Battle combines air and naval assets to deter or defeat China's antiaccess strategy within the latter's "first island chain."[38] The doctrine also foresees a closer integration of allies in this enterprise, specifically mentioning Japan and Australia. To be implemented, then, the Air-Sea Battle doctrine requires deeper alliance commitments from Tokyo and Canberra. Washington is also engaged in building the capacities of Southeast Asian armed forces (Malaysia, the Philippines, Indonesia, and Vietnam) through joint exercises that assist these states in developing multilateral strategic cooperation.[39]

Moreover, Australia and the United States are building additional military ties through Canberra's provision of new bases for the United States on its northern and western coasts, close to the SCS. The new bases combined with possible prepositioning of US equipment for joint exercises and the probable sale of up to 100 new American combat aircraft will make the United States–Australian alliance capability in SEA the strongest it has ever been.[40]

In a 2011 article written for *Foreign Policy*, Secretary of State Clinton spelled out the essentials of America's Asian position: "We are the only power with a network of strong alliances in the region, no territorial ambitions, and a long record providing for the common good. Along with our allies, we have underwritten regional security for decades—patrolling sea lanes and preserving stability."[41]

Clinton's assistant secretary of state, Kurt Campbell, in Bangkok pointed to the American repositioning of resources "from the Middle East and South Asia . . . to Asia and East Asia as a whole." For the Asia-Pacific, the Air-Sea Battle concept is about close coordination of air and maritime forces for which stealthy weapons is key. These include the F-22 and F-35 combat aircraft, Navy submarines, and even the future Air Force long-range bomber. These low-signature assets would be designed to counter China's developing antiaccess strategy along the PRC periphery. Aegis cruisers would support the air forces. Allies and partners could provide air and naval ports, command and control cooperation, intelligence and surveillance sharing, and locations for prepositioned supplies. Crafting these arrangements requires substantial military diplomacy, especially as the United States reduces the numbers of forces stationed in Asia and closes some bases in the region.[42] In effect, ally and partner facilities and cooperation become more important for America's Asian security posture.

While more US hard power is shifting to Asia, the soft power of diplomacy is also in play. With respect to the SCS, Washington has become a strong backer of ASEAN's multilateral negotiation posture, primarily because it fits best with the US goal of open sea lines of communication. Thus, Assistant Secretary Campbell speaks of the importance of the ARF "for discussions . . . of maritime security" and says that maritime sovereignty issues "need to be resolved using the criteria carefully set up in the law of the sea"—referring to UNCLOS and its 200 nm EEZ.[43]

Meanwhile, China continues to stonewall ASEAN efforts to negotiate a multilateral code of conduct on the SCS sovereignty disputes. Instead, Beijing has proposed more discussions with ASEAN on such issues as navigation safety. Meeting in Bali in July 2011, ASEAN senior officers crafted draft guidelines for their ministers that emphasized the right of Southeast Asian claimants to consult among themselves about a declaration of conduct—an ASEAN arrangement that the PRC opposes because it would violate China's insistence that ASEAN is not a party to the dispute and that China is prepared to negotiate island ownership only bilaterally with other claimants. Nevertheless, ASEAN foreign ministers have decided to proceed without China by forming a working group that will draft a code of conduct.[44]

As Sam Bateman points out:

> Due to the complex geography of the South China Sea and the multiple bordering states, a conventional system of straight line maritime boundaries will be impossible to achieve in many parts of the sea. This situation is aggravated by the difficulties of resolving the sovereignty disputes, including agreement on which insular features qualify as "islands" under international law entitled to a full set of maritime zones.[45]

Bateman goes on to say that settlement of the SCS disputes requires a "change in mind-sets" from sovereignty, sole ownership of resources and seeking "fences in the sea," to one of cooperative management of the waters and their resources. This shift in orientation can only be achieved multilaterally, using ASEAN-derived institutions such as the ARF as the venue for collaboration. Not coincidentally, should the ARF undertake this task, the forum would move directly from its current focus on "confidence building" into the next stage of its maturation, "preventive diplomacy" and perhaps over time even to the ultimate goal of "dispute resolution"—though that achievement may be many years in the future, if at all.

Notes

1. For more elaboration on SCS features and territorial claims, see Tommy Koh, "Mapping Out Rival Claims to the South China Sea," *The Straits Times* (Singapore), 13 September 2011; and Clive Schofield and Ian Storey, *The South China Sea Dispute: Increasing Stakes and Rising Tensions* (Washington, DC: The Jamestown Foundation, 2009).

2. See the discussion in Sam Bateman, "Managing the South China Sea: Sovereignty Is Not the Issue," *RSIS* [*S. Rajaratnam School of International Studies*] *Commentaries*, no. 136 (29 September 2011); and Subathra R. Periyaswamy, "The South China Sea Dilemma: Options for the Main Actors," *RSIS Commentaries* no. 137 (29 September 2011).

3. Sam Bateman, "Solving the 'Wicked Problem' of Maritime Security: Are Regional Forums Up to the Task?," *Contemporary Southeast Asia* 33, no. 1 (April 2011): 2.

4. Richard Bitzinger, "A New Arms Race? Explaining Recent Southeast Asian Arms Acquisitions," *Contemporary Southeast Asia* 32, no. 1 (April 2010): 50–69.

5. Robert Kaplan, "The South China Sea Is the Future of Conflict," *Foreign Policy*, no. 188 (September/October 2011): 83; and Agence France-Presse (AFP), 8 September 2011.

6. Bitzinger, "New Arms Race?," 58.

7. Ibid., 60–66; and Bernard Loo, "Arms Races in Asia?," *Eurasia Review*, 19 November 2010.

8. J. N. Mak, "Sovereignty in ASEAN and the Problem of Maritime Cooperation in the South China Sea" (Working Paper no. 156, RSIS, Singapore, 23 April 2008), 6–8, 16.

9. Bateman, "Solving the 'Wicked Problem' of Maritime Security," 17–21.

10. Carlyle Thayer, *Southeast Asia: Patterns of Security Cooperation* (Barton, Australia: Australian Strategic Policy Institute [ASPI], 2010), 25, 30.

11. Carlyle Thayer, "China-ASEAN and the South China Sea" (paper presented at Institute of European and American Studies and the Center for Asia-Pacific Studies Major and Policy Issues on the South China Sea Conference, Academia Sinica, Taipei, 6–9 October 2011), 3–6, 13–14. See also Robert Sutter and Chia-hao Huang, "China–Southeast Asia Relations: Managing Rising Tensions in the South China Sea," in *Comparative Connections: A Triannual E-Journal on East Asian Bilateral Relations* 13, no. 2, May–August 2011, eds. Carl Baker and Brad Glosserman (Honolulu: Pacific Forum CSIS, September 2011), 68; and Huy Duong, "Negotiating the South China Sea," *Diplomat*, 20 July 2011.

12. Cecil Morella (AFP), "Philippines Seeks ASEAN Help to Blunt China," *Yahoo!News*, 23 September 2011, http://ph.news.yahoo.com; and AFP, 23 September 2011.

13. "Alarm Bells over the South China Sea," AFP, 3 August 2011; and Huy Dong, "Negotiating the South China Sea," *Diplomat: ASEAN Beat* (blog), 20 July 2011, http://thediplomat.com/asean-beat.

14. *South China Morning Post* (Hong Kong), 23 September 2011.

15. This section draws extensively from Sheldon Simon, "US–Southeast Asia Relations: Deep in South China Sea Diplomacy," in Baker and Glosserman, *Comparative Connections*, 55–57.

16. ASEAN news, Bali, "Hard Work Ahead for ASEAN, but Indonesian President Confident of Progress," Philippine Information Agency press release, 20 July 2011, http://archives.pia.gov.ph/?m=7&r=GHQ&id=44471&y=2011&mo=07.

17. US Secretary of State Hillary Clinton (official statements, ARF, 17th Ministerial Meeting, Hanoi, 23 July 2010).

18. Statement by Indonesian president Susilo Bambang Yudhoyono, 2011 chair, ASEAN (opening speech, 18th ASEAN Summit, "ASEAN Community in a Global Community of Nations," Jakarta, 7–8 May 2011), quoted in Simon, "US–Southeast Asia Relations," 56.

19. Kurt Campbell, US assistant secretary of state for East Asian and Pacific affairs (remarks, United States–China Asia-Pacific Consultations, East-West Center, Honolulu, 26 June 2011), quoted in Simon, "US–Southeast Asia Relations," 57.

20. Secretary of State Hillary Clinton (remarks, 18th ARF, "ASEAN Community in a Global Community of Nations," Bali, 23 July 2011).

21. Quoted in Simon, "US–Southeast Asia Relations," 57.

22. Daniel Ten Kate and Nicole Gaouette, "Clinton Warns South China Sea Spats Threaten Asian Peace, Trade," Bloomberg.com, 24 July 2011, http://origin-www.bloom berg.com.

23. This section draws extensively from Simon, "US–Southeast Asia Relations," 58–59.

24. Secretary of State Hillary Clinton, remarks, joint news conference with Philippine foreign minister Albert del Rosario, State Department, Washington, DC, 24 June 2011.

25. Amando Doronila, "Spratlys Row a Test of President Aquino Mettle," *Philippine Daily Inquirer,* 13 June 2011.

26. Ibid.

27. Gus Lubin, "China Tells America to Stay Out of Its Territorial Disputes," *Business Insider,* 14 June 2011.

28. James Manicom, "Japan's Role in Strengthening Maritime Security in Southeast Asia," in *Maritime Security in Southeast Asia: U.S., Japanese, Regional, and Industry Strategies,* National Bureau of Asian Research (NBR) Special Report no. 24, ed. John Bradford et al. (Seattle: NBR, November 2010), 35–37.

29. Christopher Acheson, "Japan's Shifting Security Environment," interview with Christopher Hughes (professor, international politics and Japanese studies, University of Warwick), NBR Japan-US Discussion Forum, 13 September 2011.

30. AFP, "China's Sea Claims to Top Japan-Philippines Summit," *Bangkok Post,* 27 September 2011, http://www.bangkokpost.com; and Associated Press, "Japan Steps into South China Sea Territorial Feud," *Japan Today,* 21 September 2011, www .japantoday.com.

31. Yoree Koh, "Asian Bloc Agrees to Counter China Heft," *Wall Street Journal,* 30 September 2011, http://online.wsj.com.

32. "Japan Taking a New Role in the South China Sea?," STRATFOR (Strategic Forecasting, Inc.), 30 September 2011, http:/www.stratfor.com.

33. Walter Ladwig III, "India and Military Power Projection: Will the Land of Gandhi Become a Conventional Great Power?," *Asian Survey* 50, no. 6 (November/ December 2010): 1174–79.

34. David Brewster, "The India-Japan Security Relationship: An Enduring Security Partnership," *Asian Security* 6, no. 2 (May–August 2010): 97, 99, 110. See also Hillary Clinton, "America's Pacific Century," *Foreign Policy,* November 2011.

35. David Brewster, "The Relationship between India and Indonesia: An Evolving Security Partnership?," *Asian Survey* 51, no. 2 (March/April 2011): 231, 235, 240–42.

36. Ishaan Tharoor, "Is This How Wars Start? India and China Now Feud over the South China Sea," *Time,* 19 September 2011, http://world.time.com. See also "India, Vietnam: Testing China's Patience," STRATFOR, 26 September 2011, http:/www .stratfor.com.

37. John Bradford, "The Maritime Strategy of the United States: Implication for the Indo-Pacific Sea Lanes," *Contemporary Southeast Asia* 33, no. 2 (August 2011): 182, 192–93.

38. Robert M. Gates, *Quadrennial Defense Review* (Washington, DC: Department of Defense, February 2010).

39. See the discussion in Andrew Davies and Benjamin Schreer, *Whither U.S. Forces? U.S. Military Presence in the Asia-Pacific and the Implications for Australia*, ASPI Policy Analysis no. 87 (Canberra: ASPI, 8 September 2011), 4; and Clive Schofield and Ian Storey, *The South China Sea Dispute: Increasing Stakes and Rising Tensions* (Washington, DC: The Jamestown Foundation, November 2009), 40.

40. The 15 September 2011 Australian-US ministerial meeting is previewed by Ernest Bower and Xander Vagg in *CSIS Southeast Asia: Critical Questions—Australia-U.S. Ministerial* (Washington, DC: CSIS, 14 September 2011).

41. Clinton, "America's Pacific Century."

42. "U.S. Strategy," *Defense News*, 20 October 2011, 10; Dave Majumdar, "U.S. AirSea Battle Takes Shape amid Debate," *Defense News*, 10 October 2011; and Kurt Campbell, "U.S. Engagement in Asia," (public lecture, US Department of State, Institute of Security and International Studies, Bangkok, 10 October 2011).

43. Campbell, "U.S. Engagement in Asia," 4, 5, 8.

44. Thayer, "China-ASEAN and the South China Sea," 25–27; Barry Wain, "China Faces New Wave of Dispute," *Jakarta Post*, 17 October 2011; and Christine Tjandraniagsih, "ASEAN Working Group to Draft South China Sea Code of Conduct," *Kyodo News*, 4 October 2011.

45. Bateman, "Managing the South China Sea," 2.

Chapter 11

Nuclear-Strategic Asia

Dr. Stephen J. Cimbala
Professor, Political Science, Penn State Brandywine

Introduction

The Obama administration has endorsed a paradigm shift in military planning emphasis from Europe to Asia while acting to reassure European North Atlantic Treaty Organization (NATO) allies that they will not be abandoned or diminished. Among perceived threats both current and prospective, the existing and potential spread of nuclear weapons among states in Asia is a major peril to regional and global peace and security. Nuclear proliferation in Asia not only raises the probability and cost of wars among states but also invites nuclear handoffs to terrorists or other nonstate actors with grievances aplenty and bad manners.[1] In addition, nuclear conflict between two large states in Asia, such as India and Pakistan, has the potential to escalate into a wider regional war with possibly global consequences.[2]

Nuclear Asia is a large canvas. In the discussion that follows, we project to the year 2020 or shortly thereafter, into the latter second or early third decade of the twenty-first century. The political context of an Asian nuclear arms race is obviously different from the political context that surrounded United States–Soviet competition throughout the Cold War. Therefore, the consequences of variations in the performances of various forces may be more significant for crisis and arms race stability in a multipolar arms competition compared to the two-way street of the Cold War.

Policy Problems and Issues

US policy has been to support the Nuclear Non-Proliferation Treaty (NPT), requiring nonnuclear state subscribers to the treaty to abjure the option of nuclear weapons. Nonnuclear states have, under the NPT regime, the right to develop a complete nuclear fuel cycle for peaceful purposes (i.e., generating electricity). States adhering to the

NPT are required to make available their facilities and infrastructure for scheduled or challenge inspections by the International Atomic Energy Agency (IAEA). The IAEA has a mixed track record. Depending on the cooperation or resistance of the regime in question, inspectors may obtain an accurate road map of a country's nuclear program or be misled. In Iraq, for example, regular IAEA inspections prior to 1991 failed to detect the complete size and character of Saddam Hussein's efforts to develop nuclear weapons.

US intelligence has also performed erratically in ascertaining the extent of weapon of mass destruction (WMD), including nuclear, activities in potential proliferators. The Central Intelligence Agency (CIA) assured President Bush and his advisors that the presence of large quantities of WMDs in Iraq in 2003 was a slam dunk. However, inspectors found no WMDs after the completion of Operation Iraqi Freedom and the ousting of Hussein from power. The CIA was apparently taken by surprise in 1998 by India's and Pakistan's nearly simultaneous detonations of nuclear weapons, followed by announcements in New Delhi and Islamabad that each was now an acknowledged nuclear power. The US government signed an agreement with North Korea in 1994 freezing its nuclear development programs, but in 2002 North Korea unexpectedly denounced the agreement, admitted it had been cheating, and marched progressively into the ranks of nuclear-weapon states (NWS).

The difficulties in containing the spread of nuclear weapons and delivery systems are only compounded by the possibility that materials or technology could find a way into the hands of terrorists, to deadly effect. Reportedly, al-Qaeda has tried to obtain weapons-grade materials (enriched uranium and plutonium) and assistance in assembling both true nuclear weapons and radiological bombs (conventional explosives that scatter radioactive debris). Nuclear weapons are in a class by themselves as weapons of "mass destruction." Thus, a miniature nuclear weapon exploded in an urban area could cause much more death and destruction than either biological or chemical weapons similarly located.

In addition to the plausible interest of terrorists in nuclear weapons, there is also the disconcerting evidence of nuclear entrepreneurship resulting in proliferation. The A. Q. Khan network of Pakistani and other government officials, middlemen, scientists, and non-descripts trafficked for several decades in nuclear technology and know-how. The Khan network, described as a "Wal-Mart of private-sector proliferation," apparently reached out and touched North Korea, Libya, and Iran, among others.[3] States seeking a nuclear start-up can save enormous time and money by turning to experts in and out of government for help. Knowing how to fabricate nuclear weapons is no longer as esoteric as it was in the early days of the atomic age.

In response to 9/11 and to the possible failure of nuclear containment in Asia and the Middle East, the George W. Bush administration sought to reinforce traditional nonproliferation with an interest in preemptive attack strategies and missile defenses. US superiority in long-range precision weapons made preemption technically feasible, provided the appropriate targets had been identified. Bush policy guidance apparently also permitted the possible use of nuclear weapons in preemptive attack against hostile states close to acquiring their own nuclear arsenals.[4] Missile defenses are further behind the technology power curve compared to deep strike, but the first US national missile defense (NMD) deployments took place in 2004. The Obama administration has since embarked on an ambitious program for European-deployed land- and sea-based missile defenses (the so-called phased adaptive approach).[5] Preemption strategies and defenses are controversial in their own right.[6] For present purposes, however, they are simply talismans of US government awareness and acknowledgment that containment and deterrence can no longer complete the antiproliferation tool kit.

Uncertainty about the rate of nuclear weapons spread in future Asia is in contrast to the comparative stability of the Cold War experience. During the Cold War, nuclear weapons spread from state to state at a slower rate than pessimists projected. In part, this was due to the bipolar character of the international system and nuclear preeminence of the Soviet Union and the United States over other contenders. Both superpowers discouraged horizontal proliferation among other state actors, even as they engaged in vertical proliferation by creating larger and more technically advanced arsenals. In addition, the NPT and the regime it established contributed to limitation in the rate of nuclear weapons spread among states that might otherwise have gone nuclear.[7]

The end of the Cold War and the demise of the Soviet Union have moved the zone of political uncertainty—and the interest in WMDs and missiles—eastward across the Middle East, South Asia, and the Pacific basin.[8] North America and Western Europe, pacified or at least debellicized by an expanded NATO and a downsized Russia, regard nuclear weapons as dated remnants of the age of mass destruction. The most recent "revolution in military affairs" has created a new hierarchy of powers based on the application of knowledge and information to military art.[9] From the standpoint of postmodern westerners, nuclear and other WMDs are the military equivalent of museum pieces, although still dangerous in the wrong hands.

On the other hand, major states in Asia and also in the Middle East within reach of long-range missiles based in Asia see nuclear weapons and ballistic missiles as potential trumps. The appeal of nuclear weapons and delivery systems for these states is at least threefold. First, they enable "denial of access" strategies for foreign powers that might want to interfere in regional issues. US military success in Afghanistan in 2001 and in Iraq in 2003 only reinforced this rationale of access denial via WMDs for aspiring regional hegemons or nervous dictators. Second, nuclear weapons might permit some states to coerce others lacking countermeasures in the form of deterrence. Israel's nuclear weapons—not officially acknowledged but widely known—have appealed to Tel Aviv as a deterrent against provocative behavior by Arab neighbors and as a possible "Samson" option on the cusp of military defeat leading to regime change. Third, nuclear weapons permit states lacking the resources for advanced-technology conventional military systems to stay in the game of declared major powers. Russia is the most obvious example of this syndrome. Without its nuclear arsenal, Russia would be vulnerable to nuclear blackmail or even to conventional military aggression from a variety of strategic directions. Russia's holdover deterrent from the Cold War, assuming eventual modernization, guarantees Moscow military respect in Europe and makes its neighbors in Asia more circumspect.[10]

North Korea is another example of a state whose reputation is enhanced by its potential deployment of nuclear weapons or long-range ballistic missiles.[11] Absent a nuclear capability, North Korea is a politically isolated outlaw state with a bankrupt economy that would receive almost no international respect. But as an apparent nuclear power, North Korea has played nuclear poker with a five-nation coalition—the United States, Russia, Japan, China, and South Korea—attempting to disarm its program by peaceful means.[12]

In an agreement signed with those five powers in February 2007, North Korea promised to shut down its nuclear reactor at Yongbyon within 60 days and to admit international inspectors into the Democratic People's Republic of Korea (DPRK) to verify compliance. For taking this step, North Korea was to receive an emergency shipment of fuel oil from the United States, Russia, China, and South Korea. The first phase of this pact thus froze the North Korean plutonium-based weapons program but left for future discussions its suspended uranium-enrichment program. In September 2007, North Korea agreed to declare and disable all of its nuclear programs by the end of the year.[13] However, as is often the case in dealing with the DPRK, backsliding relations with its nuclear interlocutors and shifting sands in North Korean domestic politics have since stranded the six-party talks into diplomatic stasis and arms control uncertainty. The death of Kim Jong-il and his succession by son Kim Jong-un in December 2011 focused world attention on the implications of a power transition within a regime of uncertain stability and military-strategic provenance.[14]

Failure to contain proliferation in Pyongyang could spread nuclear fever throughout Asia. Japan and South Korea might seek nuclear weapons and missile defenses. A pentagonal configuration of nuclear powers in the Pacific basin—Russia, China, Japan, and the two Koreas (not including the United States with its own Pacific interests)—could put deterrence at risk and create enormous temptation toward nuclear preemption. Apart from actual use or threat of use, North Korea could exploit the mere existence of an assumed nuclear capability to support its coercive diplomacy.[15]

A five-sided nuclear competition in the Pacific would be linked, in geopolitical deterrence and proliferation space, to the existing nuclear deterrents of India and Pakistan and to the emerging nuclear weapons status of Iran. An arc of nuclear instability from Tehran to Tokyo could place US proliferation strategies into the ash heap of history and call for more drastic military options, not excluding preemptive war, defenses, and counterdeterrent special operations. In addition, an eight-sided nuclear arms race in Asia would increase the likelihood of accidental or inadvertent nuclear war. It would do so because (1) some of these states already have histories of protracted conflict; (2) states may have politically unreliable or immature command and control systems—especially during a crisis involving a decision for nuclear first strike or retaliation—that might permit a technical malfunction causing an unintended launch or a deliberate but unauthorized launch by rogue commanders; and/or (3) faulty intelligence and warning systems might cause one side to misinterpret the other's defensive moves to forestall attack as offensive preparations for attack, thus triggering a mistaken preemption.

The elephant in the room thus far unmentioned is the rising economic and military power of China relative to that of the United States and other nuclear-weapon states. China's growing economy and the more capable military that it will support will almost certainly, over the course of several decades, lead to more assertiveness with respect to Chinese influence in the Asia-Pacific region. Seen from the standpoint of some classical international relations theory, China is a rising power posing a potential threat to an existing hegemon, at least regionally and perhaps globally. One expert analysis of United States–China relations from this perspective of power transition identifies three sets of outcomes or scenarios that might occur between now and midcentury: (1) a deadly contest for change, (2) a peaceful changing of the guard, or (3) a reluctant accommodation.[16] This geostrategic competition need not end in war. In the short term, Chinese economic modernization requires a period of sustained development uninterrupted by major interstate war. Also, the longer perspective of a power transition as between China and the United States argues for China's application of the formula "at odds, but not at war" to the relationship between the two states. As David Lai explains, "Indeed, in a power transition process, if the upstart sees that its comprehensive national power will surpass that of the extant hegemonic power by virtue of its expected development, it will be foolish for the rising power to initiate a premature fight with the latter."[17]

A focus on power transition theory applied to the US–China relationship also ignores other possible axes of competition and conflict between China and other states in Asia. Russia and Japan are two competitors for regional influence against China, and the possibility of an outbreak of local or theater war between China and Russia or China and Japan is not precluded. Russia's large combined-arms military exercise, Vostok-2010, in the Siberian Far East was designed in part to test the readiness of its "new look" reformed armed forces, especially its brigade-based ground forces aspiring to advanced conventional operations and a Russian version of network-centric warfare. Although Russian officials designated the opponent in these exercises as hypothetical, the conclusion was difficult to escape that the Chinese People's Liberation Army (PLA) was on the minds of Russian military planners. As Jacob W. Kipp has noted, "Finally, the air and ground exercises near Chita and Khabarovsk make no sense except as responses to some force threatening the territorial integrity of Eastern Siberia and the Far East. The only forces with the military potential to carry out air and ground attacks that deep into Russian territory are the PLA in support of the so-called separatists identified in the scenario."[18]

Thus far, we have discussed the problem of an Asian nuclear arms race as an abstract, albeit sufficiently alarming, problem. Next, we want to pin down the concept by detailed interrogation of two contrasting scenarios: (1) a proliferation-constrained model in which a multilateral agreement among NWSs and others essentially freezes the status quo in long-range nuclear weapons deployments, and (2) an unconstrained Asian nuclear arms competition leading to the addition of new NWSs and potentially more instability in Asia.

States and Forces

Case 1: Constrained Nuclear Proliferation

A multilateral agreement on nuclear arms limitations and/or reductions would have to establish some rank order among existing NWSs and close the door to admission for others. Preferably, it would also negotiate the successful dismantlement of North Korea's nuclear weapons and infrastructure. A rank order among the remaining NWSs might be established as follows: for the United States and Russia, an upper limit of 1,000 operationally deployed long-range nuclear weapons for each; for China, France, and the UK, a ceiling of 500 weapons; and for India, Pakistan, and Israel, a top line of 300. States would have to count all weapons deployed on either intercontinental or intermediate-range launchers but not those on missiles or bombers of shorter range. Obviously, some agreed-upon mechanism of monitoring and verification would have to be established, perhaps through the IAEA and its program of inspections.

This solution calls for a considerable amount of cooperation among the P-5 (the permanent members of the United Nations [UN] Security Council and also the first five members of the nuclear club) and might be a difficult briefing to give in some chiefs of staff meetings. Nevertheless, the sacrifices being asked of states under this regime are small compared to an unregulated market of demand for nuclear weapons in Asia and the Middle East. With an agreement of this sort in place and enforceable, the UN and the IAEA would have additional credibility and clout in bringing pressure to bear against aspiring or nascent nuclear proliferators.

Would the preceding arrangement among existing nuclear weapons be deterrence stable and/or crisis stable? The exchange model below (fig. 11.1) provides one illustration in this regard.[19] It summarizes the numbers of weapons assigned to the various states in the constrained proliferation model.

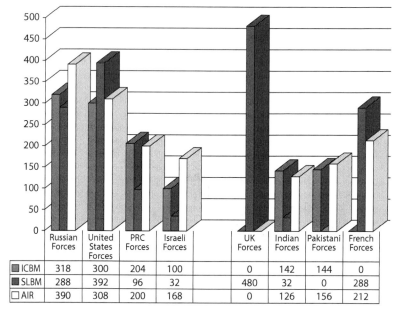

	Russian Forces	United States Forces	PRC Forces	Israeli Forces		UK Forces	Indian Forces	Pakistani Forces	French Forces
ICBM	318	300	204	100		0	142	144	0
SLBM	288	392	96	32		480	32	0	288
AIR	390	308	200	168		0	126	156	212

PRC People's Republic of China
ICBM intercontinental ballistic missile
SLBM submarine-launched ballistic missile
AIR bomber-delivered weapons

Figure 11.1. Constrained proliferation model: total strategic weapons. (The author created this figure and those following using the Arriving Weapons Stability Model [AWSM@] developed by Dr. James Scouras, who is not responsible for its use here.)

Figure 11.2 displays the numbers of second-strike surviving and retaliating weapons available to each state, given reasonable assumptions about the capabilities of attackers and defenders with notional forces and the recognition that nuclear forces are deployed primarily for the purpose of deterrence. No one really knows how they would perform under the stress of a two- or many-sided nuclear war.

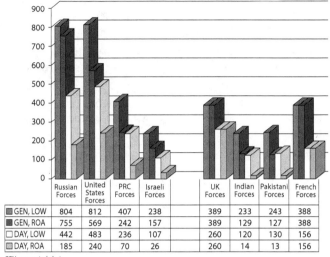

	Russian Forces	United States Forces	PRC Forces	Israeli Forces		UK Forces	Indian Forces	Pakistani Forces	French Forces
GEN, LOW	804	812	407	238		389	233	243	388
GEN, ROA	755	569	242	157		389	129	127	388
DAY, LOW	442	483	236	107		260	120	130	156
DAY, ROA	185	240	70	26		260	14	13	156

GEN generated alert
DAY day-to-day alert
LOW launch on warning
ROA riding out the attack and retaliating

Figure 11.2. Constrained proliferation model: surviving and retaliating warheads

The outcomes of figures 11.1 and 11.2 show that, although all states retain adequate numbers of surviving and retaliating warheads with the potential for stable deterrence, larger arsenals have more survivable redundancy. Whether this variety among "postattack" states would matter in a world having witnessed the first nuclear weapons fired in anger since Nagasaki is a question with both scientific and ethical components. In the best of worlds, the constrained proliferation model would provide for enough deterrence and crisis stability to retain the "nuclear taboo," or de facto abstention, from nuclear first use well into the third decade of the twenty-first century.

Figure 11.2 establishes that it is at least possible for this constrained proliferation regime to provide for deterrence stability based upon assured retaliation. Crisis stability is slightly harder to assess. Findings in figures 11.1 and 11.2 indicate that states in the constrained proliferation model can provide for sufficient degrees of crisis stability—if their nuclear-capable forces are duly responsive to authorized commands and proof against political usurpation or malfunction. At least it can be said that the results of the model do not exclude this optimistic scenario.

On the other hand, political leaders and their military advisors—not some magic system or process—will determine whether any particular multipolar nuclear regime will succeed or fail in preserving crisis stability. Given that this is so, states should provide for a margin of error in the performances of their nuclear alerting, response, and command-control networks that adds to their disinclination toward nuclear preemption. In this regard, states might prefer to emphasize force structures that are less dependent upon prompt launch for survivability—sea-based ballistic missiles compared to land-based ones, for example, or mobile land-based missiles compared to silo-based missiles. States that are contiguous to prospective enemies will be especially prone to first-strike fears unless they have well-protected forces and command systems buffered against "decapitation" attacks.[20]

Case 2: Asian Nuclear Arms Race

What would a nuclear arms race in Asia look like after the second decade of the present century? If proliferation in Asia is successfully contained or rolled back by politics or by war, speculation becomes irrelevant. Therefore, we will assume a more pessimistic future: proliferation is not contained. The second or third decade of the twenty-first century witnesses an eight-sided nuclear club, to include Russia, China, Japan, North and South Korea, India, Pakistan, and Iran. Although proliferation is not contained under this set of assumptions, it does not automatically result in war. The assumption that nuclear weapons can spread among these states without war will be questioned by some, and with some justification. For example, the United States has declared that an Iranian or a North Korean nuclear capability is presently unacceptable. The former must be prevented, and the latter must be rolled back. And some experts would surely argue that China would never accept a Japan armed with nuclear weapons.

On the other hand, the rollback of North Korea's nuclear program is not a certainty. A complicated international bargaining process may leave the DPRK as a standing nuclear power, with a trade-off including more glasnost on the part of the regime, a willingness on the part of Pyongyang to adhere to some international arms control agreements, and economic assistance from the United States and other powers to help rebuild North Korea's moribund economy. As for the Iranian nuclear case, both Israel and the United States have obliquely threatened preemption (presumably with conventional weapons) against Iran's nuclear infrastructure and against any nuclear-capable military forces. But the costs of carrying out the threat of preemption against Iran must be factored into the equation.[21] Iran is a large state and, unlike Iraq, cannot be conquered and occupied by outside powers. Iran could therefore reconstitute any destroyed nuclear power plants or other infrastructure. An additional consideration is political. An Israeli preemption against Iran becomes a recruitment poster for another holy war by jihadists against Israel. Iran has been one of the major sponsors of Hezbollah and other groups that have carried out past terror attacks in Palestine. An Israeli preemption against Tehran might reignite the intifada or otherwise destabilize the peace process headed toward political devolution and Palestinian self-rule.

The point is that many uncertainties loom, and the exclusion of any specific candidate state from the future nuclear club is not automatic. Therefore, we will include all eight in the analysis and assign to them notional forces. As a benchmark, we assume that the older and newer nuclear forces are deployed within an agreed limit comparable to the agreed ceilings of the New Strategic Arms Reduction Treaty (New START) of 2010 between the United States and Russia: a ceiling of 1,550 operationally deployed warheads on launchers of "strategic," or intercontinental, range (or intermediate range for states other than the United States and Russia, since no other states are treaty-committed to forego the deployment of intermediate-range missiles) with freedom to mix various types of launch platforms among land-based, sea-based, and air-launched weapons. While cruise missiles are omitted from this analysis for simplification, as they become smarter, stealthier, and more widely available, they could be a preferred weapon over ballistic missiles for some states if capped with nuclear charges.

States in the analysis include Russia, China, India, Pakistan, North Korea, South Korea, Iran, and Japan. Some might object to the inclusion of Japan, whose current policy abjures any nuclear weapons capability. However, unless North Korea's nuclear arsenal is verifiably dismantled, incentives for South Korea or Japan to go nuclear increase, especially if North Korea deploys additional ballistic missiles of longer range. Figure 11.3 summarizes the forces deployed and available to the various state parties under the hypothesized top limit (formal or tacit) of 1,550 operationally deployed warheads. This limit is established as a marker on the assumption that the United States and Russia will do whatever it takes to maintain the appearance of parity between their two states and the equally credible appearance of a gap between their forces and any others.

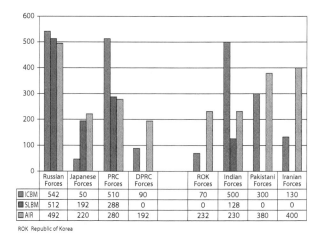

	Russian Forces	Japanese Forces	PRC Forces	DPRC Forces		ROK Forces	Indian Forces	Pakistani Forces	Iranian Forces
ICBM	542	50	510	90		70	500	300	130
SLBM	512	192	288	0		0	128	0	0
AIR	492	220	280	192		232	230	380	400

ROK Republic of Korea

Figure 11.3. Asian nuclear arms race model: total strategic weapons

Each nation would have to plan for the likelihood that only a portion of its forces would survive a nuclear first strike, retaliate, and arrive at their assigned targets. The numbers of each state's second-strike surviving and retaliating forces following notional first strikes are summarized in figure 4, below.

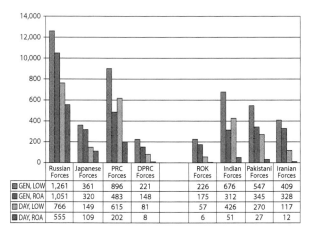

	Russian Forces	Japanese Forces	PRC Forces	DPRC Forces		ROK Forces	Indian Forces	Pakistani Forces	Iranian Forces
GEN, LOW	1,261	361	896	221		226	676	547	409
GEN, ROA	1,051	320	483	148		175	312	345	328
DAY, LOW	766	149	615	81		57	426	270	117
DAY, ROA	555	109	202	8		6	51	27	12

Figure 11.4. Asian arms race model: arriving retaliatory weapons

Several findings of significance are apparent. From the standpoint of deterrence stability, no clear metric exists to delineate that "so many additional nuclear powers equate to such-and-such a decline in deterrence." In theory, it is not impossible for a many-sided nuclear rivalry, even one as regionally robust as this case, to be stable. Provided it has the resources and the technical know-how to do so, each state could deploy ample numbers of "first strike survivable" forces to guarantee the "minimum deterrent" mission, and perhaps the "assured destruction" mission as well.

Both "minimum deterrence" and "assured destruction" are terms of art that overlap in practice. Assured destruction (or assured retaliation) forces are second-strike forces sufficient under all conditions of attack to inflict "unacceptable" societal damage. *Unacceptable* varies with the recipient of the damage and depends on cultural values and political priorities. But it would be safe to assume that the decapitation of a regime and the loss of at least 25 percent of its population and/or one-half its industrial base would satisfy the requirements of assured destruction for "rational," or at least sensible, attackers.

Minimum deterrence is a standard presumably less ambitious than assured destruction. It requires only that the defender inflict costs on the attacker that would create enough pain to make the gamble of an attack unappealing.[22] For example, during the Cold War, the French nuclear retaliatory forces were not adequate by themselves to deter a Soviet attack on NATO, but they might have deterred nuclear blackmail against France separately by threatening Moscow with the prospect of "tearing an arm off," or destroying several Soviet cities. Some expert analysts have suggested that a minimum deterrent strategic nuclear force for the United States might be maintained with as few as several hundred operationally deployable weapons.[23] Former US national security advisor McGeorge Bundy put forward the most assertive definition of minimum deterrence in his argument that 10 nuclear weapons on 10 cities would be a "disaster beyond history."[24]

Although the projection of past events into future scenarios is always perilous, something like the July 1914 crisis in Europe could erupt in Asia once nuclear weapons have been distributed among eight Asian and/or Middle Eastern states and in numbers sufficient to tempt crisis-bound leaders. National, religious, or other cultural hatreds could be combined with the memory of past wrongs and the fear of preemptive attack. This could occur not only between dyads of states but also between alliances, as it did on the eve of the First World War.

Coalitions might form among a nuclear-armed China, Pakistan, North Korea, and Iran—lined up against Russia, Japan, South Korea, and India. This would be an alignment of market democracies of various stripes against dictatorships or authoritarian regimes of sorts. Another possibility would be conflicts between dyads within, or across, democratic and dictatorial coalitions (i.e., rivalry between Japan and China, between the two Koreas, or between India and Pakistan). Russia might find itself in bilateral competition or conflict with China or Japan. Iran might use its nuclear capability for coercion against US allies, such as Saudi Arabia or Israel, drawing American political commitments and military power directly into a regional crisis.

This analysis underlines the truth of the old saying that "everything old is new again." The end of the Cold War did not repeal the nuclear revolution, although it did make deterrence calculations more complicated. It remains the case that nuclear weapons are in a class by themselves as instruments of mass destruction. Very small numbers can produce historically unprecedented destruction and social chaos almost anywhere. What is important about these differences is *not* the numbers and percentages, however, but the possible effect of leaders' *perceptions* that higher alerts and faster launches are necessary to avoid catastrophic defeat should war occur. There are no "winnable" nuclear wars depicted here nor would there be even if agreed levels among the powers were reduced to several hundreds of warheads.[25] The danger is that a war might begin not so much from deliberation but from desperation. States feeling that their nuclear deterrents were threatened might therefore be coerced to make a yes or no decision on a time line that permits neither reflection nor appropriate vetting of the information at hand.

Conclusion

Stability of a regional balance of nuclear terror resides mainly in the policies of states and in the intentions of their leaders. Thus, a catastrophic outcome from nuclear weapons spread in Asia is neither anticipated nor precluded. Nuclear complacency is ill advised. Regional rivalries, including ethno-nationalist and religiously inspired disagreements, combine dangerously with WMDs from the standpoint of international security and stability.

Nuclear forces may be deployed and operated with more or less sensitivity to the problem of provocative crisis behavior. According to Lawrence J. Korb and Alexander Rothman, the United States should adopt an unconditional "no first use" policy for its nuclear weapons and urge other NWSs to do likewise. An agreed multilateral no-first-use policy would help to prevent an outbreak of nuclear war in Asia and contain such a war if it occurred. Even short of such an agreement among all NWSs, an unconditional US no-first-use nuclear policy has other prospective benefits. Korb and Rothman suggest that it would "help the United States implement its nonproliferation agenda, promote stability between NWSs, and deemphasize the role of nuclear weapons in US defense policy, all while actually increasing Americans' security."[26]

Alternatively, a unilateral US declaration of this sort, without support from other NWSs, could weaken US extended deterrence now provided to nonnuclear allies, possibly compromising the NPT and encouraging formerly US-protected allies to develop their own nuclear weapons arsenals.

Notes

1. For contrasting perspectives on this issue, see Kenneth N. Waltz, "More May Be Better," in *The Spread of Nuclear Weapons: A Debate*, eds. Scott D. Sagan and Kenneth N. Waltz (New York: W. W. Norton, 1995), 1–45; and Scott D. Sagan, "More Will Be Worse," in Sagan and Waltz, *Spread of Nuclear Weapons*, 47–91.

2. Lawrence J. Korb and Alexander Rothman, "No First Use: The Way to Contain Nuclear War in South Asia," *Bulletin of the Atomic Scientists* 68, no. 2 (March/April 2012): 34–42, esp. 35, http://the bulletin.sagepub.com.

3. Graham Allison, *Nuclear Terrorism: The Ultimate Preventable Catastrophe* (New York: Henry Holt, Times Books, 2004), 61–63. See also, on the topic of nuclear terrorism, Brian Michael Jenkins, *Will Terrorists Go Nuclear?* (New York: Prometheus Books, 2008).

4. Lawrence Korb with Peter Ogden, *The Road to Nuclear Security* (Washington, DC: Center for American Progress, December 2004), 5.

5. Robert M. Gates, "A Better Missile Defense for a Safer Europe," *New York Times*, 19 September 2009, http://www.nytimes.com/2009/ 09/20/opinion/20gates.html. The Obama administration's phased adaptive approach to missile defense will retain and improve some technologies deployed by the George W. Bush administration but shift emphasis to other interceptors, supported by improved battle management command, control, and communications (BMC3) systems and launch detection and tracking. See unclassified statement, LTG Patrick J. O'Reilly, USA, director, Missile

Defense Agency, before the House Armed Services Committee, 1 October 2009, 111th Cong., 1st sess., http://www.mda.mil/global/documents/pdf/ps_hascl00109 .pdf. Early assessments of the revised Obama missile defense plan include George Friedman, "The BMD Decision and the Global System," *Stratfor.com*, 21 September 2009, http://www.cdi.org/russia/johnson/2009-175-30.cfm; Alexander Golts, "Calling Moscow's Bluff on Missile Defense," *Moscow Times*, 22 September 2009, http:// www.themoscowtimes.com/opinion/article/calling-moscows-bluff-on-missile -defense/383727.html; Alexander L. Pikayev, "For the Benefit of All," *Moscow Times*, 21 September 2009, http://www.themoscowtimes.com/opinion/article/for-the-benefit -of-all/383638.html; and Strobe Talbott, "A Better Base for Cutting Nuclear Weapons," *Financial Times*, 21 September 2009, http://www.ft.com/intl/cms/s/0/d32ee608-a61a -11de-8c92-00144feabdc0.html#axzz1sAW9acix.

6. See Karl P. Mueller et al., *Striking First: Preemptive and Preventive Attack in U.S. National Security Policy* (Santa Monica, CA: RAND, 2006), for an assessment of past and present US experience. Unnecessary confusion in the American policy debate about preemption and preventive war strategies is noted in Colin S. Gray, *The Implications of Preemptive and Preventive War Doctrines: A Reconsideration* (Carlisle, PA: Strategic Studies Institute, US Army War College, July 2007).

7. Joseph Cirincione, *Bomb Scare: The History and Future of Nuclear Weapons* (New York: Columbia University Press, 2007), 43. According to Cirincione, the following states have abandoned nuclear weapons programs, nuclear weapons, or both since the NPT entered into force: Argentina, Australia, Belarus, Brazil, Canada, Iraq, Kazakhstan, Libya, Romania, South Africa, South Korea, Spain, Switzerland, Taiwan, Ukraine, and Yugoslavia (ibid., 43).

8. Paul Bracken, *Fire in the East: The Rise of Asian Military Power and the Second Nuclear Age* (New York: Harper Collins, 1999), esp. 95–124.

9. Michael O'Hanlon, *Technological Change and the Future of Warfare* (Washington, DC: Brookings Institution, 2000), 7–31.

10. Nikolai Sokov, "Nuclear Weapons in Russian National Security Strategy," in *Russian Nuclear Weapons: Past, Present, and Future*, ed. Stephen J. Blank (Carlisle, PA: Strategic Studies Institute, November 2011), 187–260. See also Nikolai Sokov, "The New, 2010 Russian Military Doctrine: The Nuclear Angle," James Martin Center for Nonproliferation Studies, Monterey Institute of International Studies, 5 February 2010, http://cns.miis.edu/stories/100205_russian_nuclear_doctrine.htm.

11. North Korean military capabilities are discussed in Andrew Scobell and John M. Sanford, *North Korea's Military Threat: Pyongyang's Conventional Forces, Weapons of Mass Destruction, and Ballistic Missiles* (Carlisle, PA: US Army War College, Strategic Studies Institute, April 2007).

12. Writing in November 2011, Stephen J. Blank noted that "the Six Party process is moribund, if not dead" and referred to a "growing intransigence" among the major negotiating parties. See Blank, *Arms Control and Proliferation Challenges to the Reset Policy* (Carlisle, PA: Strategic Studies Institute, November 2011), 36–37.

13. Choe Sang-Hun, "North Korea Says U.S. Will Lift Sanctions," *New York Times*, 4 September 2007, http://www.nytimes.com/2007/09/04/world/asia/04korea .html; Bill Powell, "North Korea Has Agreed to Shut Down Its Nuclear Program: Is He Really Ready to Disarm?," *Time*, 26 February 2007, 32–33; and Glenn Kessler, "Conservatives Assail North Korean Accord," *Washington Post*, 15 February 2007, A01.

14. Historical perspective on North Korea's interest in nuclear weapons and on US relations with the DPRK appears in Richard Rhodes, *The Twilight of the Bombs: Recent Challenges, New Dangers, and the Prospects for a World without Nuclear Weapons* (New York: Alfred A. Knopf, 2010), 173–209. See also David E. Sanger and Joseph Berger, "Arms Bid Seen in New N. Korea Plant," *New York Times*, 21 November 2010, http://www.nytimes.com/2010/11/22/us/22talk.html; and Siegfried S. Hecker, *A Return Trip to North Korea's Yongbyon Complex* (Stanford, CA: Center for International Security and Cooperation, Stanford University, 20 November 2010).

15. George H. Quester, *Nuclear First Strike: Consequences of a Broken Taboo* (Baltimore, MD: Johns Hopkins University Press, 2006), 49.

16. David Lai, *The United States and China in Power Transitions* (Carlisle, PA: Strategic Studies Institute, US Army War College, December 2011), 81.

17. Ibid., 173.

18. Jacob W. Kipp, "Russia's Nuclear Posture and the Threat That Dare Not Speak Its Name," in *Russian Nuclear Weapons: Past, Present, and Future*, ed. Stephen J. Blank (Carlisle, PA: Strategic Studies Institute, US Army War College, November 2011), 459–503, n. 489.

19. Grateful acknowledgment is made to Dr. James Scouras for use of his Arriving Weapons Stability Model (AWSM)@ for making calculations and drawing graphs in this study. Dr. Scouras is not responsible for any analysis or arguments herein.

20. Unfortunately, the old Cold War–style recipes for nuclear decapitation are now complicated by the possibility of cyberwar and related information operations. US government and other definitions for *cyberspace* and related concepts are reviewed in Daniel T. Kuehl, "From Cyberspace to Cyberpower: Defining the Problem," in *Cyberpower and National Security*, eds. Franklin D. Kramer et al. (Washington, DC: National Defense University Press and Potomac Books, Inc., 2009), 24–42. See also Martin C. Libicki, *Cyberdeterrence and Cyberwar* (Santa Monica, CA: RAND Corporation, 2009); Timothy L. Thomas, *Cyber Silhouettes: Shadows over Information Operations* (Fort Leavenworth, KS: Foreign Military Studies Office, 2005); and David S. Alberts et al., *Understanding Information Age Warfare*, 3d ed. (Washington, DC: Department of Defense [DOD] Command and Control Research Program, US DOD, October 2004). On influence operations, see John Arquilla, *Worst Enemy: The Reluctant Transformation of the American Military* (Chicago, IL: Ivan R. Dee, 2008), 132–55. On the role of information operations in Russian military policy, see Timothy L. Thomas, *Recasting the Red Star: Russia Forges Tradition and Technology through Toughness* (Fort Leavenworth, KS: Foreign Military Studies Office, 2011), esp. chap. 6 and app. 1.

21. On this topic, see Alexander Wilner and Anthony Cordesman, *U.S. and Iranian Strategic Competition: The Gulf Military Balance* (Washington, DC: Center for Strategic and International Studies [CSIS]), 2 November 2011), esp. 102–28; and David Albright, Paul Brannan, and Jacqueline Shire, *Can Military Strikes Destroy Iran's Gas Centrifuge Program? Probably Not* (Washington, DC: Institute for Science and International Security, ISIS Report, 7 August 2008), http://isis-online.org/isis-reports /category/iran. For US intelligence community thinking on Iran, see Director of National Intelligence John Negroponte, *DNI Annual Threat Assessment 2006*, cited in Anthony H. Cordesman, *Iran's Nuclear and Missile Programs: A Strategic Assessment*, rev. ed. (Washington, DC: CSIS, 31 August 2006), 23. For force projections and sce-

narios for the Middle East, see Anthony H. Cordesman, *Warfighting and Prolifera-tion in the Middle East*, rev. ed. (Washington, DC: CSIS, 17 April 2007).

22. On minimum deterrence, see Hans M. Kristensen, Robert S. Norris, and Ivan Oelrich, *From Counterforce to Minimal Deterrence: A New Nuclear Policy on the Path toward Eliminating Nuclear Weapons* (Washington, DC: Federation of American Sci-entists and Natural Resources Defense Council, April 2009).

23. James Wood Forsyth Jr., B. Chance Saltzman, and Gary Schaub Jr., "Mini-mum Deterrence and Its Critics," *Strategic Studies Quarterly* 4, no. 4 (Winter 2010): 3–12.

24. McGeorge Bundy, "To Cap the Volcano," *Foreign Affairs* 48, no. 1 (October 1969): 10, http://www.jstor.org/stable/20039419.

25. This point is made in the larger context of an argument for further Russian and American nuclear arms reductions and for strengthening the nuclear nonproliferation regime in Wolfgang K. H. Panofsky, "Nuclear Insecurity; Correcting Washington's Dangerous Posture," *Foreign Affairs* 86, no. 5 (September–October 2007): 109–18, http://www.foreignaffairs.com/articles/62832/wolfgang-k-h-panofsky/nuclear-insecurity.

26. Korb and Rothman, "No First Use," 37.

Chapter 12

Aspects of Korean Unification

Planning for US Involvement on the Korean Peninsula

Dr. Kimberly Gill
Assistant Professor, Political Science, and Director, Master of
Public Administration Program, Columbus State University

Dr. Thomas P. Dolan
Professor and Chairman, Department of Political Science and
Public Administration, Columbus State University

Introduction

Russia's ambassador to the United States, Sergey Kislyak, observes that the expansion of the North Atlantic Treaty Organization to include some former Warsaw Treaty Organization members has begun to sway the military balance in Eastern Europe, leaving Russia feeling outnumbered. The research presented in this chapter stems from his remarks, made at a 2010 nuclear disarmament conference.[1] A parallel situation could result in East Asia if and when Korean unification occurs; a unified Korea could unbalance the security relationships among China, Japan, and Russia and would have major implications for US presence in the region.

Background of Korean Separation

The Korean Peninsula has been separated since 1945 into the Republic of Korea (South Korea) and the Democratic People's Republic of Korea (North Korea). The history of this separation is well documented, although the North's version of events differs significantly from that of the rest of the world. Both sides accept that the partitioning of the Korean Peninsula resulted from the defeat of Japan, which had colonized Korea in 1910, but they dispute the motivations of the United States and Soviet Union in establishing a presence there. While the Soviet Union no longer exists, the United States has maintained a presence in South Korea as part of the United Nations Command, established in 1950 to counter the North Korean invasion of the South.

Studies over the last several decades have examined the scenarios, costs, and long-term results of unification/reunification of North and South Korea.[2] There is no agreement on any of these aspects of Korean unification. Scenarios of unification compare the Koreas with East and West Germany, essentially the absorption of the East by the West, and with Vietnam, or the North's military conquest of the South. In the case of the Koreas, researchers have examined the scenarios of managed, contested, and failed succession in North Korea.

Most Western (i.e., American) researchers have assumed that the failure of the North Korean regime will occur in the short term, generally within 10 years of their studies. This time period, used in the 1980s and '90s, is still referenced today. Assessments by South Korean researchers tend to take a longer view of 30–50 years. These estimates generally assume that a unified Korea will be one in which the North is absorbed by the South, much as East Germany was integrated into a unified Germany that operates as West Germany did. North Korean proposals tend to foresee a confederation in which the North would maintain its current political structure in a confederation of the two sides.

American research, especially that funded by many think tanks (the Hudson Institute, Council on Foreign Relations, American Enterprise Institute), is largely based on a belief that the failure of the regime in the North is imminent. This research stresses the need for a strong American involvement and military presence on the Korean Peninsula once the government of North Korea fails. Others, like Selig Harrison of the Woodrow Wilson International Center for Scholars and Martin Hart-Landsberg, point out that what might be best for American interests is not best for the welfare of a reunified Korea and that an American presence would make successful reunification less likely.[3]

Scenarios for Korean Unification

Estimated costs of Korean reunification vary widely, from $200 to $300 million annually to tens of trillions of dollars over many decades. Low-end estimates appear to be based on the assumptions that after reunification neither side will need large military expenditures and that large savings could be made from military cutbacks. A major problem with this rationale is that if the estimated 1 million North Korean military personnel were demobilized and simply lost their jobs, a situation like that which occurred in postinvasion Iraq could result. An insurgency that might follow would make successful re-unification impossible. Some dismiss this scenario with a prediction that the newly unemployed former military personnel would make up a large labor force, bringing down labor costs and thus stimulating the Korean economy.

The alternative to demobilization—integrating the military forces of the North and South—would result in a unified military of over 1.6 million people armed with vast amounts of artillery, sophisticated aircraft, large numbers of submarines, and nuclear weapons. This option would be unacceptable to China, especially if the United States remained involved militarily on the peninsula. Conservative American researchers use this as the justification for a "stabilizing" American presence in postunification Korea. Others, like Harrison, counter that this is why the United States must be prepared to leave.

With all the possible scenarios and variables involved in answering the question of how a reunified Korea would play out, no single study can hope to come up with a final answer. Among studies already completed, the most common belief is that the failure of the Kim dynasty in North Korea is imminent. Considering the longevity of this regime—begun in President Truman's time (1948) and continuing through the administrations of Presidents Eisenhower, Kennedy, Johnson, Nixon, Ford, Carter, Reagan, George H. W. Bush, Clinton, George W. Bush, and Obama—perhaps failure should not be assumed, at least in the short term. The North Korean regime was established 14 years before Fidel Castro led the Cuban revolution.

A premise of this study is that Korean unification will take place at some point in the future. Although the regimes of Kim Il-sung and Kim Jong-il were maintained for over 60 years, the stresses brought about by failed socialism, nature, and a growing awareness in North Korea of its situation relative to other countries continue to pressure the regime. Nevertheless, a transition to the third generation—leadership by Kim Jong-eun—has begun.

The "Arab Spring" of 2011 demonstrates that regimes long in power can be brought down through popular uprising, as seen in Tunisia, Egypt, and Libya. However, other regimes (Iran and Syria) have resisted such internal pressure. The successful popular movements have generally credited social communications networks for the ability to coordinate group actions; these networks are not widespread in North Korea. Earlier domestic uprisings against authoritarian governments (e.g., the 1989 overthrow of Nicolae Ceausescu in Romania) took place without modern communications but in societies far freer than North Korea.

Other partitioned countries have reunited, including Vietnam, Germany, and Yemen. The means by which these reunifications have occurred vary widely, from military defeat in the case of Vietnam, to political collapse in the case of Germany, to political accommodation in the case of Yemen. A variety of scenarios under which the Koreas would unite have been proposed. Many of these include the collapse of the Kim dynasty in North Korea involving "managed succession," "contested succession," and "failed succession."[4] In the early 1990s, the former foreign minister of the Republic of Korea, the Honorable Choi Kwang-Soo, wrote of the consequences "if Kim Jong-Il fails to secure a stable power basis in the post Kim Il-sung period and a power struggle erupts."[5] As with many of the more recent predictions of North Korean regime failure, Minister Choi has been proven wrong.

The Vietnamese model of unification—military conquest of one side by the other—would be the most destructive, least desired, and probably least likely scenario. A commonly cited casualty figure is that the first 24 hours of open conflict in Korea would bring hundreds of thousands of casualties in the South and billions of dollars in damages.[6] While a renewal of the Korean War is possible, the resulting devastation would set back the progress made in the South and lead to the defeat of the North in short order. Rather than China supporting the North Koreans as it did in the 1950s, China would more likely attempt to discourage them from overt military action.

The German model of reunification entails regime failure on the part of either North Korea or South Korea. Given the economic and diplomatic successes of the South as compared with those of the North, only regime failure in the North is addressed in this study. Such failure could occur over a relatively short period, as postulated by many American researchers, or over a protracted period, as envisioned by most South Korean researchers.[7] Assuming that South Korea would remain intact to assist the North, a nonviolent reunification would result in dealing with the issues of the assimilation of North Koreans: education, conflicting ideologies, nutrition, and, of course, the costs of bringing about long-term stability.

Most observers believe that North Korea's economy has significantly deteriorated since the 1990s. Famines have exacerbated the problems and further withered the state. Despite numerous economic and social problems, North Korea continues to spend a large amount of its budget on its military and nuclear weapons program. Along this unsustainable path, some researchers believe that North Korea may soon be forced to economically integrate or reunify with South Korea. This study identifies several methodologies that estimate the costs of possible scenarios for reunification of North Korea and South Korea. It does not address the humanitarian issues of famine in North Korea or the internment of hundreds of thousands of North Koreans in prison camps there.

Cost Estimates of Korean Unification

A review of research reveals many methodologies to calculate the costs of Korean reunification, and these methods and their predictions have changed over time. In 1993 Kang Suk Rhee estimated that a sudden collapse of the North Korean government would require "$816.7 billion (in 1990 dollars) over the ten-year period 2001–10" to raise North Korean productivity to 60 percent of South Korea's, with South Korea spending between $46.05 billion to $47.88 billion annually for the first four years.[8] As Rhee notes in another study, this figure is based on a Korea Development Institute estimate of a German-style collapse of the North Korean regime, a scenario Rhee finds unlikely.[9] Rhee observes that while the two Germanys accepted American and Soviet involvement in their movement toward unification, both Koreas have rejected foreign interference. The North sees such involvement by the United States (which it identifies as an imperialist aggressor) and by Japan (which colonized the Korean Peninsula from 1910 to 1945) as intolerable, and the South wishes to avoid having this issue as a barrier toward any progress that might be made.[10] Rhee points out that each Korea has proposed its own plan for reunification: the North desires a Democratic Confederal Republic of Koryo (DCRK), while the South wants a Korean National Community Unification Formula (KNCUF). One fundamental difference between these approaches is that the DCRK would be a state, while the KNCUF would be a process.[11] Of course, each side is suspicious of the other.

Writing soon after Rhee and Ian Jeffries, Hong-Tack Chun employed a "gradual integration approach" to examine the implications of Korean unification. Like Rhee, Chun did not foresee any success in a sudden unification in Korea. Chun indicates that while the economies of the Germanys were very different, the economies of North and South Korea are even more disparate. For this reason, he proposes a more gradual process. He suggests that a measured integration of North and South Korea would decrease the fiscal burden of reunification because North Korea is considerably worse off than South Korea, adding that it will take a considerable amount of time for North Korea's wage levels to reach those of South Korea.[12]

Chun uses the following equation to calculate the income ratio in a given year: $X_T = X_o e^{VT}$. In this equation, X_o stands for the initial ratio of income between the North and the South, X_T for the income ratio in year T, and V for the growth rate differential between the two states. If the growth rate differential equals V, then the initial income ratio will be raised to X_T in T years. Under the assumption that X_o equals 0.15 (Bank of Korea), Chun solves for T in the following equation: $T = 1/V (\ln X_T - \ln X_o)$. With this equation, one may project how many years it will take to reach a certain income ratio between North and South Korea. For example, per capita incomes in North Korea must grow faster than those in South Korea for the ratio to decrease.[13]

However, Chun maintains that targeting for a zero income gap is unrealistic. He cites the European Union as an example of regional integration; within it, per capita income disparities exist. Chun asserts that the Korean economies could be integrated without serious economic problems with North Korean per capita income only 40–60 percent of the levels in South Korea. According to Chun, it would take approximately 20 years for the income ratio to increase to 0.4 and 28 years for the income ratio to increase to 0.6. Therefore, a smooth economic integration of North and South Korea would take about 20–30 years.[14]

The vast differences in the economies of the two Koreas and the steady progress of the South relative to the North were the bases of Marcus Noland's "Some Unpleasant Arithmetic Concerning Unification" in 1996. Noland raises the concern that following an economic collapse in North Korea, migration to the South could result in problems. He calculates that "assuming that a person carrying some belongings could travel 20 miles a day, 40 percent of the population of North Korea lives within a 5 day walk of the DMZ." His recommendation to the South Korean government was to maintain the Military Demarcation Line as a barrier and to "encourage capital investment in the North to lessen the incentive to migrate."[15] This reinforcement of the Military Demarcation Line is, in fact, what the South foresees in the event of a collapse in the North.

As others have observed, the economic success of South Korea has far outpaced that of the North. This mounting gap will lengthen the time required for unification and increase its cost. Noland proposes various scenarios to reduce the gap; South Korea should plan for massive capital inflows to North Korea, which would greatly increase its productivity while simultaneously reducing South Korean economic growth. These scenarios include capital investment of as much as $3 trillion over 10 years, leading to economic growth in the North of 30 percent a year. The increased growth rate in the North, when combined with the slowing of South Korean growth, would then make economic integration easier. What Noland did not address in this short essay is that the operationalization of such scenarios would involve severe taxes on the South Korean population. The prospect of reduced economic growth is, to those younger South Koreans beginning their careers, less desirable than unification with North Koreans they do not see as family.

Marc Piazolo, in a 1997 article, echoes Rhee's concerns regarding any comparison of Korean unification to German unification. The relative scales of the German economies were not as divergent as the economies of the Koreas: personnel interchanges were much more frequent between East and West Germany, and trade between the German states was much higher than that on the Korean Peninsula. Piazolo also repeats the concern that the longer Korean unification is delayed, the more it will cost. Using the 10-year prediction, he estimates a cost to South Korea of $270 billion annually. He further calculates that easing of tensions could result in military cutbacks of $10 billion a year to South Korea. Nevertheless, he concludes that Korean unification will be much more costly than German unification was.[16]

Also writing in 1997, Nicholas Eberstadt conveys that "the North is soon likely to implode, its economy deteriorating as its weapons of mass destruction accumulate."[17] While not providing any quantitative estimate of the cost of Korean unification, Eberstadt states that unification can greatly reduce the military expenditures on the peninsula since massive demobilization on both sides will "releas[e] hundreds of thousands of military personnel for economically productive undertakings."[18] He suggests that the greatest contribution the United States will be able to make will be in security: "Just as the US military commitment to the South has been the sine qua non of deterrence on the peninsula, a vibrant United States–South Korean security relationship in a united Korea will be critical to the success of reunification."[19]

In his thorough study of Korean culture, *Korea and Its Futures: Unification and the Unfinished War*, Roy Richard Grinker goes beyond methodological estimations of the cost of unification and examines some of the basic assumptions about what unification would mean to each side. His assessment is that that while the South sees unification as "the southern conquest and assimilation of the north," the North envisions a joining of the two Korean cultures as they exist now.[20] Grinker also examines the generational differences as South Koreans see the results of unification. Older South Koreans see unification as "an endpoint, something to achieve before death," while younger South Koreans see it not as "an event, but as a place from which to launch an autonomous and authentic Korean history."[21] This bifurcation raises a major issue between the generations. Older (South) Koreans see the opportunity for unification decreasing as they near the end of their lives. Younger South Koreans would take the more pragmatic approach of delaying unification until the North Korean economy has improved to the stage where the cost would be lower, since it is the South that will have to bear the bulk of the financial burden.

In 1998 Noland, Sherman Robinson, and Li-Gang Liu addressed alternate scenarios affecting the costs and benefits of Korean unification. Applying a present discounted value (PDV) of income approach to study scenarios of Korean reunification, these authors use this behavioral model to maximize both South Korean and peninsular income. This model allows them to examine the distributional effects within South Korea. Their ideal scenario of unification produced positive net benefits to South Korea, "characterized by low levels of South Korean private investment in North Korea and high levels of North-South labor migration."[22]

To measure the net benefits of economic integration, these authors use their Korean Integration Model (KIM) to generate baseline projections of North and South Korean economies and eight alternative reunification scenarios. KIM is described as a "simple dynamic two-country computable general equilibrium (CGE) model linking North and South Korea."[23] It is supposed to evaluate the impact of trade liberalization and the formation of free trade areas, customs unions, and monetary unions. The authors include other world actors by showing fixed world prices for North and South Korean exports and imports and countries linked by trade.

This model identifies eight sectors: agriculture, forest, and fisheries; mining; light manufacturing; industrial intermediates; capital goods; construction; public administration; and services. The "demanders" include a single aggregate household that buys consumer goods, a government that spends on goods and public administration, and an aggregate capital account that purchases investment goods. Primary factors of production include capital, agricultural labor, and high- and low-skill urban labor. Land is included under agricultural capital.[24]

Noland, Robinson, and Liu assert that this model is meant to determine trends over the long run. They calibrated the model for 1990 and ran it out to 2007, using the scenarios in table 12.1. The results of these scenarios are summarized in table 12.2.

Table 12.1. Scenarios used for applying Korean Integration Model

Scenario	Description
1A	Labor migration is "high," capital and technology transfers are "low," and capital transfers take the form of grants.
1B	Same as Scenario 1A, except capital transfers take the form of private investment.
2A	Labor migration is "low," capital and technology transfers are "low," and capital transfers take the form of grants.
2B	Same as Scenario 2A, except capital transfers take the form of private investment.
3A	Labor migration is "low," capital and technology transfers are "high," and capital transfers take the form of grants.
3B	Same as Scenario 3A, except capital transfers take the form of private investment.
4A	Labor migration is "high," capital and technology transfers are "high," and capital transfers take the form of grants.
4B	Same as Scenario 4A, except capital transfers take the form of private investment.

Adapted from Marcus Noland, Sherman Robinson, and Li-Gang Liu, "The Costs and Benefits of Korean Unification: Alternate Scenarios," *Asian Survey* 38, no. 8 (August 1998): 809.

Table 12.2. Summary of alternative income streams

Base Scenario	PDV of South Korean Income (1990 PPP[a] $billions)	PDV of Total Peninsular Income (1990 PPP $billions)	Ratio of North to South Korean Per Capita Income, 2002 (percent)
Scenario 1A	5,519	6,201	55
Scenario 1B	5,695	6,201	38
Scenario 2A	5,338	6,113	64
Scenario 2B	5,524	6,113	46
Scenario 3A	5,119	6,116	91
Scenario 3B	5,503	6,116	52
Scenario 4A	5,293	6,173	79
Scenario 4B	5,659	6,123	41

Reprinted from Marcus Noland, Sherman Robinson, and Li-Gang Liu, "The Costs and Benefits of Korean Unification: Alternate Scenarios," *Asian Survey* 38, no. 8 (August 1998): 812.
Note: PDVs calculated assuming annual discount rate of 5 percent
[a] purchasing power parity

If reunification had happened in 1998, North Korean income would have dropped in seven of the eight cases. However, it would have risen after capital transfers and technological changes took effect in North Korea. According to the authors, scenario 3A would be the worst case due to an inflated PDV of the South Korean income stream. South Korea would be better off in scenario 1B in which reunification produces a relatively low PDV of its income stream.

These authors determine that economic integration may result in higher levels of income and wealth inequalities in the South. However, they add that redistribution provides for higher incomes; thus, people in South Korea would be better off with unification than without it. This scenario is produced by low levels of South Korean private investment in North Korea and high levels of North-South migration. The authors stress the importance of these factors in ensuring that the economic interests of the North don't conflict with those of South Korea. As with the other estimations, this scenario takes place without military conflict.

In 1999 Noland and Robinson joined with Tao Wang to build upon the work they had done the year before with Liu to examine the implications of Korean reunification. Similar to their earlier work, they used a CGE of Korean integration to produce a Korean integration model. The researchers used an updated version of the KIM in this study, allowing them to generate conclusions based on only limited data. Building on the 1998 work of Noland, Robinson, and Liu, they recalibrated the base year from 1990 to 1996 and used data from the International Monetary Fund, the Food and Agricultural Organization, and the World Food Program. With 1996 as the base year, they used data from macroeconomic and microeconomic social accounting matrices for North and South Korea since it provides a "consistent array of economic transactions among agents that reconciles the input-output and national accounts." The base gross domestic product (GDP) of North Korea was calculated to be approximately 32 billion (North Korean) won ($14,545,440,000 at the official exchange rate of the time).[25]

Noland, Robinson, and Wang studied integration under two scenarios. The first was the formation of a customs union that would eliminate North Korean quantity rationing of trade, remove intra-Korean barriers to trade, and adopt South Korea tariffs as the common external barrier. This scenario assumes product market integration between North and South Korea.

The second scenario includes four variants on exchange rate unification with a fixed exchange rate between the two states. In the first variant, capital flows freely from South to North Korea until North Korean per capita incomes reach 60 percent of levels in the South. In the second variant, per capita income in the North reaches 60 percent of levels in the South by allowing labor migration from the North to the South. In the third variant, the target per capita income level is reached by moving labor and capital. In the fourth variant, capital flows into North Korea from the world instead of from South Korea.[26]

This study examines the effects of a complete North Korean economic collapse and concludes that migration to the South would effectively depopulate the North, with approximately 90 percent of the population leaving North Korea. This is, of course, improbable because of the physical barriers in place, including minefields, as well as South Korean desires to avoid such an influx of refugees. The authors propose that avoiding this situation would require massive aid to North Korea—either from South Korea or from foreign sources—of up to $700 billion. In either case, the capital flow would be far greater than that in German reunification.[27]

Norman Levin examines South Korean public opinion in a 1999 RAND report, *The Shape of Korea's Future: South Korean Attitudes toward Unification and Long-Term Security Issues*. Comparing data from 1996 and 1999, he notes a diminishing level of regard toward Americans and increasing respect for the Chinese. He also found that South Koreans were becoming less enthusiastic about the idea of swift unification. In 1999 more than 45 percent of respondents felt that unification would be more than 10 years away or would never happen; this has been proven true.[28] At the time of the report (five years after the death of Kim Il-Sung and two years after Kim Jong-il had assumed full power as ruler in the North), South Koreans had begun to feel less insecure about threats from the North, and concerns were developing about the United States provoking insecurity through its hard line toward Pyongyang. By 1999 South Koreans were becoming somewhat doubtful of their country's long-standing security relationship with the United States.[29] The following year, South Korean president Kim Dae-jung surprised the United States by traveling to Pyongyang for a summit meeting with Kim Jong-il, after which Secretary of State Madeleine Albright also visited Pyongyang with an American delegation.

As these events occurred, Robert Dujarric wrote that "the nature of the North Korean state makes it difficult to affirm with any certainty that it can survive the next decade or even the next 12 months. Therefore, policy-makers should be prepared for a sudden collapse." He advised that the United States should prepare for a "large and prolonged U.S. military presence in Korea and Japan after Korean unification."[30] Dujarric envisioned the collapse of North Korea as a situation in which farmers are able to increase productivity but where factory workers and the North Korean military are unemployed.[31] The American experience with the demobilized Republican Guard in Iraq during the second war there indicates that simply releasing a large military force is unwise.

Dujarric makes the interesting comparison of Korean unification to the Union victory in the American Civil War, pointing out that the Civil War is a better model than German unification because East and West Germany never fought each other. Citing Grinker, Dujarric feels that unification will be seen in the South as a victory over the North; others see that maintenance of some degree of separation between the two sides after the collapse of the northern regime would be advisable.

Addressing the challenge of dealing with the ousted leadership, Dujarric asks, "Should the leaders of the ruling party be prosecuted for their crimes? How should torturers, camp guards, and other lesser criminals be punished? Should some, or all, members of the party be banned from politics?"[32] Other states have faced this situation; South

Africa has dealt with its apartheid past through its Truth and Reconciliation Commission, and the new governments brought into power
during the Arab Spring of 2011 will have to confront similar issues.
Other concerns, such as property entitlement requests by Koreans on
both sides wanting a "right of return," more closely parallel claims
Palestinians make against Israel.

Dujarric determined that some agencies in the United States (the
Pentagon, etc.) will advocate a strong US military role in a unified
Korea, while others (Congress, the Department of Commerce, and
the Office of the US Trade Representative) will focus on economics
and trade.[33] The end of a military threat may lead some to seek reductions in military spending in the way a "peace dividend" was expected
in the United States in the 1990s after the collapse of the Soviet Union.
Dujarric believes that the financial burden to the South after unification will likely bring any Korean support to US forces (host nation
support, etc.) to an end.[34] If US forces are not permitted to remain in
Korea, Dujarric states, they would have to relocate to Japan. The Japanese would neither welcome nor likely permit this. Although Dujarric does not specifically address expected costs, his analysis provides
some guidance on which models and scenarios to consider.

In their 2004 study, *The Fiscal Burden of Korean Reunification: A
Generational Accounting Approach*, Alan J. Auerbach, Young Jun
Chun, and Ilho Yoo employ a time-phased approach to examine how
the potential costs of fiscal changes would be apportioned between
different populations. The generational accounting approach is useful
because it allows the researcher to examine government policies and
project how reunification will affect Korea's finances.[35]

Through an elaborate set of equations using such variables as GDP,
aggregate capital stock, aggregate labor represented by the economically
active population, capital income share, and level of multifactor productivity (expressed in labor-augmenting units), the authors project the
costs of reconstruction after reunification. They estimate that reconstruction costs will amount to approximately 10 percent of the GDP of
South Korea for 20 years. They assume that the government and the
private sector will each cover half of the costs. Therefore, the costs of
reconstruction that will fall on the South Korean government will
amount to approximately 5 percent of its GDP for 20 years after unification. The study does not mention military expenditures or transition
from a large defense establishment to a more moderately sized one.

Auerbach, Chun, and Yoo conclude that most unification costs are likely to fall on the shoulders of current and future generations of South Koreans due to the disparities between North and South Korea. Fortunately, they further ascertain that the gap between the two states should decrease as North Korea adopts South Korea's fiscal policies and its economy grows.

In 2002 Charles Wolf gave an optimistic prediction of the costs of reunification, stating that "if the process of reunification is negotiated sensibly and managed carefully, the ensuing cost burden imposed on the South and its allies can be limited to a sum that is less than one-tenth of the conventional estimates!" He reports that the literature has projected costs as high as $2–3 trillion, about five or six times South Korea's GDP in 2002 figures. However, he points out that these costs may be reduced by pursuing several principal offsets and economic goals based on the assumption of significant military downsizing after unification. With North Korea employing over 1 million people in the armed forces (about 30–40 percent of the North Korean GDP), Wolf calculates that $13–15 billion could be saved annually after reunification due to military downsizing.[36]

South Korea's substantial military of approximately 600,000 troops brings the total force on the Korean Peninsula to about 1.7 million. Wolf suggests that an additional $2–3 billion could be saved annually if the unified Korean military downsizes. Ideally, he envisions a total military force of approximately 400,000 to garner the given amount of savings. While nice in theory, downsizing on this scale would at first cause widespread unemployment in the unified nation, leading to a labor surplus and downturn in wages. Writing in 2002, Wolf did not know the results of demobilization of the Iraqi military after the US invasion and the resultant insurgency that developed.

Wolf cautions that economic growth after reunification requires realistic goals that are sufficient but not excessive. For example, while the goal of doubling per capita income in North Korea over five to seven years is reasonable, an equalization of per capita income between North and South Korea over the same amount of time is excessive. He argues that if realistic goals are set early in the reunification process, total capital costs of achieving those goals should not exceed four or five times North Korea's GDP.

Some $75 billion could be saved in his proposed military build-down; he estimates the costs of reconstruction in the North at $200 billion, arriving at a net reunification cost of $125 billion. He assumes that half of this total may come from private foreign capital and that the other half would be paid for by public capital transfers from South Korea, Japan, the United States, the World Bank Group, and the Asian Development Bank.[37]

Building on this research, in 2005 Wolf and Kamil Akramov employed a simple simulation model to address possible Korean reunification. Noting that previous studies propose a vast array of unification costs, they assert that several considerations may reduce the costs that have been projected. First, they indicate that North Korea's large military places a burden on its economy. Second, military expenditures—ranging from 20 to 30 percent of its GDP—may decrease after reunification. Third, North Korean attitudes may limit the amount of migration from North to South Korea upon reunification.

Next, the simulation model attempts to double North Korea's GDP using the following parameters:

1. South Korea's preunification GDP is denoted by G_s = \$477 billion.

2. North Korea's preunification GDP scaled to that of South Korea's GDP is $G_N = \alpha_i G_s$ (α_i is the scaling factor), with i = .03, .04, .05.

3. Incremental capital coefficient (ICOR) is δ_j, (j = 3, 4, 5).

4. Preunification military spending in South Korea is M_s, which is scaled as a share, β_k, of South Korea's GDP: $M_s = \beta_k G_s$ (k = .025, .03).

5. Postunification military spending in South Korea is a (reduced) share of South Korea's GDP, (β_l = .02).

6. Preunification military spending in North Korea is M_n, which is scaled as a share, Υ_m, of North Korea's GDP: $M_n = \Upsilon_m G_N$, (m = .25, .30).

7. Υ_n is North Korea's postunification military spending share, (n = .04, .05).

8. μ_o denotes the effectiveness of the market-oriented institutional reform strategy (IRS): μ_o = IRS, with (o = 1, 2, 3), indicating very effective, moderately effective, and relatively ineffective, respectively.

9. Finally, we specify that the target, (T_p), or goal for North Korea's postunification economy is to double its GDP in four to five years. T_p = doubling North Korean GDP, with (p = 4, 5).

10. The capital build-up costs of unification are ($\delta 2\alpha G_s$).

11. Annual savings realized from the military build-down in North and South Korea are, respectively, $S_n = \alpha G_s(\Upsilon_m - \Upsilon_n)$, and $S_k = G_s(\beta_k - \beta_l)$.

12. Total capital costs of doubling North Korean GDP = C_r; $C_r = \mu_o \delta_j 2\alpha_i G_s - (\alpha_i G_s (\Upsilon_m - \Upsilon_n)) - G_s(\beta_k - \beta_l)$.[38]

Wolf and Akramov ran roughly 200 tests with these given parameters. The capital costs of doubling North Korean GDP in four or five years ranged from $50 billion to over $670 billion in 2003 US dollars. Table 12.3 exemplifies this range of projected costs in 2003 US dollars:

Table 12.3. Estimates of reunification costs: selected simulation results (assuming four-year doubling of North Korean GDP)

Preunification North-South GDPs	Incremental Capital Coefficient	Capital Buildup Costs (billions)	Military Build-Down Savings (billions)	Institutional Reform Effectiveness (1–3)	Reunification Costs (billions)
.03	3	$86	$36	1	$50
.04	3	$114	$42	2	$186
.05	4	$191	$49	3	$524
.05	5	$239	$48	3	$667

Reprinted from Charles Wolf, Jr., and Kamil Akramov, *North Korean Paradoxes: Circumstances, Costs, and Consequences of Korean Unification* (Santa Monica, CA: RAND, 2005), 39.

Wolf and Akramov maintain that total reunification costs may be shared by different sources. If North Korea adopted economic reform policies, investment could increase there. If private commercial transfers increased, public transfers from South Korea and the world could decrease. This would decrease the fiscal burden that would rest on South Korea after reunification. The sources Wolf and Akramov envision include private capital flows from South to North Korea P_s, private capital flows from the rest of the world P_r, public transfers from South Korea T_s, and public transfers from the rest of the world T_r. These costs are denoted in the equation $C_r = P_s + P_r + T_s + T_r$.

However, without knowing what these public and private investments might be, this equation is only as useful as the famous Drake Equation used to calculate the likelihood of intelligent life in the universe: $N=N^*fp^*ne^*fl^*fi^*fc^*fL$, where N is the number of stars in the Milky Way galaxy; fp is the fraction with planets; ne is the number of planets per star capable of supporting life; fl is the fraction of planets where life evolves; fi is the fraction where intelligent life evolves; fc is the fraction that communicates; and fL is the fraction of the planet's life during which the communicating civilizations live. Without knowing what the variables are, the Wolf and Akramov formula is, at best, only a way to make a guess. The same could be said of most of the purely mathematical formulae proposed to estimate the cost of Korean unification.

An example of this can be found in the work of Michael Funke and Holger Strulik (2005), which employed a two-region (North and South Korea) endogenous growth model to examine the implications of Korean reunification. The authors used the modeling they had applied to German unification, which, as identified above, is an imperfect comparison.

Funke and Strulik identify government policies as key aspects of unification. They assume that the government of a unified Korea would utilize the same tax policy but might have different expenditure policies in each region. The government would impose a flat tax rate on all income earners. Tax revenues would be spent on regional infrastructure: income redistribution within a region and income redistribution between the two regions. The authors assume that the government would run on a balanced budget. They note that the effect of infrastructure on regional productivity in the literature is modeled so that the macroeconomic production function exhibits constant returns to scale in private and public capital and long-run growth.

Using this assessment as an example, Funke and Strulik go on to assume that as a region's level of public capital per capita increases, its level of technology improves. However, regional disparities are not spontaneously equalized with private capital investment because regional infrastructure is immobile. Regional productivity disparities are determined by regional contributions controlled by the government.

To attract enough capital for convergence, the unified government would have to temporarily spend more on infrastructure in the North than in the South. The authors assume that the postunification government desires regional convergence and thus would choose a fiscal policy for smooth convergence.

Continuing their assumption that Korean unification can be compared to German unification, Funke and Strulik further develop their model without addressing the fundamental differences between the events in Germany versus Korea. They suggest that under the right conditions, people from the North would not have an economic incentive to migrate to the South and conclude that North Korea is "in a poverty trap."[39]

In their study, Funke and Strulik make several questionable assumptions. For instance, they state that "since private capital moves freely between the two regions, infrastructure is the limiting factor for convergence and it is more important to match production elasticity accurately" and that because "the government fully compensates lower wages in northern Korea through lump-sum transfers . . . there is no economic incentive for the abundant North Korean labor force to migrate."[40]

Why Germany Is the Wrong Model for Korean Unification

Although Funke and Strulik apply the German model to the Korean case, they do observe differences. First, North Korea's backwardness is more severe than was the case in East Germany. Second, North Korea's population is approximately half of South Korea's, while East Germany's population was a quarter of West Germany's population. Third, South Korea spends more on infrastructure than did West Germany, meaning that more money would have to be spent on infrastructure in North Korea for any level of backwardness. Fourth, taxes, as a share of GDP, are lower in South Korea than in Germany. Lastly, the South Korean economy grows with a higher equilibrium rate than West Germany (5 percent versus 1.75 percent), which, the authors mention, may ease the burden of reunification.[41]

More recently, writing for the Council on Foreign Relations, Paul B. Stares and Joel S. Wit address the various scenarios under which Korea would be unified, focusing on unification without war. They also discuss the issues of refugee assistance and humanitarian needs in the North, making the policy recommendation that the United States not attempt to undermine the Kim regime in the North but instead try to encourage that regime toward behavioral change.[42]

Many of the assumptions in the studies cited above overlook the tenacity of the regime currently in power in North Korea. Daniel Byman and Jennifer Lind address this in "Pyongyang's Survival Strategy: Tools of Authoritarian Control in North Korea." They point out that the Kim regime has developed institutions to limit public dissent, making any popular uprising (such as those seen in the Arab Spring) virtually impossible. They compare North Korean society to that of Middle Eastern states, suggesting that North Korean nationalism is much stronger because of the long-standing restrictions imposed there. The anti-American inculcation begins in primary school. Byman and Lind quote a mathematics textbook: "The brave uncles from the Korean People's Army destroyed six tanks of the wolf-like American bastards. Then they destroyed two more. How many did they destroy altogether?"[43] This level of public indoctrination—generally ignored or overlooked in many of the purely methodological analyses of Korean unification—must be recognized as a barrier to any idea of public uprising against the Kim regime in the North.

Scott Snyder, director of the Center for US-Korea Policy at the Asia Foundation, writing in 2011 about the differences between German unification and the possible Korean scenarios, portrays how German unification was a negotiated process in which East German authorities accepted that they had "lost legitimacy in the eyes of the East German people to govern effectively."[44] This is very different from the North Korean survival strategy that Byman and Lind describe. Snyder sees the United States and China as key players in any set of circumstances that would bring about Korean reunification. He comments that China was willing to support the government of the North even after the military provocations of 2010 (the sinking of the South Korean warship *Cheonan* and the artillery shelling of Yeonpyeong-do) because China values peace and stability in the region as a means to further its economic interests.

Many of the analyses reviewed above have been disproven by events since they were prepared, so one generalization that can be made is that predictions are usually unreliable. One more detailed and recent analysis comes from the Republic of Korea Ministry of Unification. Consisting of a set of estimates, this report provides short-term (10-year), midterm (20-year), and long-term (30-year) scenarios and expectations.[45] They are based on the assumption of North-South agreements on the elimination of nuclear weapons and a peace agreement between the two sides.

In the short term—assuming that the per capita GDP in the North is 21 percent of that in the South and that the South will have to provide living expenses and medical support to the North—this study estimates that the first year of unification would cost between $47 and $213 billion.[46] The upper-level projection equates to 6.8 percent of the South's GDP and 59.9 percent of the North's GDP, considerably higher than the percentage cost to East and West Germany.

This study reveals that public support for unification in South Korea is decreasing. In 2007 21 percent of respondents in a survey saw "no need" for unification; by 2011 this had risen to 70 percent, based largely over concern for the cost to South Koreans.[47] The study details past unification cost estimates, ranging from a few hundred billion dollars to Marcus Noland's 1996 estimate of $3.172 trillion. It does point out that some of the estimates of German unification were wrong because East German assets were overestimated.

The Unification Ministry study does forecast significant long-term savings in defense spending. South Korea spends nearly 3 percent of its GDP on defense; the study estimates this could be cut to 1.5 percent. The annual defense budget could be reduced by $585.3 million by 2040 if unification occurred in the short term.

Another publication by the Korea Institute for Unification echoes the declining South Korean interest in national unification, citing studies showing that 91.4 percent of South Koreans surveyed in 1994 supported it, with this number falling to 83.9 percent in 2005 and 76.6 percent in 2010. In particular, younger South Koreans believe unification would have a negative impact on them personally.[48]

Conclusion

Collectively, these studies fall into three broad categories: (1) methodological analyses that provide frameworks into which estimates can be input to derive cost estimates, (2) short-term estimates of what will be required in the event of sudden regime failure or regime change in North Korea, and (3) longer-term estimates of the eventual cost of Korean unification. Some broad comments can be made of these three types.

The purely methodological estimates (Chun, 1995; Piazolo, 1997; Noland, Robinson, and Liu, 1998; Noland, Robinson, and Wang, 1999; Auerbach, Chun, and Yoo, 2004; Wolf, 2002; Wolf and Akramov, 2005; Funke and Strulik, 2005) generally dismiss concerns over military demobilization, seeing a reduction in military expenditures as a cost savings without addressing the problems of having hundreds of thousands of unpaid trained soldiers unemployed. While they could eventually be used in a workforce, in the short term these soldiers would be a security threat and the possible basis for an armed insurgency.

These methodological descriptions generally attempt to apply the German model to Korean unification. There are problems with this: the two German states had never fought against each other, the borders were relatively open, and German unification was supported by the major powers (the United States and the Soviet Union). While the two German states were unequal in their economic development, they were not as far apart as the two Koreas. Nonetheless, integration of the two German states has not been painless. Many former East Germans perceive that they are considered second-class citizens. However, the divergence has not been as great as that seen by North Korean defectors to South Korea.

In the second case, the likelihood of North Korean regime failure has been broadly disproven over time and is challenged by Byman and Lind. One of Samuel Huntington's measures of governmental success is regime duration. As noted above, the Kim regime in North Korea has survived 12 American presidencies. Nevertheless, Eberstadt, Dujarric, and many others see the failure of the regime in the North as inevitable and coming in the short term.

The third category of studies, generally made by the South Korean Unification Ministry but also supported by a few Western researchers, takes a longer view of Korean unification. These studies (Grinker, 1998; Snyder, 2011; Republic of Korea Ministry of Unification, 2011; Choi, 2011) see Korean unification neither as a repeat of German unification nor as a process that will necessarily happen in the short term. The Unification Ministry addresses a broader set of needs (humanitarian, medical, and security) than the others discussed and accounts for the very real fact that the date of Korean unification is not known. Examining a range of time periods is much more useful. Unfortunately, its study has not been released in any language other than Korean at the time of this writing.

Overall, the methodologies to calculate the costs of Korean reunification vary significantly. Estimates range from hundreds of millions to trillions of dollars, and calculations are speculative due to the lack of reliable data on North Korea's economy. However, some scholars manage to generate models with little data. While Korean unification shares some similarities with the German model of unification, distinct differences include lower relative wages and a higher relative population. However, Korea can learn from Germany's mistakes to make economic integration or reunification run smoother and decrease the fiscal burden on South Korea and other world players.

The US role in a unified Korea is not certain. In the short term, the United States can expect to remain on the Korean Peninsula as part of a deterrent force against North Korean aggression. Conversely, North Korea cannot be expected to give up its nuclear capability because the leadership of the North sees this nuclear capability as its guarantee of security. The plans of the South Korean Unification Ministry set North Korean denuclearization as a precondition to movement toward unification, resulting in an impasse that precludes any short-term solution.

As the Korean population ages, the portion of South Koreans who hold unification as a necessary achievement continues to diminish. This view will reduce popular pressure for unification and the sacrifices it would require. In the 30- to 50-year time frame envisioned by South Korea's Unification Ministry studies, popular support for unification will further erode.

At the time of this writing, the third generation of the modern Kim dynasty is establishing itself in Pyongyang without any of the contention predicted by those observers who foresaw a collapse of the regime. Although Kim Jung-eun did not have as long to be groomed for his leadership role as had his father, Kim Jong-il, he does appear to have the support of the North Korean military and political leadership. Although this youngest Kim received a foreign education in Switzerland, there appears to be no reason to expect that he will digress from the policies of his father and grandfather in terms of maintaining North Korean security.

Under these conditions, the most significant change in the role or status of the United States on the Korean Peninsula will likely come from the South Korean populace as the generation that remembers the role of the United States in protecting Korea ages and dies and is replaced by a generation that, to some extent, sees the United States as an occupying force left over from a Cold War that Korea did not cause.

Notes

1. Remarks by Amb. Sergey Kislyak, Georgia Tech's Sam Nunn Bank of America Policy Forum, "The Path toward a World Free of Nuclear Weapons: The Euro-Atlantic Challenge," Atlanta, GA, 29 March 2010.

2. The terms *unification* and *reunification* are often used interchangeably; their significance is that older Koreans see the joining of the two Koreas as a return to the status quo, while younger South Koreans see it as a new condition. The Republic of Korea Ministry of Unification uses 통일, which translates as *unification*.

3. Selig Harrison, *Korean Endgame: A Strategy for Reunification and U.S. Disengagement* (Princeton, NJ: Princeton University Press, 2003); and Martin Hart-Landsberg, *Korea: Division, Reunification, and U.S. Foreign Policy* (New York: Monthly Review Press, 1998).

4. Paul B. Stares and Joel S. Wit, *Preparing for the Sudden Change in North Korea*, special report (New York: Council on Foreign Relations, 2009).

5. Choi Kwang-Soo, "Korea Unification: Problems and Future Prospects," in *Korea in the 1990s: Prospects for Unification*, ed. Steven W. Mosher (St. Louis, MO: Transaction Publishers, 1992), 48.

6. Donald Oberdorfer, *The Two Koreas: A Contemporary History* (Reading, MA: Addison-Wesley, 1997), 313–14.

7. Daniel Byman and Jennifer Lind, "Pyongyang's Survival Strategy: Tools of Authoritarian Control in North Korea," *International Security* 35, no. 1 (2010): 44–74.

8. Ian Jeffries, *North Korea: A Guide to Economic and Political Developments* (London: Routledge, 2006), 748.

9. Kang Suk Rhee, "Korea's Unification: The Applicability of the German Experience," *Asian Survey* 33, no. 4 (April 1993): 360–75.

10. Ibid., 364.

11. Ibid., 367.

12. Hong-Tack Chun, "Rapprochement Model for Economic Integration," in *Economic Systems in North and South Korea: The Agenda for Economic Integration* (Seoul: Korea Development Institute, 1995), 306.

13. Ibid., 304.

14. Ibid., 306.

15. Marcus Noland, "Some Unpleasant Arithmetic Concerning Unification," in *Eleventh Annual Conference on U.S.-Korean Security Studies*, 23–25 October 1996 (Seoul: Peter G. Peterson Institute for International Economics, 1996), 2.

16. Marc Piazolo, "Could South Korea Afford German-Style Reunification?," *The Economics of Korean Reunification* 2, no. 2, quarterly journal of the Hyundai Research Institute (Summer 1997): 48–63.

17. Nicholas Eberstadt, "Hastening Korean Unification," *Foreign Affairs* 76, no. 2 (March/April 1997): 77–92.

18. Ibid., 86.

19. Ibid., 91.

20. Richard Roy Grinker, *Korea and Its Futures: Unification and the Unfinished War* (New York: St. Martin's Press, 1998), 10.

21. Ibid., 20.

22. Marcus Noland, Sherman Robinson, and Li-Gang Liu, "The Costs and Benefits of Korean Unification: Alternate Scenarios," *Asian Survey* 38, no. 8 (August 1998): 801–14.

23. Ibid., 805.

24. Ibid., 806.

25. Marcus Noland, Sherman Robinson, and Tao Wang, "Modeling Korean Unification," Institute for International Economics, Working Paper 99-7, 1999.

26. Ibid., 11–12.

27. Ibid., 18–21.

28. Norman Levin, *The Shape of Korea's Future: South Korean Attitudes toward Unification and Long-Term Security Issues* (Santa Monica, CA: RAND, 1999).

29. Ibid., 44.

30. Robert Dujarric, *Korean Unification and After: The Challenge for U.S. Strategy* (Indianapolis, IN: Hudson Institute, 2000), ii.

31. Ibid., 14.

32. Ibid., 17.

33. Ibid., 68.

34. Ibid., 78.

35. Alan J. Auerbach, Young Jun Chun, and Ilho Yoo, *The Fiscal Burden of Korean Reunification: A Generational Accounting Approach*, National Bureau of Economic Research (NBER) Working Paper no. 10693 (Cambridge, MA: NBER, Inc., 2004).

36. Charles Wolf, "Managing the Costs of Korean Unification—*If* It Occurs," chap. 38 in *Straddling Economics and Politics: Cross-Cutting Issues in Asia, the United States, and the Global Economy* (Santa Monica, CA: RAND, 2002).

37. Ibid.

38. Charles Wolf, Jr., and Kamil Akramov, *North Korean Paradoxes: Circumstances, Costs, and Consequences of Korean Unification* (Santa Monica, CA: RAND, 2005), 63.

39. Michael Funke and Holger Strulik, "Growth and Convergence in a Two-Region Model: The Hypothetical Case of Korean Unification," *Journal of Asian Economics* 16, no. 2 (April 2005): 263.

40. Ibid., 262, 264.

41. Ibid., 265–66.

42. Stares and Wit, *Preparing for the Sudden Change*, 2009.

43. Byman and Lind, "Pyongyang's Survival Strategy," 54.

44. Scott Synder, "Value and Significance of Korean Reunification within the Dynamics of Northeast Asia," *SERI [Samsung Economic Research Institute] Quarterly* 4, no. 1 (January 2011): 41–47.

45. Republic of Korea Ministry of Unification, 통일, 어떻게 준비할 것인가 [*Unification, How Will It Be Achieved?*] (Seoul: National Research Council for Economics, Humanities and Social Sciences, 2011).

46. Ibid., 22.

47. Ibid., 27.

48. Choi Jinwook, ed., *Korean Unification and the Neighboring Powers* (Seoul: Neulpum Plus Co. Ltd., 2011), 23.

Chapter 13

Building Positive Relationships
in the Asia-Pacific

Dr. Adam Lowther
Research Professor, Air Force Research Institute

Introduction

Calling the twenty-first century the "Asia-Pacific Century" is becoming common. With Asia's dramatic transformation, sustained economic growth, and widespread military modernization, it is understandable why so many see Asia as a region on the rise and why it is increasingly at the center of US foreign policy. As the 2011 *National Military Strategy* states, "The Nation's strategic priorities and interests will increasingly emanate from the Asia-Pacific region."[1] Former secretary of state Hillary Clinton underscores this point in her *Foreign Policy* article, saying that "harnessing Asia's growth and dynamism is central to American economic and strategic interests."[2] That is, US foreign policy will follow the shifting winds that carry the nation's interests around the globe.

Why the Asia-Pacific Matters

A look at trade between the United States and the Asia-Pacific offers considerable insight into this growing focus on the region. Over the past three decades, Asia-Pacific nations—with China leading the way—have experienced long-term economic growth rates that were, on average, double and triple those of the United States.[3] With half the world's population, the region consumes 60 percent of American exports. In fact, since 2001 US exports to the Asia-Pacific have grown 89 percent—twice the rate of export growth to Europe.[4] A look at American imports tells a similar story. Simply stated, the region is critical to American prosperity. With the Asia-Pacific serving as the United States' largest trading partner and the destination for a majority of American exports, security concerns are not the only reason the United States is increasingly looking to Asia. As a vital national interest, US trade takes a central role in shaping US foreign and defense policy. However, economic interests are not the sole reason for pivoting toward the Asia-Pacific.

The US *National Military Strategy* also states that "we expect to maintain a strong military presence in Northeast Asia for decades." It adds, "As our presence and alliance commitments remain the key to preserving stability in Northeast Asia, we must also invest new attention and resources in Southeast and South Asia."[5] Clinton echoes this theme in declaring that "strategically, maintaining peace and security across the Asia-Pacific is increasingly crucial to global progress, whether through defending freedom of navigation in the South China Sea, countering the proliferation efforts of North Korea, or ensuring transparency in the military activities of the region's key players."[6]

In other words, regional stability remains a vital interest of the United States and a pivotal reason for our growing interest in the region. This increased focus on the Asia-Pacific presents a set of strategic challenges and opportunities for the US Air Force.

Covering almost one-third of the earth's surface, the Pacific Ocean is the single largest geographic feature on the planet. With the distance from Los Angeles to Beijing twice the distance of Washington, DC, to Berlin, airpower is the only means of transiting the Pacific's vast expanses rapidly. Every nation in the Asia-Pacific profits from continued growth and stability in the region. But ensuring that competing interests among nations do not derail three decades of developmental progress will require the participation of the region's leading powers.

As the United States seeks to play a positive role in promoting growth and stability, the military and some civilian departments can expect to be called on to leverage the nation's diplomatic, informational, military, and economic capabilities for the benefit of the United States and nations across the Asia-Pacific. Continuing to play a largely benevolent and stabilizing role will prove central to American success in the region. Overly assertive policies will only work to the detriment of US interests.

One of American history's great lessons is that the nation's economic and military success often result from gaining and maintaining the proverbial high ground. For the United States Air Force, air, space, and cyber power come together in the single concept of airpower—the service's principal contribution to national defense. Whether it is conventional or nuclear deterrence, long-range strike, air superiority, airlift, or surveillance and reconnaissance, American airpower has played a central role in stabilizing the Asia-Pacific for over half a century—defending the lines of commerce and communication. This is unlikely to change in the near future.

As the 2010 *Quadrennial Defense Review* notes, "The role of the Department of Defense [DOD] is to field, sustain, and employ the military capabilities needed to protect the United States and its allies and to advance our interests."[7] Over the next two decades, geography alone will ensure that airpower's role in the Asia-Pacific grows as the United States looks to promote its economic interests, assure long-standing allies of continued American commitment, promote regional stability, and build relationships with new allies and friends. Whether American forces are based in the continental United States or the region, it will take significant airpower assets to reach zones of conflict and disaster. Only the USAF can provide those capabilities.

While economic analysis suggests that the dynamism of the Asia-Pacific will continue to outpace growth in the West, the 49 countries of the region often have competing interests. Thus, the United States has an opportunity to play a stabilizing role, with American airpower playing a leading role in ensuring US credibility.[8] But to do this, the United States must clearly demonstrate that it is willing to serve as an impartial arbiter when intraregional disagreements arise and that it has the staying power required to effectively balance a rising and increasingly confident China. Few would disagree that states throughout the region will seek to avoid domination by China or the United States. And when one of the region's great powers acts overly assertive or appears too dominant, countries within the Asia-Pacific may look to balance against that power. Airpower is particularly well suited to such missions because it is both an area of strength for the United States and is often accepted with less reservation among host nations than other forms of military power.

As a relative newcomer to the Asia-Pacific, the United States finds itself in the midst of a broad renaissance across a region that once led the world in culture and wealth.[9] While a young country like the United States may have a short memory, many in the Asia-Pacific have forgotten neither the glories of the past nor old animosities. Navigating the Asia-Pacific's turbulent skies is certain to prove difficult for the United States because of the cultural, linguistic, philosophical, and religious differences that often underpin the thinking and actions of Americans and their Asia-Pacific partners.

China

As the Chinese look to return their country to its traditional role as the leading power in the region and countries across the Asia-Pacific search for a place within a changing economic and security environment, American political and military leaders must continue to unravel the complex web of interests shaping the region. This will not prove an easy task.

With scholars such as Alastair Iain Johnston offering valuable insight into Chinese strategic culture, historical evidence suggests that the region's other great power will resort to appeasement when it is weakest, defend when possible, and act aggressively when it has the upper hand. To ensure that China and the United States avoid coming to blows, American leaders will need to focus on their shared interests.[10] These areas may include fighting transnational threats such as pandemic disease and climate change, preserving regional stability, and ensuring the free flow of goods.

China may also oppose the United States at other times. The extraction of resources in the South China Sea, a peaceful reconciliation with Taiwan, and the reunification of Korea are areas where our interests may diverge.[11] However, conflict is not a foregone conclusion when two nations do not share the same interests.

It is also possible that the relationship may be something in between. China and the United States may consistently compromise when a divergence of interests threatens to undermine the Sino-American relationship.[12] Neither the United States nor China stands to profit from a conflict or a new cold war that could undermine the region's dramatic gains over the last three decades. Nonetheless, there can be little doubt that both the United States and China will seek access to markets, energy supplies, and natural resources around the globe, potentially stressing the relationship. Conversely, the United States and China may be able to use the common pursuit of shared aspirations and objectives as an opportunity to overcome their differences.

As the United States marches steadfastly into the future, the nation must never forget that the Asia-Pacific is not a playground for great powers. It is home to allies and friends—whom we should not take for granted.

Airpower in the Asia-Pacific

With American foreign policy increasingly focused on maintaining stability in the Asia-Pacific, airpower will play a central role in achieving American objectives. The range, speed, and flexibility the US Air Force provides are unmatched elsewhere. When Air Force chief of staff Gen Norton Schwartz wrote in his "CSAF Vector 2011" that the principal role of the Air Force is "consistently and reliably delivering *Global Vigilance, Reach, and Power* for America—in what is likely to be a very challenging future" (emphasis in original), he was absolutely right.

With the Asia-Pacific the regional hub of American interests in coming decades, the challenge before the service is unprecedented. While the need for nuclear deterrence; conventional long-range strike; air, space, and cyber superiority; airlift; aerial refueling; and surveillance and reconnaissance is well understood, one Air Force capability is often overlooked and deserves greater attention—building partnerships.

Early in his administration, President Obama sought to shift the focus of American foreign policy from one centered on hard power to one that increasingly emphasized the United States' considerable soft power.[13] For the Air Force, this gave new energy to a wide range of existing programs that fell within the building partnerships core function. Often disparate and difficult to neatly place within the context of a defined capability, building partnerships span a wide range of what may be called "soft power" missions. As secretary of state, Clinton described the administration's approach to building partnerships as "forward deployed diplomacy."[14] It has also been described as "airpower diplomacy."[15] Whatever term is preferred, building partnerships is a capability that the Air Force provides the nation for the defense of its interests. Some further explanation is helpful.

Within the Air Force, Air Education and Training Command (AETC) serves as the core function lead integrator for all building partnership activities. Essentially, this means that AETC is responsible for coordinating approximately 60 programs that employ airpower assets and personnel in nonkinetic ways.

Although not defined in either Air Force or joint doctrine, the term *building partnerships* may most easily be understood as a proactive approach to preventing and prevailing in conflict by employing airpower (air, space, and cyber) in nonkinetic operations as an instrument of national power. This definition incorporates a wide range of security cooperation activities such as training, equipping, and exercising; bilateral talks, workshops, and conferences; and much more.[16] As a soft power capability, partnership building can play a critical role in strengthening security alliances, deepening our working relationships with emerging powers, engaging with regional multilateral institutions, expanding trade and investment, forging a broad-based military presence, and advancing democracy and human rights—the very foreign policy objectives described by Clinton.[17]

The United States and its military will achieve their objectives in the Asia-Pacific over the coming years as much from the building of partnerships and related activities as from the application of hard power. Accomplishing this will require the US Air Force to gain an increasingly sophisticated understanding of the region and to make a dedicated effort to building young relationships.

Given the persistent fiscal constraints the DOD faces, the criticality of effectively utilizing soft power cannot be sufficiently underscored. Because building partnerships is often less resource- and manpower-intensive than using hard power, it presents an attractive option during fiscally constrained times.[18] A fundamental premise of the Air Force's recently released *Air Force Priorities for a New Strategy with Constrained Budgets* is the importance of carefully exercising airpower.[19] If this philosophy is executed effectively, the nation will defend its interests while realizing cost savings.

For example, the White House estimates that the average annual cost of maintaining a single American service member in Afghanistan is $1 million.[20] With partnership-building activities taking place in phase zero (before a conflict), the fiscally demanding circumstances of a conflict zone are not present—making building partnerships both proactive in preventing conflict and a more cost-effective approach.[21] Focusing on conflict prevention using soft power presents an opportunity to preserve limited resources for circumstances where hard power must be employed if soft power fails.

This strategy is particularly useful in the Asia-Pacific, where the United States maintains some of its most costly bases and where distances make transporting people and materiel expensive and difficult—thus making a proactive approach to conflict prevention an attractive option.[22] Simply put, building partnerships employs existing Air Force capabilities to further the nation's interests through the use of soft power. It serves as a key enabler in the Asia-Pacific, offering greater flexibility for the United States and its friends than is possible through formal alliances. This flexibility is often desirable when dealing with nations that—because of domestic or strategic concerns—may be reluctant to formalize a relationship with the United States.[23]

For Airmen who are equally skilled at the application of hard and soft power, building partnerships is but one side of a coin—with kinetic operations being the other. As the US Air Force increasingly includes building partnerships as a core capability, the service will shift from its often ad hoc approach to soft power missions to a comprehensive approach guided by the Air Force's Global Partnership Strategy and Air Force Campaign Support Plan.

One article recently suggested that the Air Force partnership-building program is actually a form of "air diplomacy." If thinking in terms of the broader diplomatic impact of building partnerships, it is easy to see how central these activities are to US foreign policy.

Some may ask whether diplomacy and soft power are the State Department's role. Diplomatic historian Elmer Plischke's description of diplomacy is instructive:

> Diplomacy is the political process by which political entities (generally states) establish and maintain official relations, direct and indirect, with one another, in pursuing their respective goals, objectives, interests, and substantive and procedural policies in the international environment; as a political process it is dynamic, adaptive, and changing, and it constitutes a continuum; functionally it embraces both the making and implementation of foreign policy at all levels, centrally and in the field, and involves essentially, but is not restricted to the functions of representation, reporting, communicating, negotiating, and maneuvering, as well as caring for the interests of nationals abroad.[24]

Although an expansive description of diplomacy, it illustrates the wide array of activities that fall within the diplomatic realm. For states, diplomacy and soft power are employed to promote economic interests (trade), protect citizens abroad, propagate culture and ideology, enhance national prestige, promote friendship, and isolate adversaries. Moreover, diplomacy is often the least expensive means of exercising power in international affairs.[25] Building partnerships is intended to do just that. It is important to keep in mind that the use of hard or soft power is but a means to an end—a tool for achieving American objectives—not an end in itself.

Many readers may not be familiar with the US Air Force's long and successful history of conducting public diplomacy, humanitarian operations, military diplomacy, and commercial diplomacy—all aspects of building partnerships. Dating to the earliest days of aviation, decision makers have employed airpower for diplomatic purposes. Some past examples illustrate the breadth of the Air Force's contribution to furthering national interests.

When aviation enthusiasts in the Army first attempted to convince service leaders, Congress, and the American people that aviation deserved their support, they undertook a large-scale public diplomacy campaign. In perhaps the earliest example of air diplomacy, members of the fledgling Aviation Section sent its small fleet of aircraft on a successful cross-country tour in 1910—eventually leading to widespread support for military aviation.[26]

Throughout the first three decades of its existence, the Army's Aviation Section (1914–18), Air Service (1918–26), and Air Corps (1926–41) became adept at conducting diplomacy at home, as leading aviators such as Brig Gen William "Billy" Mitchell and Maj Gen Mason Patrick worked tirelessly to increase the support and prestige of military aviation. At a critical time in the history of airpower, public diplomacy began at home.[27]

Well before the establishment of an independent air force, the Army Air Corps conducted what may well have been the first overseas air diplomacy mission. In an effort to showcase the new B-17, demonstrate American power, and counterbalance growing German and Italian influence in Latin America, six B-17s under the command of Lt Col Robert Olds flew a public diplomacy mission from the United States to Buenos Aires for the inauguration of Pres. Roberto Ortiz in February 1938.[28] This mission opened engagement between the US Air Force and Latin American air forces that continues today.

It is, in part, due to these early efforts that the US Air Force maintains strong relations with the leaders of Latin American air forces, for example, despite the often contentious politics that dominate the public debate. This relationship is maintained through the partnership-building programs in which US and Latin American air forces participate. Through conferences, academic engagement, officer exchanges, and the publishing of *Air and Space Power Journal* in Spanish, the US Air Force invests in its relationships with Latin American air forces that began more than three generations ago. Over that time, trust between airmen has grown and created a more stable relationship between the United States and its southern neighbors. Developing similar relationships in the Asia-Pacific is a principal objective of partnership-building programs.

Other public diplomacy missions include regularly participating in international air shows, hosting international conferences, transporting foreign dignitaries and media aboard Air Force aircraft, and conducting "show the flag" flights to foreign air bases. The 89th Airlift Wing may conduct the most well-known of the US Air Force's public diplomacy missions—flying Air Force One. It is said to be the most widely recognized symbol of the United States in the world.[29]

Humanitarian relief operations are a particular specialty of the US Air Force because of the speed with which it can respond to a crisis. For example, during the Berlin Airlift (24 June 1948–12 May 1949)—perhaps the best-known relief operation in American history—the Air Force responded to a call for food, water, and fuel for the people of West Berlin. Initially led by the US Air Force, the operation included airmen from the United States, Britain, and the Commonwealth who supplied Berlin with more than enough necessities for survival. Operation Vittles managed to deliver 13,000 tons of fuel and provisions per day. A resounding success, the Berlin Airlift highlighted the ability of the Allies to provide humanitarian assistance on a massive scale while avoiding a conflict between the United States and Soviet Union.[30]

More recent examples of the US Air Force's participation in humanitarian diplomacy include Operations Provide Hope (1992–94) in the former Soviet Union, Provide Promise (1992–96) in Bosnia-Herzegovina, and Support Hope (1994) in Rwanda.[31] When a 7.9-magnitude earthquake struck a remote region of Sichuan Province, China, on 12 May 2008, two US Air Force C-17s deployed from Hickam AFB, Hawaii, and Elmendorf AFB, Alaska, with desperately needed relief supplies, arriving on 18 May.[32]

One example of a humanitarian relief operation dramatically improving relations between the United States and a formerly reticent country is American efforts in the wake of the 2004 Christmas tsunami. Whereas Indonesia and the United States once had limited relations, a much more collaborative relationship now exists.

Because of its ability to deploy rapidly to locations around the world, the Air Force is undoubtedly the United States' best tool for providing immediate assistance. These relatively low-cost missions build goodwill with governments and citizens around the globe and provide an intangible benefit to the United States. They can also serve to open doors previously closed and to establish military-to-military relations with nations that may be skeptical of US intentions. Public diplomacy and humanitarian relief operations conducted by the military are, however, not enough.

For decades the DOD and US Air Force have employed a combination of military, commercial, and traditional diplomacy across the globe.[33] Current efforts are by no means the first for the Air Force. During World War II, for instance, the Army Air Forces equipped Britain and the Allies with a number of aircraft and supplies under the auspices of the Lend-Lease program (1941–45)—providing similar support to the Chinese government during the Japanese occupation.[34]

Current efforts often fall within the "train, advise, and equip" realm of military diplomacy. Although the sale of weapons systems to foreign governments—through an embassy's Office of Defense Cooperation—often receives the most attention, this example of commercial diplomacy is not the most significant partnership-building program of the US Air Force.[35]

The service often directs its effort toward training and assisting foreign air forces as they build their capacity to operate as a professional force and join the global community of airmen. In doing so, professional training and education programs can operate as part of a broader security cooperation strategy as the US Air Force is expanding the quantity and quality of air forces with which it can operate. In any given year, about 11,000 members of partner air forces will participate in USAF developmental education, professional military education, technical education, and flight education programs.[36]

The Inter-American Air Forces Academy (IAAFA) at Lackland AFB, Texas, is one example of these programs. By offering Latin American officers and enlisted airmen a range of training courses in Spanish, IAAFA assists in creating a professional officer and noncommissioned officer corps while strengthening ties between the United States and Latin America and building relationships with future Latin American leaders.[37] Such a program does not exist for Asia-Pacific nations and may be one area where the Air Force can aid in strengthening the relationship between the United States and countries in the region.

Officers who attend IAAFA may also receive additional professional military education at the US Air Force's graduate school, Air University, further developing the skills necessary to lead a professional air force. In 2011, 24 officers from the Asia-Pacific were attending Air University's Air Command and Staff College and Air War College. Such students attend these schools as part of AETC's effort to support the US Pacific Command—for which it has provided training to airmen from 22 Asia-Pacific nations.[38] Because of their time in the United States, these officers are also more adept at reading the many cultural and linguistic nuances of US diplomatic and political signals.[39]

While these examples of soft power are not an exhaustive list of the Air Force's partnership-building enterprise and its extensive set of programs, activities, and organizations, they offer a sense of what the service has achieved in the past through taking a decidedly different approach to the use of military power. They also offer a glimpse into what is possible if the service looks beyond its traditional war-fighting role—with a particular focus on building trust through relationships that require a significant investment of time.

Conclusion

In the years ahead, AETC and the US Air Force are likely to continue refining the service's partnership-building capabilities and the role they play in advancing American interests and promoting stability across the region.[40] For nations across the Asia-Pacific, partnership-building programs may prove particularly attractive. Focusing on building capacity, trust, and interoperability—rather than on a place to base large numbers of American forces—these programs do not put host governments in the difficult position that often occurs with some initiatives. Nations working with America's friends and allies in ways that they and their publics find acceptable makes possible the strengthening of common bonds, through shared interests, that may be otherwise overlooked. In the end, it is American ideals and values that the nation seeks to export. Often, it is the US military that provides the country's best sales staff and, in many instances, is its only salesman.

In the not-too-distant future, the United States may find that its Air Force provides the nation global vigilance, reach, power, *and* partnering. But for this to become a reality, the service will need to develop a successful strategy that effectively employs Air Force capabilities across the Asia-Pacific.

Notes

1. Michael Mullen, *National Military Strategy* (Washington, DC: Office of the Chairman of the Joint Chiefs of Staff, 2011), 13.

2. Hillary Clinton, "America's Pacific Century," *Foreign Policy* 189 (November 2011): 56–63, http://www.foreignpolicy.com/articles/2011/10/11/americas_pacific_century.

3. International Monetary Fund, *Regional Economic Outlook: Asia and Pacific: Leading the Global Recovery: Rebalancing for the Medium Term* (Washington, DC: International Monetary Fund, 2010).

4. White House, Office of the Press Secretary, "Fact Sheet: APEC [Asia-Pacific Economic Cooperation] Outcomes on Jobs, Growth, Economic Opportunity," 13 November 2011, http://iipdigital.usembassy.gov/st/english/texttrans/2011/11/20111113205755su0.3971171.html#axzz1lFqwqukk.

5. Mullen, *National Military Strategy*, 13.

6. Clinton, "America's Pacific Century."

7. Robert Gates, *Quadrennial Defense Review Report* (Washington, DC: DOD, 2010), 10.

8. Jacob Bercovitch and Karl DeRouen, Jr., eds., *Unraveling Internal Conflicts in East Asia and the Pacific: Incidence, Consequences, and Resolution* (New York: Lexington Books, 2011), chap. 2.

9. Rhoads Murphey, *A History of Asia*, 6th ed. (New York: Prentice Hall, 2008).

10. Alastair Iain Johnston, *Cultural Realism: Strategic Culture and Grand Strategy in Chinese History* (Princeton, NJ: Princeton University Press, 1998).

11. Aaron Friedberg, "The Future of U.S.-China Relations: Is Conflict Inevitable?," *International Security* 30, no. 2 (Spring 2005): 7–45.

12. Michael Swaine and Zhang Tousheng, *Managing Sino-American Crises: Case Studies and Analysis* (Washington, DC: Carnegie Endowment for International Peace, 2007).

13. Mark Lagon, "The Value of Values: Soft Power under Obama," *World Affairs*, September/October 2011, http://www.worldaffairsjournal.org/article/value-values-soft-power-under-obama.

14. Clinton, "America's Pacific Century."

15. Adam Lowther, "Why U.S. Needs Airpower Diplomacy," *Diplomat*, 22 November 2011, http://the-diplomat.com/2011/11/22/why-u-s-needs-airpower-diplomacy.

16. Jennifer Maroney et al., *A Framework to Assess Programs for Building Partnerships* (Santa Monica, CA: RAND Corporation, 2009), xiii.

17. Ibid.

18. For a discussion of hard power, see Kent E. Calder, *Embattled Garrisons: Comparative Base Politics and American Globalism* (Princeton, NJ: Princeton University Press, 2007), 188–208.

19. Michael Donley and Norton Schwartz, *Air Force Priorities for a New Strategy with Constrained Budgets*, white paper (Washington, DC: Department of the Air Force, 2012).

20. Mary Louise Kelly, "Calculating the Cost of War in Afghanistan," *NPR (National Public Radio) News*, 29 October 2009.

21. Barbara Starr, "Adding Afghanistan Troops Could Cost $500,000 per Person," *CNN.com*, 30 October 2009, http://www.cnn.com/2009/POLITICS/10/30/afghanistan.costs/index.html.

22. Stephen Hagel, Adam Lowther, and Chad Dacus, *The Future of Global US Air Force Basing 2010–2040*, Air Force Research Institute Paper no. 2010-3 (Maxwell AFB, AL: Air University Press, 2010), 37–41.

23. Michael Evans, "Power and Paradox: Asian Geopolitics and Sino-American Relations in the 21st Century," *Orbis* 55, no. 1 (Winter 2010): 94.

24. Quoted in Harvey J. Langholtz, "The Psychology of Diplomacy," in *The Psychology of Diplomacy*, ed. Harvey J. Langholtz and Chris E. Stout (Westport, CT: Praeger Publishing, 2004), 1.

25. A. F. K. Organski, *World Politics* (New York: Alfred A. Knopf, 1968), 401.

26. Warren Kozak, *LeMay: The Life and Wars of General Curtis LeMay* (Washington, DC: Regnery, 2009), 1–5.

27. Bruce Bingle, *Building the Air Force: Major General Mason Patrick and the Army Air Service* (Maxwell AFB: Air University Press, 1995), 42–54.

28. Irwin F. Gellman, *Good Neighbor Diplomacy: United States Policies in Latin America, 1933–1945* (Baltimore: Johns Hopkins University Press, 1979), 127–28; and Frank McCann, *The Brazilian-American Alliance, 1937–1945* (Princeton, NJ: Princeton University Press, 1974), 108–13.

29. Tom Baldwin and Gerard Baker, "Behind the Story: On Board Flying Virility Symbol," *London Times*, 11 June 2008.

30. Roger G. Miller, *To Save a City: The Berlin Airlift, 1948–1949* (Washington, DC: Air Force History and Museums Program, 1998).

31. Air Force Doctrine Document 1, *Air Force Basic Doctrine*, 17 November 2003, 24.

32. Public Affairs Office, "US Air Force to Deliver PRC Relief Supplies," United States Pacific Command, 16 May 2008.

33. See Gordon England, *Building Partnership Capacity: QDR Execution Roadmap* (Washington, DC: DOD, 2006); and Bruce Lemkin, *Global Partnership Strategy* (Washington, DC: Department of the Air Force, 2008).

34. Thomas Parrish, *To Keep the British Isles Afloat: FDR's Men in Churchill's London, 1941* (New York: Smithsonian Books/Collins, 2009).

35. This office is not found in every American embassy.

36. Gen Edward Rice, commander, Air Education and Training Command (address, conference, "The Asia-Pacific Century: Overcoming the Strategy Gap," Maxwell AFB, AL, 7 December 2011).

37. See "Inter-American Air Forces Academy," Lackland AFB website, http://www.lackland.af.mil/IAAFA.

38. Rice, address.

39. See Jovan Kurbalija and Hannah Slavik, eds., *Language and Diplomacy* (Msida, Malta: DiploProjects, Mediterranean Academy of Diplomatic Studies, University of Malta, 2001).

40. Rice, address.

Abbreviations

A2AD	anti-access/area denial
ADMM+	ASEAN Defense Ministers Meeting Plus
AETC	Air Education and Training Command
AFRI	Air Force Research Institute
AIS	automated identification system
AOR	area of responsibility
APEC	Asia-Pacific Economic Cooperation
ARF	ASEAN Regional Forum
ASEAN	Association of South East Asian Nations
BAMS	Broad Area Maritime Surveillance
bcm	billion cubic meters
BEA	Bureau of Economic Analysis
C4ISR	command, control, communications, computer, intelligence, surveillance, and reconnaissance
CAP	combat air patrol
CBO	Congressional Budget Office
CGE	computable general equilibrium
CIA	Central Intelligence Agency
DARPA	Defense Advanced Research Projects Agency
DCRK	Democratic Confederal Republic of Koryo
DIME	diplomatic, information, military, and economic
DOC	Declaration on the Conduct of Parties in the South China Sea
DOD	Department of Defense
DPJ	Democratic Party of Japan
DPRK	Democratic People's Republic of Korea
EAS	East Asia Summit
EEZ	exclusive economic zone
EI	economic integration
EU	European Union
GDP	gross domestic product

GNP	gross national product
GPS	Global Positioning System
IAAFA	Inter-American Air Forces Academy
IAEA	International Atomic Energy Agency
ICBM	intercontinental ballistic missile
IISS	International Institute for Strategic Studies
IMF	International Monetary Fund
INF	Intermediate-Range Nuclear Forces (Treaty)
IRBM	intermediate-range ballistic missile
ISR	intelligence, surveillance, and reconnaissance
ITCZ	intertropical convergence zone
JMSU	Joint Marine Seismic Undertaking
JSTARS	Joint Surveillance Target Attack Radar System
KIM	Korean Integration Model
KNCUF	Korean National Community Unification Formula
LOC	line of communication
LOCC	line of commerce and communication
LRASM	long-range antiship missile
NATO	North Atlantic Treaty Organization
nm	nautical mile
NMD	national missile defense
NPT	Nuclear Non-Proliferation Treaty
NWS	nuclear-weapon state
OECD	Organization for Economic Cooperation and Development
ONGC	Oil and Natural Gas Corporation
OTH	over the horizon
PDV	present discounted value
PID	positive identification
PLA	People's Liberation Army
PLAN	People's Liberation Army Navy
PPP	purchasing power parity

PRC	People's Republic of China
REE	rare earth element
ROC	Republic of China
RPA	remotely piloted aircraft
SAM	social accounting matrix
SCS	South China Sea
SEA	Southeast Asia
SECC	Scan Eagle Compressed Carriage
SIPRI	Stockholm International Peace Research Institute
SLOC	sea line of communication
SPR	strategic petroleum reserve
START	Strategic Arms Reduction Treaty
TPP	Trans-Pacific Partnership
UN	United Nations
UNCLOS	United Nations Convention on the Law of the Sea
USPACOM	United States Pacific Command
UTC	Coordinated Universal Time
WMD	weapon of mass destruction
WTO	World Trade Organization

The Asia-Pacific Century
Challenges and Opportunities

Air University Press Team

Chief Editor
Jeanne K. Shamburger

Project Editor
James S. Howard

Copy Editors
Tammk K. Dacus
Sandi Davis
Sherry Terrell

Cover Art and Book Design
Daniel Armstrong

Illustrations
L. Susan Fair

Composition and Prepress Production
Vivian D. O'Neal

Print Preparation and Distribution
Diane Clark